RUBBISH THEORY

The creation and destruction of value

MICHAEL THOMPSON

RUBBISH THEORY

The creation and destruction of value

With a Foreword by E. C. Zeeman

Oxford New York Toronto Melbourne

OXFORD UNIVERSITY PRESS

1979

Oxford University Press
Walton Street, Oxford OX2 6DP

OXFORD LONDON GLASGOW
NEW YORK TORONTO MELBOURNE WELLINGTON
KUALA LUMPUR SINGAPORE JAKARTA HONG KONG TOKYO
DELHI BOMBAY CALCUTTA MADRAS KARACHI
IBADAN NAIROBI DAR ES SALAAM CAPE TOWN

© Michael Thompson 1979

British Library Cataloguing in Publication Data

Thompson, Michael
  Rubbish theory.
  I. Social values
  I. Title
  301.2′1   HM73   78–40942

ISBN 0–19–217658–7

Printed in Great Britain by
The Bowering Press Ltd
Plymouth and London

Contents

Contents

Foreword

by E. C. ZEEMAN, FRS, Professor of Mathematics,
University of Warwick

In 1971 I wrote an article in the *Times Literary Supplement* describing René Thom's new geometric method of modelling called catastrophe theory, and suggesting that it might be useful in the social sciences. Michael Thompson was one of the first social scientists to take advantage of this new method, and since he credits my article for first drawing his attention to it, I have a particular pleasure in welcoming the publication of this book. I also had the privilege of being one of the examiners of his doctoral thesis, out of which this book has grown. Being a mathematician, I had never examined a PhD in social anthropology before, and I confess I was somewhat hesitant, but I felt it was an academically important occasion because not only was Thompson bringing together two very different disciplines, but he was also making essential use of both of them.

As a general rule, whenever mathematics is applied to science the minimum possible mathematics should be used, and it should play a subservient role to the matter being modelled. For some writers the mathematics is not essential, because they can describe the heart of their matter in ordinary language; they use mathematics only in a cosmetic role for making their arguments look more elegant. However, for Thompson the mathematics is an essential ingredient, for it is part of the very language without which he cannot describe his main sociological conclusions.

The appearance of a geometric language, that can be used in conjunction with, but not replaced by, ordinary language, is a new phenomenon—indeed Thom claims that his theory is the first coherent attempt (since Aristotelian logic) to give a theory on analogy. However, there is a striking difference between symbolic logic and catastrophe theory: symbolic logic is a convenient tool for checking certain arguments, just as Venn diagrams (such as those used by Thompson in Chapter 5) are a convenient tool for displaying those arguments, but neither symbolic logic nor Venn diagrams are linguistically essential, since both can be replaced by their verbal equivalents in ordinary language. This is because the mathematics behind symbolic logic and Venn diagrams is elementary; hence their verbal equivalents were well understood and incorporated into spoken language when language first evolved, long before the advent of mathematics. By contrast the mathematics behind catastrophe theory is non-elementary, and the proof of the significance of the geometry is sophisticated. The resulting geometric language was unknown until recently, and consequently no verbal equivalent exists.

The geometric language offers a new method of expressing relationships, and synthesizing into a comprehensible whole a variety of observations that would otherwise appear disconnected or paradoxical. This then is Thompson's long-term objective: to tackle some of the central problems and paradoxes of the social sciences, such as the relationships between values and behaviour, between world view and action, and between culture and society.

He begins gently, disarming us with his wit and his anecdotes about the paradoxes of rubbish. But when he passes from things to ideas we begin to perceive the full scope of his enquiry. I like the way he jolts us out of habits of thought and reveals to us the underlying structure of other societies—indeed, opens our eyes to our own society. This must be partly due to the rich variety of his own experience, from Sandhurst and the regular army to lecturing at art colleges, from building jobs in London to climbing Everest and living amongst the Sherpas in Kathmandu. But his main strength is his depth of insight. Not that I can judge the importance of his general ideas, since I am not a social scientist. However, when he begins to make specific use of catastrophe theory, as in the model of curriculum change in Chapter 8, or in the model of the pig cycle in Chapter 9, then I am sure he is on the right track. He has grasped Thom's central idea and uses it with originality and imagination.

Let us digress for a moment, and compare physics with the social sciences. One of the features illuminated by catastrophe theory is when something can behave in two different ways under the same constraints: for example, if a flat spring is compressed then it may bend to the left or bend to the right. In physics it is usually quite easy to see the different configurations that a physical system may take up under the same physical constraints. Moreover, the physicist is lucky because the phenomena that he observes in his laboratory are very similar to those that occur outside; thus he is justified in iso-lating his experiments in order to make accurate predictions and measurements. The social scientist on the other hand has no such luck: he can seldom isolate his phenomena from the rest of the world because of their very nature. He resigns himself to accepting para-doxes. One of Thompson's major insights is to observe that a paradox may in fact be none other than the existence of two different con-figurations of the same system under the same social constraints. The analogy with physics is made precise by using the same universal mathematical model for both, namely the cusp catastrophe. So, he argues, we should try to resolve the paradox by embedding it in a cusp catastrophe. This in turn suggests a variety of related phenom-ena, a synthesis of ideas that would not have been possible without the geometry. Nor is this synthesis expressible without the geometry.

Of course, this type of modelling is still very much in its infancy, and has yet to be tested against the touchstone of prediction and experiment. So far Thompson is using his models as sociological *hypotheses*, frameworks within which, in support of which, and from which, he can argue by conventional methods. This procedure is already scientific because it reduces the arbitrariness of description. But the heart of science involves prediction; and the design of suitable experiments to test the models, and the collection and fitting of data, are yet to come.

October 1978

Preface

It is difficult for the author of a book on rubbish to thank adequately those who have helped him in his endeavour. Rubbish, when all is said and done, remains pretty repulsive stuff and has a tendency to adhere to people who come into contact with it. It is for this reason that not all those whom I wish to thank may thank me for doing so in too public a manner.

But I do owe a great deal to the many colleges of art (particularly Hull, Winchester, Falmouth and The Slade) which over the years have given me encouragement and financial support. The same is true of the School of Architecture at Portsmouth Polytechnic. I should also like to thank the following institutions for their financial support: the Nuffield Foundation (9 months' research assistantship at University College, London), the Massachusetts Institute of Technology (14 months' post-doctoral fellowship), the International Institute for Environment and Society, Berlin (4 months' visiting fellowship). The intellectual climate in schools of art and architecture is ideally suited to the germination and growth of tender plants but, sooner or later, they must be transferred from the art hothouse into the cold-frame of the academic—and the wider—world. That both I and my ideas have, I hope, survived this traumatic journey, and that thoughts about rubbish led to wider considerations and to involvement with catastrophe theory, is largely thanks to the stringent yet helpful criticism of my colleagues in the Anthropology Department at UCL and in the Mathematics Institute at the University of Warwick.

It is proper to record that some parts of the argument in the early chapters of the book appeared in a somewhat different form in *New Society*; and that part of Chapter 8 was first published in *Studies in Higher Education*, vol. 1, no 1 (1976).

1 The filth in the way

Riddle: What is it that the rich man puts in his pocket that the poor man throws away?

Answer: Snot.

Whilst children usually find this extremely amusing, the normal adult reaction is to regard it as unfunny, childish, disreputable, rather revolting and altogether unworthy of serious attention. Rubbish theory stands this response on its head, regarding this joke as particularly worthy of attention precisely because the normal adult response in Western culture is to disregard it. Thus right from the word go rubbish theory is faced with the near-impossibility of taking a detached, objective, scientific approach to its subject matter. The serious adult is a serious adult because he avoids childish rubbish and so a serious adult approach to childish rubbish is a contradiction, requiring a stance as schizophrenic as that of a communist stockbroker (or, perhaps, a Young Conservative or an art-educationist).

This childish riddle provides a convenient, if vulgar, outline of my main area of concern. First of all it sets out a relationship between status, the possession of objects, and the ability to discard objects. The impeccable and quite unentertaining paradigm which is set up in the riddle may be stated thus: there is a status difference between the condition of being rich and the condition of being poor, the former being higher than the latter. The condition of richness or poorness is determined by the quantity of objects one possesses: a poor person possesses few objects, a rich person many objects. But how can one tell whether a person is rich or poor? Apart from tramps, most people choose not to carry all their possessions around with them and really rich people would be physically incapable of doing so even if they wanted to and even assuming they could overcome the problems of security and insurance that such ostentatious behaviour would entail. Well, the answer is that one cannot always be sure of recognizing a rich or poor person, but one sure indication of status which one may sometimes be fortunate enough to witness is how many objects people are able to discard. A poor man, since he has few possessions, can afford to discard very little; a rich man will be able to discard much more.

This paradigm is evidently correct since, at least in Western culture, people recognize this riddle as a riddle. That is, it claims that there is a situation which, on the face of it, would seem to deny the whole basis of our social order: namely that a person who is poor discards more than a person who is rich. We are puzzled by the riddle, rack our brains for an answer, cannot find one, and when we hear the answer 'snot' feel cheated since we assumed that the object discarded was valuable. Obviously a poor man who discards more valueless objects than a rich man, in no way threatens the social order. For the social order to be maintained there has to be some measure of agreement as to what is of value. People in different cultures may value different things, and they may value the same things differently, but all cultures insist upon some distinction between the valued and the valueless.

The riddle succeeds by playing upon that which is residual to our system of cultural categories. When, in the context of wealth and poverty, we talk of possessable objects we unquestioningly assume that we are talking about valuable objects. The category 'objects of no-value' is invisible and we only notice its existence when it is pointed out to us by the riddle. But the riddle contains much more than this. If the answer is simply 'an object of no-value' (say, pebbles or sweet papers) it is not very funny. What makes it funny is that the answer 'snot' is an object, as it were, of negative value; something that should be thrown away. Thus we can identify three categories of possessable object: valuable, valueless, and negatively valued. The rich man and the poor man according to the cultural paradigm should both discard their snot, yet the rich man does not, and in pointing this out the riddle is genuinely subversive and does threaten the social order. Hence the serious adult response which seeks to suppress this subversion by refusing to see it: a conspiracy of blindness.

Rather than join this conspiracy of blindness, let us poke our noses right into the rich man's snotty handkerchief. When one thinks of it, it really is quite extraordinary that a fastidious person, who regularly changes his socks and underwear, has a bath each day, keeps his hair neatly trimmed and brushed, cleans his fingernails, and stems any undesirable body smells by using a deodorant, should quite happily discharge a stream of opaque mucous fluid, liberally studded with darker more solid fragments, not to mention the millions of germs and bacteria which although invisible he knows to be present, into a porous handkerchief and then place the whole soggy parcel, none too carefully folded, in his trouser pocket on top of his small change and cigarette lighter which he will later use to pay for his gin-and-tonics and to light his and his companion's cigarettes. Yet this is exactly what he does, though one can only assume, in view of his otherwise extremely hygiene-conscious behaviour, that this is not how he sees his actions. One can only assume that in discharging his snot into his handkerchief and then folding it, he has in some way transferred that same snot from the category of negatively-valued object to the category of valueless object. That is, whilst he evidently feels he must get rid of it from his nose, he does not feel any such compulsion to get rid of it from his pocket. Nor, on the other hand, does he go home and put the handkerchief in his desk, or place it in the safe deposit at his bank: once in his handkerchief it is evidently neither positively nor negatively valued.

In contrast, the rude peasant cheerfully discharging his snot on to the ground, first through one nostril and then through the other (sometimes called a 'docker's hankie'), has no need of these conceptual acrobatics. Such category manipulations are hard to spot in our own culture, obscured as they are by the residues from our cultural categories and our conspiracies of blindness, but they often appear more prominent, and occasionally much more spectacular, when we look at other cultures. Consider this Trinidad Indian's view of his previously unvisited Motherland:

Indians defecate everywhere. They defecate, mostly, beside the railway tracks. But they also defecate on the beaches; they defecate on the hills; they defecate on the river banks; they defecate on the streets; they never look for cover.

Indians defecate everywhere, on floors, in urinals for men (as a result of yogic contortions that can only be conjectured). Fearing contamination they squat rather than sit, and every lavatory cubicle carries marks of their misses. No one notices.

These squatting figures—to the visitor, after a time, as eternal and emblematic as Rodin's Thinker—are never spoken of; they are never written about; they are not mentioned in novels or stories; they do not appear in feature films or documentaries. This might be regarded as part of a permissible prettyfying intention. But the truth is that *Indians do not see these squatters* and might even, with complete sincerity, deny that they exist. A collective blindness arising out of the Indian fear of pollution and the resulting conviction that Indians are the cleanest people in the world. They are required by their religion to take a bath every day. This is crucial and they have devised minute rules to protect themselves from every conceivable contamination. There is only one pure way to defecate; in love-making only the left hand is to be used; food is to be taken only with the right. It has all been regulated and purified. To observe the squatters is therefore distorting; it is to fail to see through to the truth.[1]

Yet, total though it might appear, this conspiracy of blindness is not extended to the non-Indian. I was told by one of the most eminent Indians of Nehru's generation that there were no flies in the Kulu Valley in the Indian Himalayas until the Tibetan refugees came there. As it happens, I had been there thirteen years previously, just before the Tibetan refugees arrived, and can vouch that, so far as one can estimate these things, the fly population had remained unchanged throughout the period. Yet I was told that the Tibetans had brought them, that 'the whole forest is their latrine'. Only the Tibetan excrement was visible to the Indian. Only the outside observer can see that all India is the Indians' latrine. It is all too easy as an outsider to spot the Indians' conspiracy of blindness. To see one's own is altogether a more difficult and uncomfortable feat. The particular version of this feat that I wish to perform is to make visible the conspiracy of blindness that is imposed by the social sciences.

Now sociology, our formalized area of enquiry concerned with the understanding and explanation both of our own society and of societies in general, is very much a serious and adult occupation and, consequently, very much predisposed to such conspiracies of blindness. The questions I will ask are: first, is this in fact the case? And second, if it is, does it matter? I will argue that the answer to each of those questions is yes: that serious adult thought in general, and sociology in particular, constitute a form of discourse that, of its very nature, is unable to make contact with certain regions of social life and, more important, that what goes on in those regions is crucial for any understanding of society.

This inevitable circumspection that so distressingly distances the

[1] V. S. Naipaul, *An Area of Darkness* (1964), ch. 3.

social scientist from the object of his study places him within the first of the Three Species of Mortal Men identified by the founder of Rubbish Theory: Jonathan Swift. According to Swift, a member of this Species proceeds 'with the Caution of a Man that walks thro' Edenborough Streets in a Morning, who is indeed as careful as he can, to watch diligently, and spy out the Filth in his Way, not that he is curious to observe the Colour and Complexion of the Ordure, or take its Dimensions, much less to be padling in, or tasting it: but only with a Design to come out as cleanly as he may.'[2]

If this were the end of the matter then rubbish theory would seem to be doomed from the start. For the social scientist who wishes to study rubbish must, at the very least, 'padle' in it. Yet if he does this what chance is there that he will 'come out as cleanly' as his fellows? How can he remain a member of the social scientific community if, in order to study rubbish, he has to abandon the form of discourse which is the defining criterion of that community? How can he wallow in the ordure in Edenborough streets throughout the morning and contribute to post-graduate seminars at Edinburgh University in the afternoon? Yet this seemingly impossible and revolting course of action is the defining characteristic of one type of social scientist: the anthropologist. It is called Participant Observation.

The simple fact is that most (I will not presume to speak for all) social scientists do not remain trapped for life inside their defining form of discourse—they can shout abuse at the referee, camp it up at the gay disco, or terrorize their children, as well as the next man or woman. It is just that when they are being social scientists these other forms of discourse are excluded. The student of rubbish cannot do this. The fundamental irreconcilability of a serious adult approach and rubbish subject-matter means that the rubbish theorist has to deal in different forms of discourse simultaneously. And since they cannot be mixed they must be juxtaposed. The joke, the paradox, the shock technique and the journalistic style, far from being unscholarly devices to be avoided at all costs, become rubbish theory's inseparable accompaniments.

Of course, the anthropologist doing his fieldwork on Skid Row remains different from those he studies, for he has access to his

[2] Jonathan Swift, 'A digression concerning criticks' (1696) in *A Tale of a Tub*, reprinted 1949 (Nonesuch Press, London), p. 308.

university seminars whilst they do not. It is a nice irony that those who do the best fieldwork and actually merge with their subjects must at the same time sever totally their links with their discipline. In consequence, theory can only be built up from the second-rate—from sadly incomplete insights into other realities—and this gives rise to a formidable problem, which is: how do we make allowance for this incompleteness? Do we adopt a crude positivism and assume that what we have gained access to is all that there is—that, if we can't get at it, it doesn't exist? Or do we accept that our insights are incomplete, that we have no way of knowing how incomplete they are, and that, in consequence, we might as well abandon the whole enterprise? Though these pessimistic polar alternatives can each exert a powerful attraction, there does exist another course which lies not so much between, as in calculated opposition to, these twin counsels of despair. It seems to me that the real significance of the form of discourse associated with serious thought is that, suitably developed, it holds out the possibility of recognizing the existence of, and of making some allowances for, this incompleteness. In other words, what I propose to do is, by juxtaposing immiscible forms of discourse, to take a very serious adult approach to our disgracefully childish riddle.

An advertisement in *The Times* promoting *The Times*' classified advertisement columns, and the service provided by *The Times* staff who advise on the best wordings for the classified ads, shows a pair of identical vases of oriental style. One is labelled, in crude block capitals, 'Secondhand'; the other, in elegant copperplate within a black border, 'Antique'. The inscription above the vases reads: 'It's not what you say, it's the way that you say it.'

Our appreciation of the advertisement is adequate proof that objects may be seen in two very different ways, one aesthetically and economically superior to the other, and moreover that in certain circumstances we may be able, to our considerable advantage, to control the way in which we ourselves and others see an object. The pair of vases has been chosen to illustrate this flexibility. The label 'Secondhand' leads us to see the vase on the left as a worthless piece of tat; a grotesque present from a grotesque relative. The label 'Antique' leads us to see its mate as the real thing; a beautiful, delicate, valuable, old, Chinese ceramic *objet d'art*.

This flexibility does not extend to all objects. Most objects are only visible in one or other of these two ways, and their identities are so certain that the labels 'Secondhand' and 'Antique' are superfluous. The used car in the back street car mart and the Queen Anne walnut tallboy advertised in *Country Life* are perhaps more typical, in their unequivocal natures, of objects in general, than *The Times*' border-line vases.

Let us start by identifying two very different ways in which objects can be seen. They form an element in our perception of the physical and social environment, our world view. The element can be described like this. In our culture objects are assigned to one or other of two overt categories which I label 'transient' and 'durable'. Objects in the transient category decrease in value over time and have finite life-spans. Objects in the durable category increase in value over time and have (ideally) infinite life-spans. The Queen Anne tallboy, for example, falls into the durable category, the used car into the transient category.

The way we act towards an object relates directly to its category membership. For instance, we treasure, display, insure, and perhaps even mortgage the antique vase, but we detest and probably destroy its secondhand mate. Obviously, when it comes to objects, there is a relationship between our view of the world and our action in that world, but what is the nature of this relationship? Does the category membership of an object determine the way we act towards it, or does the way we act towards an object determine its category membership? So far as the unequivocal Queen Anne tallboy and the used car are concerned simple observation of the market in these objects reveals that their category membership determines the way we act towards them: that is, world view is prior to action. They are located within a region of fixed assumptions. But when we look at the two vases we find that the way we act towards them, that is whether we treat them as antique or secondhand, determines their category membership: that is, action is prior to world view. They lie in a region of flexibility somewhere between the inflexible regions inhabited by Queen Anne tallboys and used cars (see Fig. 1 on page 8).

This is an obvious example of what I feel is a general phenomenon and as an anthropologist I should be able to provide a formal des-cription—an adequate theory—to account for what is going on here. For categories are not free just to float about. They are closely tied to the social situation that they render meaningful. A common response for the theorist is to treat the data *as if* the category framework determined the social action, and then to treat it again *as if* the social action determined the category framework—rather like physicists who can treat light as made up of waves or of particles and who choose whichever approach is best suited to their particular problem. The trouble is that neither approach is much help in understanding the conceptual equivalent of 'muddling through' that must go on when, despite the clear separation between them, equivocal objects become unequivocal and *vice versa*. I have to come at it from a different direction altogether.

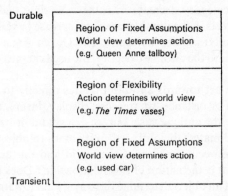

Durable

Region of Fixed Assumptions
World view determines action
(e.g. Queen Anne tallboy)

Region of Flexibility
Action determines world view
(e.g. *The Times* vases)

Region of Fixed Assumptions
World view determines action
(e.g. used car)

Transient

Fig.1

Innovation and creativity arise within the region of flexibility, but access to innovation and creativity is not freely available to all members of our society. Differential access is imposed through the social order. For those near the bottom there really is no region of flexibility; for those near the top there may be a wide range of manipulative freedom (and, of course, *The Times* is a paper for top people!).

By relating these differences in the breadth of the region of flexibility to the various social levels, we can uncover the control mechanism within the system: the manner in which durability and transience are imposed upon the world of objects. This is perhaps the first stumbling block in presenting rubbish theory, for we all tend to think that objects are the way they are as a result of their intrinsic physical properties. The belief that nature is what is there when you check in is reassuring but false: the belief that it is made anew each afternoon is alarming but true. We have to recognize that the qualities objects have are conferred upon them by society itself and that nature (as opposed to our idea of nature) plays only the supporting and negative role of rejecting those qualities that happen to be physically impossible.

The operation of this control mechanism would seem inevitably to give rise to a self-perpetuating system. Briefly: it is decidedly advantageous to own durable objects (since they increase in value over time whilst transient objects decrease in value). Those people near the top have the power to make things durable and to make things transient, so they can ensure that their own objects are always durable and that those of others are always transient. They are like a football team whose centre-forward also happens to be the referee; they cannot lose.

A paradoxical question now arises. How can such a self-perpetuating system ever change itself? How, as it were, can the other side ever score a goal? In this case the equivalent of such a goal is the transfer of an object from the transient to the durable category: a transfer which defies the powerful control mechanism that results from combining the roles of centre-forward and referee yet nevertheless does happen. We are all familiar with the way despised Victorian objects have become sought-after antiques; with bakelite ashtrays that have become collectors' items; with old bangers transformed into vintage motor cars. So we know the changes take place, but how? The answer lies in the fact that the two overt categories which I have isolated, the durable and the transient, do not exhaust the universe of objects. There are some objects (those of zero and unchanging value) which do not fall into either of these two categories and these constitute a third *covert* category: *rubbish.*

My hypothesis is that this covert rubbish category is not subject to the control mechanism (which is concerned primarily with the overt part of the system, the valuable and socially significant objects) and so is able to provide the path for the seemingly impossible transfer of an object from transience to durability. What I believe happens is that a transient object gradually declining in value and in expected life-span may slide across into rubbish. In an ideal world, free of nature's negative attitude, an object would reach zero value and zero expected life-span at the same instant, and then, like Mark Twain's 'one hoss shay', disappear into dust. But, in reality, it usually does not do this; it just continues to exist in a timeless and valueless limbo where at some later date (if it has not by that time turned, or been made, into dust) it has the chance of being discovered. It may be discovered by a creative *Times* reader and successfully transferred to durability.

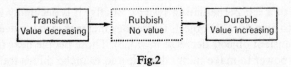

Fig.2

The delightful consequence of this hypothesis is that, in order to study the social control of value, we have to study rubbish.

Rubbish theory, with its bizarre subject-matter and engaging paradoxes, is often smiled upon by economists, sociologists, and physical scientists as if it were some Wodehousean corner of Academia: an amusing backwater, like The Drones' Club or Lord Emsworth's estate, far removed from the mainstream of social life. There is the assumption that, though it may hold for Victoriana and bakelite ashtrays, it does not, of course, hold for major components of the economy such as housing. There is also the assumption that, though the qualities of durability, transience, and rubbishness may be subject to a certain social malleability, this variation takes place within severe natural limits. Both these assumptions are mistaken.

This social malleability is apparent even when we examine the hard-core rubbish of body products. We can draw up a list of body products and then distinguish between those that are rubbish and those that are not. The rubbish items would include excrement, urine, finger and toe-nail clippings, pus, menstrual blood, scabs and so on. . . . The non-rubbish items would include milk, tears, babies (except in extreme ecological circles with the slogan: 'babies are pollution') and, sometimes, sperm. If rubbishness were self-evident and derived from the intrinsic physical properties of objects then this division of body products into rubbish and non-rubbish items would be fixed and unchangeable. Yet, in recent years, some body products have crossed from one side to the other. Phlegm is now clearly seen as rubbish but, until quite recently, it had a noble connotation. English phlegm was expectorated from splendidly stiff upper lips. The loss of empire rendered the English upper lip flaccid and English phlegm ceased to be the magical substance that kept the little brown native in his place, and became instead a repulsive green lump in the mouth during the later stages of Asian 'flu.

It is the same with sweat. Once it was good, honest, and noble. In 1940 Churchill could rally the Dunkirk spirit with offers of 'blood, toil, tears and sweat'. Today sweat is firmly in the rubbish category helped on its way by the deodorant explosion—products like Us and Femfresh: 'Is vaginal odour, your problem? Don't make it his too.'[3]

Only if one remains within severe cultural and temporal confines can one sustain the commonsense belief that rubbish is defined by intrinsic physical properties. Step outside these limits and one sees that the boundary between rubbish and non-rubbish moves in response to social pressures.

There are profound consequences to this realization that rubbish is socially defined, and there are strong incentives for the anthropologist to uncover the social forces that determine these boundary dynamics. The politicized ecologist, for instance, may pronounce *ad nauseam* that there is no waste in nature or that there is no such thing as a free lunch, the implication being that there is something wrong, something unnatural, about our society because it creates waste and insists on believing that there really are such things as free lunches. With a little more work the anthropologist can do much better. He can show that waste is a necessary condition for society, that society can exist only if we insist that there are such things as free lunches. He can show these supposedly objective scientific statements for what they really are—puritanical moral judgements on our society;

[3] One advantage of being published by the world's largest purveyors of dictionaries is that you are soon made aware of the sort of criticism that runs: 'Just a minute; words aren't the same as things, you know', or 'There is a difference between literal and metaphorical usage'. I would reply that, whilst words and things are indeed different, there is still a connection between them. It is precisely because there is a connection that things, once assigned to cultural categories, can be transferred. The same is true of metaphors. Those that are apt gain acceptance; those that are not apt are rejected, or, in most cases, not even considered in the first place. Those metaphors that are becoming more apt and those that are becoming less apt reveal the direction of change in the qualities of the object to which, however obliquely, they refer. I have a genteel aunt who could never live in Papcastle, Maidenhead, Cockfosters, or Pratt's Bottom. Try telling her that there is no connection between words and things!

and he can predict the sort of social changes that will ensue if these judgements should gain wider currency.

The less strident economist uses the concept of scarcity to define his field. If something is scarce then it lies within his orbit; if it is not scarce it does not interest him. Thanks largely to this stern limitation of its field, economics has enjoyed a high level of credibility and some predictive success. But of course the fact that the boundary between rubbish and non-rubbish is not fixed but moves in response to social pressures means that new elements may suddenly appear within his field, whilst others may suddenly disappear in an equally distressing and inexplicable manner. All he can do is sit there and marvel, 'like some watcher of the skies when a new planet swims into his ken'. Again, with a little more work the anthropologist can do much better than this. For if he can unravel the social forces behind the boundary shifts, he can write the equations for these new planets and predict their appearances and disappearances within the economic sky.

There are at present many millions of pounds and many millions of votes in the Environment and in the Quality of Life. Whichever academic discipline can lay the most convincing claim to these fields will reap a rich harvest indeed.

2 Stevengraphs—yesterday's kitsch

The basic idea in rubbish theory—the initial hypothesis—is contained in the diagram of the three categories to which objects can be assigned and of the controlled transfers between them. What is needed now is a good worked example: a detailed description of the progression through this category system of some particular physical objects. Victorian woven silk pictures recommend themselves to me for three reasons. First, since they have only recently arrived in the durable category, the aesthetic and financial somersaults that people have had to perform, either in bringing the transformation about or in coming to terms with it once it had happened, are still quite fresh in their memories. Second, I have, quite fortuitously, some personal experience of the earlier stages of their transformation. Third, they have quite recently been the subject of a detailed study by Mr G. A. Godden. His excellent book[1] relieves me of the tedious task of having to collect most of the historical data before I analyse it.

At the York Exhibition in 1879 an enterprising Coventry manufacturer, Thomas Stevens, exhibited a Jacquard loom in full working order and on which were woven, before the very eyes of the assembled visitors, brightly coloured silk pictures depicting Dick Turpin's ride to York on his bonnie Black Bess and the London to York stage coach. Those anxious to carry away a souvenir of the exhibition were able to purchase these woven pictures, complete with card mount, for a shilling each.

There was nothing particularly novel at that time in either the Jacquard loom or the mechanical weaving of pictures. As early as 1840 elaborate woven pictures featuring both the Jacquard loom and its inventor were being produced in France. However, most of these early pictures were in black and white, and it was not until the success of Mr Stevens's gimmick at York encouraged him to start producing

---

[1] Geoffrey A. Godden, *Stevengraphs* (London, 1971).

a steady stream of brightly coloured silk pictures, both nostalgic and topical, that textilographs (or Stevengraphs as they soon came to be called) began to appear on the market in any quantity.

Between 1879 and 1940, when the Stevens factory was totally destroyed by German bombs, about 70 different scenic pictures and more than 80 different portraits were produced. Also something in the region of 900 different designs of bookmarkers, postcards, Valentines, and Christmas cards. The total number of Stevengraphs produced and passed into circulation during these sixty-odd years must reach into the tens or hundreds of millions.

The scenic Stevengraphs were retailed at one shilling each, the smaller portrait silks at sixpence each. In 1902 the 66 subjects then available would have cost £2.55. In 1973 this same set of Stevengraphs would have cost over £3,000. Of course, we must allow for inflation (which increased prices by about 6½ times between 1909 and 1970), but even so, this is a very substantial increase, and it becomes quite staggering when we realize that it is restricted to the last ten years. Until the early sixties Stevengraphs were virtually unsaleable. Dealers would not buy them because they could not sell them, so there was no market for Stevengraphs, and their value was, in effect, zero.

From this very brief sketch of the history of Stevengraphs we can isolate the simple economic facts that when new in, say, 1879 a Stevengraph would cost one shilling, in 1950 it would be unsaleable, and in 1971 it would be sold in auction by Knight, Frank and Rutley for £75. The problem is deceptively simple: how can we explain these transformations of value?

Whilst it is legitimate to speak of the sequence of value transformations in relation to all Stevengraphs, since all were originally retailed for very small sums and all now fetch hundreds of times their original price, it is more convenient initially to select one particular Stevengraph and examine its history in detail and then to expand the analysis to cover Stevengraphs in general. So let us take the scenic Stevengraph entitled 'Dick Turpin's Ride to York On his Bonnie Black Bess, 1739', which was one of the original pair of subjects produced at the York Exhibition in 1879, the other being 'The London and York Royal Mail Coach'.

The Dick Turpin Stevengraph proved quite popular and continued in production until 1881 by which time Thomas Stevens had already expanded his range to twenty different titles which included three hunting scenes, six of other equestrian sports, Lady Godiva riding naked through the streets of Coventry complete with a brightly woven Peeping Tom in an upper-storey window, disasters both on land and sea (a fire-engine and lifeboat scene, respectively), a football match, a bicycle race (Coventry was, and still is, the centre of the bicycle industry), and a baseball match (the first bid in his ultimately successful attempt to open up the big American market). As Mr Godden points out, had the Queen's Award to Industry existed in those optimistic days of Victorian technology and trade, Thomas Stevens would undoubtedly have been a worthy recipient.

However, the year 1881 seems to have marked a decline in interest in highway robbery, trotting racing, and bicycle racing, for in that year the Dick Turpin Stevengraph along with three others was discontinued and Stevens pinned his hopes for the future on the growing popularity of lawn tennis by introducing a new title: 'The First Set'. The other casualty was the baseball match so we can assume that his first transatlantic venture met with failure. It was not until 1887 that he finally broke into the American market with no fewer than six new titles: 'A Souvenir of the Wild West' featuring Buffalo Bill Cody, seven Indian chiefs, Mr Nate Salsbury the director of the Wild West Show, the crossed stars and stripes, and the American Eagle; and portrait silks of President Cleveland; Mrs Cleveland; Buffalo Bill Cody; Sergeant G. H. Bates (who marched, carrying the Union flag, through the Confederacy and later from Gretna Green to London in the belief that by so doing he would help reunite the people of the United States); and H. M. Stanley, the Welsh-American journalist who uttered those immortal words to Dr Livingstone.

Various minor alterations were made to the silk picture itself during its period in production and several alterations were made to the wording on the card mount, the most important being the change to the geographically less specific title 'Dick Turpin's Last Ride on His Bonnie Black Bess' once the York Exhibition ended. We must assume that, unlike present-day purchasers, those who bought this Stevengraph were quite unconcerned about, and indeed unaware of, these slight variations and were quite happy to pay one shilling for whichever version happened to be current at the time of purchase. Thomas Stevens's enormous success at the York Exhibition can be deduced from the fact that examples of these earliest Stevengraphs actually woven in the York Exhibition are still, more than ninety years later, relatively common and certainly more plentiful than many of the titles he introduced in subsequent years.

Very little is known concerning the prices paid for this picture between 1881, when it went out of production, and 1963, when the revival of interest in Stevengraphs stimulated an exhibition at the Frank T. Sabin Gallery in Albemarle Street, London W.1. At this exhibition scenic Stevengraphs were priced at eight guineas. Throughout the rest of the sixties prices rocketed. Between November 1968 and July 1969 twenty-eight of the Dick Turpin Stevengraphs were sold by auction by the London firm of Knight, Frank and Rutley. Prices ranged from £5 (for a soiled example) to £42, and one bright example still in its original envelope realized £100. Now, just a few years later, it is no longer meaningful to speak of the price of Dick Turpin Stevengraphs. The high level of scholarship and the meticulous research devoted to Stevengraphs over the last few years has revealed the existence of numerous varieties, some very much rarer than others, and prices vary accordingly. For example, the very earliest pictures woven at the York Exhibition did not have the signpost 'To York' to the right of the toll-gate cottage, and examples of this variety are of *extreme rarity* and may be expected to fetch well in excess of £100 if in reasonable condition. Later in the exhibition, the mount was altered and the original eight-line poem replaced by a more decorous six-line version which avoided giving offence to the Temperance Movement.[2] Examples of this early mount but with the signpost to York are *very rare* and may be expected to fetch considerably more than those in the later mount.

It is most unlikely that there was ever any real market in second-

[2] Original bibulous version:
Here's a health to her memory; shirk it who dare—
If you love what is noble, pledge Turpin's brave mare;
And the draught will be welcome, the wine will be good;
If it have half the spirit and strength of her blood.
May the steed that comes nigh her in courage and fire
Carry rider more worthy to make her heart tire;
Though she saved him, and died to prove what she could do,
Yet *her* life was precious by far of the two.
In the temperate version the first four lines were replaced by the following two:
Right onward she went till she staggered and dropped,
But her limbs only failed when her heart pulse had stopped;

hand Stevengraphs until, at the earliest, the 1950s. This would mean that between 1881, when the production of Dick Turpin silks ceased, and about 1960, when a market emerged, their value was effectively zero. The career of such a Stevengraph in terms of economic value can be illustrated by the following graph:

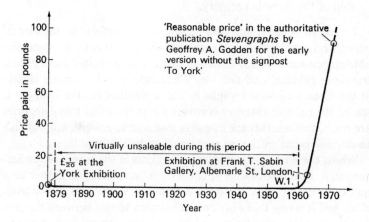

Fig.3 Career of the Stevengraph 'Dick Turpin's Ride to York on his Bonnie Black Bess, 1739'. (If this graph is corrected in an attempt to allow for inflation, its essential features, steady initial decline, long period of zero value and subsequent steep increase, are unaltered. Such a correction, by increasing the 1879 price and decreasing the 1971 price, would simply make the initial decline a little steeper and the final increase a little less steep.)

This career is consistent with the formal requirements of my hypothesis though its shape is rather distorted from what might perhaps be considered a 'typical' career. In terms of qualitative criteria this career may be resolved into three sequential stages:

1. An initial stage bounded by the Stevengraph's entry into circulation at a retail price of 5p and the moment in time shortly afterwards when its value is zero. Over this stage the value decreases with time, so this stage is consistent with the Stevengraph's membership of the transient category.

2. A long subsequent period when the value of the Stevengraph is

effectively zero and neither increases nor decreases with time. This stage is consistent with membership of the rubbish category.

3. A final stage from a rather vaguely defined point somewhere round about 1960 up to and, presumably, beyond the present. At the start of this stage the item acquires some value and the value continues to increase with time. This stage is consistent with membership of the durable category.

There can be no doubt that Stevengraphs conform to the central generalization on which my argument rests. That is that communicable objects are assigned to one or other of three cultural categories, transient, rubbish, and durable. We should now look more closely at the history of Stevengraphs to check whether (as the hypothesis states) the rubbish category is covert whilst the other two categories are overt, and whether the transfers transient to rubbish and rubbish to durable occur in the manner specified by the hypothesis.

Whilst the initial stage undoubtedly exists in the career of the Stevengraph, since the change in value from 5p to zero, no matter how quickly effected, must involve a decrease in value, it is rather truncated and it seems that only one transaction stands between the new item's entry into circulation and its entry into the rubbish category. This corresponds to the transaction habitually reversed by the dealer in rubbish, and the range of transactions appropriate to dealers in general is excluded from this particular career. The reasons are not hard to find. Stevengraphs were never functional in the sense that people bought them because they wanted to use them in the way they might use a frying-pan or an ashtray. They were small, decorative, and inexpensive. Pretty as a picture, they embodied those attributes of the Victorian age—the superiority of British technology, cosy nostalgia, and cloying sentimentality—and in consequence they were eminently suitable for the small gift or the housewife's harmless little self-indulgence.

As such they must have represented the kitsch of their time, as repulsive to those with cultured tastes as present-day Tretchikoff reproductions and plastic pineapple ice-containers are to their mid-twentieth-century equivalents. It is ironic that these individuals, who would never permit a garden gnome to dangle his rod and line in their lily ponds, should choose to titillate their Good Tastebuds by accumulating what are, in effect, the plaster ducks of yesteryear.

At present, despite the demand created by the practitioners of high camp, there is little, if any, market in secondhand Tretchikoffs, cocktail bar requisites, plaster ducks, and garden gnomes, and similar conditions, one presumes, must have prevailed for secondhand Stevengraphs, as long as new examples were readily available.

A more typical picture of the decline from transience to rubbish (one which includes a considerable sequence of transactions and the intervention of several dealers) is provided by the career of a relatively modern motor car. The following graph shows the career (to date[3]) of the Austin Countryman Estate Car, registration number 313 WBH:[4]

Fig.4 Career of Austin Countryman Estate Car, registration number 313 WBH

The interesting point about this graph is that whilst the trend is obvious enough—an inexorable decline towards zero value—there

[3] This chapter was written in 1972 and, despite some later modifications, is itself a little time capsule: the turbulent aesthetics of 'swinging London' preserved in aspic.

[4] Details taken from an article in the Automobile Association's magazine *Drive*, Autumn 1971.

are stages in the sequence where, temporarily, the trend is reversed and for a moment the value appears to increase. Each of these points of reversal represents the intervention of a used car dealer. The lower price is what he pays for the car (a figure virtually fixed by *Glass's Guide*, the trade publication obtainable only by subscription) and the upper price what he manages to sell it for. The whole of this difference may not be the dealer's profit since it may well include certain 'improvements' such as a mechanical overhaul or a respray. One dealer's profit, that after the very first transfer of ownership, is quite remarkable in that he has managed by expending probably not more than £40 to sell the car for £200 more than he paid for it, and for £100 more than it cost when new. This was achieved by heeding the advice of *The Times'* advertisement, 'It's not what you say, it's the way that you say it', and altering the category membership of the item in question, in this case by shifting an estate car from the 'domestic' to the 'sports' category, through the fitting of a sunshine roof and the respraying of the roof in 'go-faster' black. Other points to note are the automatic loss involved in the transition from 'new' to 'secondhand' and the soundness of the advice: 'cut out the middleman'.

The most convincing proof that the rubbish category occupied by the Stevengraph between about 1881 and 1960 is indeed covert lies in the fact that when one comes to look at the history of the Stevengraph during this period there isn't any. If rubbish is always covert, in that we strive quite successfully at all times to deny its existence, then its absence from the historical record, even when dressed up as the respectable latin 'detritus', is only to be expected.

The situation is a little complicated as one shifts from the particular to the general, in that the Dick Turpin Stevengraph went out of production in 1881 whilst Stevengraphs in general continued to be produced until well into the twentieth century and indeed production was not completely terminated until November 1940 when the Stevens factory was totally destroyed in an air raid. This destruction of the means of production is a most important factor in determining the subsequent turning point marking the transition from rubbish to durable. It corresponds to the death of the great artist which often gives a useful boost to the economic value of his works, to the lost secret of certain processes such as that concerning the manufacture of medieval stained glass, or to the Phylloxera epidemic which swept the vineyards of Europe in the 1870s and which eventually gave rise to the incredibly high prices paid for examples of those few pre-Phylloxera vintages of sufficiently high quality to be still drinkable today.[5]

The decline into rubbish of the Dick Turpin silk, once it had ceased to be new, was probably repeated in the case of all the other Stevengraphs but, since their production is spread over a period of fifty years or more, we cannot represent the career of Stevengraphs in general very clearly in graph form, since some individual pictures were in the rubbish category decades before others even entered into circulation.

Some indication of the 'invisibility' of Stevengraphs during their period in the rubbish category can be inferred by tabulating the known references to them in the press and in various articles and books and also the occasions when they were 'relevated',[6] that is, particularly prominently displayed, for example in trade fairs or in art galleries. Such a tabulation must inevitably be incomplete but, even so, a chronological sequence of interest, disinterest, and interest is clearly discernible. Of course the very first occasion on which Stevengraphs were relevated was the York Exhibition of 1879. This was one of a number of minor provincial exhibitions emulating the great international exhibitions of the Victorian period. Thomas Stevens was primarily concerned to display that great entrepreneurial virtue, technological innovation, and his idea of keeping his modified Jacquard loom at work producing attractive little pictures was nicely conceived to do just that.

The extent to which he succeeded in focusing the attention of the general public on his enterprise is evident in the numerous press

[5] For example, the world record price of £4,661 paid for one jeroboam of Château Mouton Rothschild 1870, in an auction sale conducted by Sothebys simultaneously in Paris, London, and Los Angeles in telephone-linked salerooms on 21 November 1972.

[6] I borrow this neologism from two physicists, Bohm and Schumacher, who explored (in a paper that, so far as I know, has not been published) certain contradictions between the formal and informal language codes of Bohr and Einstein. Their argument is that scientists, like the rest of us, do not see things with the naked eye. They are predisposed, by their theory or world view, to notice some things and to ignore others. As theory or world view changes, so the things that are noticed or ignored change. That is, the process is dynamic. They use the term 'relevate' to describe the way a theory makes things noticeable and 'irrelevate' to describe the way other things are pushed into the background.

B

references of the day, in the vast number of silk pictures which he sold in the exhibition, and in the ninety-odd years of economic life which the firm of Thomas Stevens (Coventry) Limited enjoyed as a fortunate sequel to this novel example of Victorian publicity.

Over the subsequent years the firm continued to promote its products in the press, in trade journals and, in particular, through the printed labels listing all the Stevengraphs currently in production. These were glued to the back of all silk pictures, so providing a form of free advertising reminiscent of those car dealers who affix a prominent plastic label to the back window of every vehicle they sell proclaiming: 'Another new car from Kutthroats of Kilburn'.

Despite all these efforts, Stevengraphs were never to recapture the heights of attention they received at the York Exhibition until the second half of the twentieth century, more than twenty years after they had ceased production: a salutary reminder that a thing of beauty is a joy for a fortnight. (Only a thing of beauty that happens to be in the durable category is a joy for ever.)

In order to recall the attitude, or rather, lack of attitude towards Stevengraphs during their long sojourn in the rubbish category we are forced to rely upon anecdote, upon the personal reminiscences of those whose memories extend so far into the past that they can remember the days when Stevengraphs were not auctioned in the salerooms of London's West End, and possibly even the days when new Stevengraphs were sold in a different milieu by, for instance, newsagents and the hot-potato-seller Charlie Satchwell at his pitch outside the Whitmore Head public house in Hexton.

The lack of any market in secondhand Stevengraphs during this period is made clear by Mr Godden, who is an antique dealer and a member of the long-established firm of Goddens of Worthing. Alongside his concern for antiques in general he has developed a special interest in Stevengraphs, becoming at one and the same time a discerning collector, a prominent dealer, and a leading authority on these woven silk pictures. Describing the way in which the present interest in Stevengraphs developed he says:

My own experience, as a partner in a family antique business, is that my grandfather had no interest whatsoever in Stevengraphs—not surprisingly seeing that he was an antique dealer at a period when some of these silks were still being made. Nor had my father any interest in them before the Second World War, and in the 1940s when he began to specialise in the

export market, mainly to the United States of America, there was again
no interest in such things as Stevengraphs.[7]

Speaking of things Victorian in general, he says:

... it is true to say that until the 1950s there was very little interest in
Victorian objects. They excited little sympathy and often suffered ridicule.[8]

He goes on to describe his own experience concerning the development in the 1960s of the market in Stevengraphs:

During the 1950s ... we did have in stock some examples which were
probably parts of 'mixed-lots' bought at auction sales. I remember that
these hung fire for many years, nobody showing the slightest interest in
them, until one day in the early 1960s an American buyer purchased the
five or six we had available. I do not remember now if my father had talked
him into buying them, for this American was a friend of long standing
and ... if my father ever suggested that this buyer should purchase an
article he would do so, even if it were far from being in his own line. Having
sold our 'stock' of Stevengraphs we heard nothing more about them and
I concluded that this was one of our suggestions that had fallen on stony
ground. However a year or more later, our friend was writing for 'more of
those little silk-work pictures you sold me some time back'. Needless to
say, in the interval their growing popularity had become more widely
known, with a consequent increase in price.[9]

My second piece of anecdotal evidence is based on my own personal experience. As a child I was fascinated by the silk pictures of
Dick Turpin and the London to York stage coach which hung in
little gothic frames on the back stairs of my parents' house and I can
remember questioning my grandmother about them and, in particular, wanting to know how they had been made. My grandmother, a
formidable lady who always wore jet beads and a pair of gold
lorgnettes on a black silk ribbon and walked with the aid of an ebony
stick, was the widow of a Northumbrian sheep-farmer and it is
probably safe to assume that her response was fairly typical of middle-
class opinion during the early years of this century. She showed little
concern for stimulating my interest in Stevengraphs and briefly
explained that her parents had bought them as souvenirs of the
family's visit to the Exhibition at York. They had been woven, she

[7] Godden, op. cit. p. 28.
[8] Ibid. p. 27.
[9] Ibid. p. 29.

said disparagingly, on a machine and in consequence were of no interest. If only they had been made a year or two earlier before the machine had been invented, she pointed out (erroneously), they would have been woven by hand and would be objects of both aesthetic and financial value. My mother's attitude was similar to that of my grandmother and the Stevengraphs' survival to the present day can only be ascribed to a combination of inertia and good luck. They were near to being thrown out on several occasions, and I suspect it was only my childish attachment to them that prevented this from happening. The final chapter of this saga is that it turns out that my great-grandparents must have visited the Exhibition at York very soon after its opening, for their Stevengraphs are the extremely rare varieties, the Dick Turpin one having no signpost to York and being in the early mount with the eight-line poem, and the London to York coach having the wording 'Stage-coach' as opposed to 'Royal Mail Coach' in the title, and the inscription in the bottom left-hand corner: 'Manufactured in York Exhibition 1879', whilst later versions of the mount carry the much commoner: 'Woven in the York Exhibition'. They have now been insured, placed in new frames, and moved from their insignificant position on the back stairs into the prominence of the front hall. Their transfer from rubbish to durable is complete.

Turning to this final stage of the sequence, the transition from rubbish to durable, we can clearly see from the exhibitions and publications the manner in which Stevengraphs became 'visible' once more and the way in which their increasing value was accompanied by their relevation, first in short articles in collectors' magazines and later in more substantial definitive tomes. Most significantly, the very forms taken by the literature devoted to the Stevengraph display a parallel transition for, as we go from the early transient stage to the later period of durability we go from journalism to scholarship, the former being essentially ephemeral and disposable: news one day, forgotten the next, the latter being essentially persistent and cumulative: the careful refining, reappraising and building-up upon what has gone before. The journalist has only the by-line, the scholar has the bibliography.

Although, as we have seen, the market in Stevengraphs did not emerge until the 1960s, the first scholarly article about them appeared almost thirty years earlier when Mary Dunham published 'A Check

List of Stevens' Silk Pictures' in the *Antiques Magazine* of March 1933. This magazine was published in New York and the appreciation of Stevengraphs in the United States has always slightly preceded interest in Britain. This would seem to be a fairly common state of affairs: for instance, the sporting and animal paintings of such eighteenth and nineteenth-century English artists as Stubbs, the Herrings, and Seymour have enjoyed a very much higher reputation in the United States than they have in Britain and in consequence many have crossed the Atlantic. Various reasons might be advanced for this tendency, the most attractive, since it hints at the inherent superiority of the Old World over the New, is that the States, having been in existence for a much shorter period of time than Europe, has a much smaller repertoire of rubbish to choose from. Alternatively, it can be seen as one example of the general principle of a prophet being without honour in his own land. The most likely, and much less palatable, reason is that the power of the United States is very much greater than that of Britain, that durables are always in the hands of the most powerful, and that when there is a shift in power there is a shift in durables as well.[10] If this is the case, the only defence for the weak is either to reject durability entirely or to ensure that their durables come in inalienable form, like Scotch mist or the sun going down o'er Galway Bay. This is more easily said than done. Witness the way in which American and German buyers have acquired much of Killarney, despite the wording of the song ('You cannot buy Killarney'), and the fact that London Bridge, far from falling down, now spans a stagnant artificial lake in the middle of the Arizona desert.

The rubbish to durable transition is an all-or-nothing transfer. An object cannot gradually slide across from one category to the other as is the case with the transient to rubbish transfer. The transition involves the transfer across two boundaries, that separating the

---

[10] For example, the following report in *The Times*, 12 May 1973:

'The Indian Government has discovered that one of its greatest works of art (the 12th-century bronze of the god Siva dancing in a circle of flames, from the village temple at Sivapura), stolen from a Hindu temple, is now in the collection of Mr. Norton Simon, an American millionaire.

'Following the intervention of the Indian ambassador to the United States, a gentlemen's agreement has been reached that ensures its eventual return.'

See also Hugh R. Trevor-Roper, *The Plunder of the Arts in the Seventeenth Century* (Thames & Hudson, London, 1970).

worthless from the valuable and that between the covert and the overt. Things may drift into obscurity but they leap into prominence. For an item to cross these boundaries it must begin to acquire value and it must emerge from its obscurity. It must leave its timeless limbo and acquire a real and increasing expected life-span, and since it has become visible it must also discard its polluting properties.[11] Either an item is invisible or visible, is timeless or has an expected life-span, is polluting or is pure, is an eyesore or a sight for sore eyes. So how can the transfer be effected?

In aggregate, the transfer can, under certain circumstances, be effected quite smoothly as a concatenation of individual creative leaps. Let us postulate that initially one individual suddenly in a blinding flash, as it were, sees an item not as rubbish but as a durable and that his example is followed by another and another and so on, until eventually everyone is agreed that the item is durable. From a logical point of view such a transfer might appear rather unlikely yet in practice it does happen, though not without difficulty, opposition, and confusion. The fact is that individuals are continually making bizarre and eccentric evaluations, the great majority of which do not even trigger off a second such evaluation or, at best, initiate a chain which is soon snapped into pieces by those whom it aspires to encircle and constrain. The reason why we tend not to see this seething mass of contradictory and threatening evaluations is that inevitably we must, most of the time, belong to that massive majority whose prime concern is to suppress such possibilities by simply refusing to admit to their existence. At either extreme of this vast mid-ground of eccentric evaluations that are suppressed simply by being ignored, there are those few that manage to gain currency and there are those others so intrusive and so threatening that not only must they be suppressed but must be seen to be suppressed. For instance, those individuals who make eccentric positive evaluations with respect to certain body-products and fill their chests of drawers with neatly wrapped parcels of their own excrement, far from being ignored, are emphatically categorized as insane.

So, out of this vast range of possible value transformations a tiny

---

[11] The way in which an object in the covert category that for some reason or other becomes 'visible' is seen as polluting and consigned to the cultural category 'rubbish' is set out in Chapter 5.

fraction actually gain acceptance. When looked at in detail one of these transformations is seen to be effected by a cumulative sequence of eccentric evaluations which, as they accumulate, become progressively less eccentric.

The human life-span and the time taken for an item to pass from the transient, through the rubbish, to the durable category are of the same order, and this both facilitates the rubbish to durable transfer (as those to whom it is unacceptable die off) and obscures our understanding of it. For instance, it is now generally agreed that Chippendale chairs are durable and a person expressing this view is unlikely to be suffused with excitement by his discovery or to be admired or despised by others for his originality. Yet, when they were new, Chippendale chairs were transient—good quality chairs for sitting on —and the often battered state of those that have survived is evidence that they were treated as transient by their owners. Dilapidation, obsolescence, and changing fashions ensured the decline in value and expected life-span which characterize transient items and they entered the rubbish category, being banished from the Victorian salon to the timeless limbo of the servants' attic. Those few eccentrics who first discovered these rubbish chairs and, by 'seeing' them, moving them into their drawing-rooms and extolling their aesthetic qualities, initiated the first links in the long chain of individual creative leaps, must have appeared to their staid contemporaries as absurd as the present-day collector of Festival of Britain ephemera or the preservationist campaigning to prevent the landscaping of a gaunt and derelict slag-heap.[12]

At some point along this sequence of individual creative leaps the aesthetic judgements will become sufficiently centric for a market to emerge. At first it will be a most imperfect market. The sort of situation where sellers say to themselves, 'I won't throw that away, I might just be able to sell it', and buyers offer, for a nominal sum, to take it off the owner's hands. Consequently it is most unlikely that one will ever be able to point to an exact moment in time, or to a particular transaction, and say that is when such and such an item became

---

[12] I do not claim to have given here an explanation of taste formation, but rather a tentative description. The explanation, a theory of taste formation, requires a full account of the circumstances under which eccentric evaluations gain acceptance, or, more modestly, an account of the extent to which it is possible to specify these conditions.

durable. We have seen that in the case of Stevengraphs this initially most imperfect market situation arose in the early 1960s in England. The demand, which was little developed, came at first from the United States so it is safe to assume that the market emerged marginally earlier there than here. We can take the year 1960 as the turning point, and regard all favourable aesthetic valuations in the rubbish phase before this date as eccentric.

As might be expected, there is not a great amount of historical evidence concerning the activities of these eccentrics, as they assiduously sifted their way through what most people considered to be rubbish. The earliest record is Mary Dunham's check-list in the *Antiques Magazine* in 1933, which is really quite remarkable in that Stevengraphs were still being produced at that time and about thirty years were to elapse before they finally emerged from rubbish. Miss Dunham had been collecting Stevengraphs in England for some years before she published her article, but things moved slowly in those days and it was not until 1937 that she was joined by a fellow eccentric, Mr Lewis Smith, who years later, in October 1965, was to become the founder and president of the Stevengraph Collectors' Association. Mr Smith had been given a horse-racing Stevengraph as a present, and shortly afterwards, whilst on his honeymoon in Nassau, found some more and was stimulated into carrying out some research, and in so doing came across Miss Dunham's article, corresponded with her, and eventually purchased her collection. He has since built up what is believed to be the finest collection of Stevengraphs in the world.

Another American collector during these early years was Mrs Wilma Sinclair Le Van Baker, who in 1957 published the first book devoted to Stevengraphs, entitled *The Silk Pictures of Thomas Stevens*. Her initial interest in Stevengraphs came about in typically serendipitous fashion when, having seen four of them on the walls of her married son's house, she shortly afterwards found four more in a shop at Cape Cod and bought them as a present for her daughter-in-law. However, as befits a mother-in-law, she decided not to give them away after all, but to keep them as the basis for her own collection.

An English collector, Mrs Therle Hughes, must have been active during this period, since her book *More Small Decorative Antiques*, published in 1962, devotes a chapter to Thomas Stevens, his silk-work pictures and his book-markers. In 1959 a small booklet, *Thomas Stevens and his Silk Ribbon Pictures,* by Alice Lynes, was published by the Coventry City Library. This reflected the local interest in the silk industry which has always been associated with Coventry, but at the same time it helped advance the durability of Stevengraphs and so paved the way for the presentation of the Stevens pattern books to the City Museum.

This is really all that is known concerning the activities of the eccentric Stevengraph collectors but throughout the 1950s, as Mr Godden points out, 'It is probable . . . that there were a few discerning people quietly collecting them for their decorative charm, although such buyers were in the minority and must have enjoyed ideal collecting conditions—availability of supply coupled with a low price brought about by a general lack of demand.'[13] This is a perfect description of the circumstances surrounding eccentric aesthetic valuations within the realm of rubbish. First, they are a small minority who, we can see with the benefit of hindsight, were 'discerning', though few would have used quite this adjective to describe their interest at the time. Secondly, they were collecting Stevengraphs 'quietly' and for their 'decorative charm', which indicates that their activities were not noticed and that they assessed their silk pictures in terms of aesthetic rather than economic value, as is only to be expected if there is no market and the rubbish category is covert. What is more, no great load of aesthetic value is imposed—the interest is pleasant and light-hearted—the objects are 'decorative' and 'charming' rather than 'beautiful' and 'awe-inspiring'. Thirdly, the ideal collecting conditions of availability of supply coupled with a general lack of demand describe a situation of no scarcity—a situation therefore which lies outside the terms of reference of modern economics. The system does not enter the realm of scarcity until 1960, but when it does the effects are spectacular.

To modify Oscar Wilde, every man destroys or makes durable the thing he loves, and this delightful period of low-key aesthetic values and the innocent enjoyment of decorative charm, and of an enterprise undarkened by Mammon's shadow, was not to last for ever. For, just as Gray's and Wordsworth's eulogizing of Grasmere's 'perfect Republic' where 'no flaring gentleman's house . . . breaks in upon

[13] Godden, op. cit. p. 27.

the repose of this . . . unsuspected paradise'[14] virtually guaranteed the construction of the gothic mansions of the Cotton Barons and the Toffee Magnates, so the harmless collecting, the fascinating research, and the labour-of-love publications of the Stevengraph-fanciers ensured the museum, the saleroom, and the hedge against inflation in the air-conditioned vault.

The astonishing rise in value of Stevengraphs from virtually zero in 1960 to eight guineas in 1963 and to over £100 by 1971 has already been described, as have several of the events which accompanied and gave impetus to this career. Most significant is the rapid development of the market, first by American dealers in the early sixties who placed advertisements for Stevengraphs in newspapers and magazines (also explaining how they should be packed for airmailing and that the frames were of no value and could be discarded), and later, in December 1967, the first sale at Knight, Frank and Rutley devoted entirely to Stevengraphs. Since then, the sales have become a regular monthly occurrence, many thousands of silks have been disposed of, and escalating prices have ensured many 'records'. For example:

March 1967	'The First Touch'	£52
April 1969	'The Mersey Tunnel Railway'	£220
1969	'Leda'	£290
Sept. 1969	'View of Blackpool'	£520

Such a rapid record-breaking sequence inevitably attracted the attention of the press, and the literature on Stevengraphs has been swollen by numerous articles, both in specialist magazines such as *The Antique Finder*, *Collector's Guide*, and *Country Life*, and in the heavier dailies and weeklies—the *Daily Telegraph*, *The Times*, and the *Sunday Times*.

Similarly, the amount of research and scholarship devoted to

---

[14] Wordsworth describes Grasmere as a 'perfect Republic of Shepherds and Agriculturalists' and goes on to quote approvingly from Gray's *Journal in the Lakes*:

'Not a single red tile, no flaring gentleman's house or garden wall breaks in upon the repose of this little unsuspected paradise; but all is peace, rusticity and happy poverty, in its neatest and most becoming attire.'

William Wordsworth, *A Guide Through the District of the Lakes*, 5th edn, reprinted 1926 (Oxford University Press, London), pp. 67 and 70.

woven silk pictures, the number of serious collectors, and the degree of organization amongst those who collect, have all mushroomed. Alongside the regular sales at Knight, Frank and Rutley and the emergence of the specialist dealers, there is the formation in 1965 of the Stevengraph Collectors' Association, and the publication in 1968 of the reference book *Stevengraphs* by Austin Sprake and Michael Darby and in 1971 of the amazingly detailed 500-page reference book *Stevengraphs* by Geoffrey A. Godden. In this book the scenic and portrait silks are dealt with fairly exhaustively but the direction of future research and development is indicated by those areas the treatment of which is as yet quite cursory. We can expect the publication of detailed monographs on such items as Stevens's book-markers, Grants (silks by a rival, less prolific, manufacturer), postcards, and silks by continental manufacturers.

It so happened that on the night the Coventry factory was destroyed in the air raid, Mr Henry James Stevens (the nephew of Thomas Stevens) took home with him one of the two pattern books kept at the factory. The factory was totally destroyed as were the houses on either side of Mr Stevens's home, and so, by a combination of remarkably lucky escapes, just one almost complete set of the unmounted silk pictures of Thomas Stevens has survived to the present day.

The existence of this collection, whilst invaluable as far as research was concerned, must have presented something of a threat to the health of the market, since it seems likely that if it were ever offered for sale and dispersed, it might have a depressing effect (such a depression has recently occurred in the market for English glass, following the sale of a superb collection). Such a depression is by no means certain: sometimes the dispersal of a particularly fine collection actually stimulates the market; but nevertheless, so long as there was a possibility of the Stevens pattern book coming on to the market there must have been some feelings of uncertainty and insecurity amongst collectors. However, after the death of Mr Stevens in August 1960, the pattern book was presented to the Coventry City Museum. This simultaneous removal from circulation for all time and increase in status conferred upon Stevengraphs by their relevation in a museum, removed any uncertainty which may have been nagging the more timid collectors and gave to the market a buoyancy which has easily survived two major dispersals: the Nicoll collection in October 1968 and the Austin Sprake collection in September 1969.

To generalize, we can say that the increasing economic value of objects, once they have entered the durable category, is accompanied by an increasing aesthetic value. Thus we should expect an increase in research and scholarship and in the learned publications resulting from these activities. Accompanying this, there should be an increase in interest and acquisitions among museums, either in the form of individual purchases or bequests. The exact form which these manifestations of increasing aesthetic value take will vary from item to item. For example, among buildings it is expressed first by inclusion on the Supplementary List, and then by promotion through the grades of historic buildings and perhaps, eventually, acquisition by the National Trust. Other, rather less desirable, indicators of this increasing economic and aesthetic value are the first reproduction,[15] the first fake, the first planned robbery, the first dealers' ring, and the first refusal of an export licence.

Now it may be that the history of Stevengraphs, though it provides a neat demonstration of rubbish theory, also serves to emphasize the essentially trivial nature of that theory. When all is said and done, Stevengraph-fancying, unlike, say, coal-mining, remains a pretty esoteric pursuit, and most people manage to get through life all right without even being aware of its existence. Yet it would be a mistake to take this tempting escape route back into the world of comfortingly familiar and seemingly more relevant concerns. For the fact is that world view is continually tested in the fire of social action. We act in many, often overlapping, situations and those areas of overlap enforce some degree of consistency between the different fragments of world view that we use to model these different situations. As a result, no specific instance is trivial and no one concern is more relevant than another; for there comes a point beyond which culture is indivisible.

The transfer of Stevengraphs to durability happened only a few years before the great upsurge of concern for women's rights. Could it be that the subtle cultural controls involved in this transfer of the

---

[15] In 1974 I bought a greetings card (world copyright, Parnassus Gallery) which reproduced (on paper and without the mount and its inscription) the early Stevengraph 'For Life or Death. Heroism on land', depicting a horse-drawn fire engine hastening to a burning house (Godden, p. 141).

Stevengraph were but one instance of what is now seen as an intolerable level of male domination? And could it be that the fact that these controls are now visible—the fact that I am now able to give some sort of description of them—means that they are no longer fully operative? For such controls to be successful, is it not essential that they remain invisible, that the cultural categories through which they operate appear to us all as natural and as unnoticeable as the air we breathe?

Though the evidence is far from conclusive, there does appear to be a shift from women to men as the Stevengraph goes from rubbish to durable. In the early days Stevengraph-collecting, like knitting, was largely a feminine occupation. The great names are Mary Dunham, Mrs Wilma Sinclair Le Van Baker, Mrs Therle Hughes, and Alice Lynes, but as the transition proceeds so Stevengraphs are transferred to male control. For instance, Mr Lewis Smith buys Mary Dunham's collection, the authoritative books are written by men, and the monthly sales at Knight, Frank and Rutley are in the capable hands of Mr J. E. Guy. It seems probable that women were excluded from durability by a double mechanism. Items controlled by women were transferred to the durable category by transferring control to men and, when this transfer of control did not occur, nor did the transfer from rubbish to durable. So much for petticoat power! Women have been excluded from durability just as they have been excluded from the Stock Exchange and from Great Art.[16]

---

[16] An example, linking women to journalism and transience (and, by implication, men to scholarship and durability), is provided by the words sung by that greatest of male chauvinists, Mick Jagger:
Who wants yesterday's newspaper:
Who wants yesterday's girl?

3 Rat-infested slum or glorious heritage?

Between 1966 and 1971 I was living in North London and working as a carpenter for a small (and now bankrupt) building firm. Like all my colleagues, I also 'did foreigners' (moonlighting—taking on other jobs, theoretically in one's spare time), installing a cast-iron grate and marble surround here, building a Georgian pipe-box to conceal the gas-fired central heating there. Essentially our work consisted of transforming dilapidated early-Victorian artisans' cottages into trendy residences for *Observer* journalists, and we were all piratically engaged in the early stages of a process that has since been christened 'gentrification'.

'Carpenter' is perhaps too grand a title for my activities as a wood-butcher which, appropriately, were very crudely dovetailed with the desultory pursuit of my Ph.D. at London University. And it was this Swiftian regime of wallowing in the ordure of blocked drains in the basements of Ripplevale Grove in the morning and contributing to seminars on cognitive economics at University College in the afternoon that led me to the realization that even so major a component of the economy as housing is subject to exactly the same social dynamics as are bakelite ashtrays.

The kinds of societies traditionally studied by anthropologists have little or no recorded history and this means that when, more recently, they have started to look at Western society, anthropologists have found it difficult to take account of the historical record: not surprisingly, since they operate within a set of techniques that has been evolved specially to cope with situations where such an historical record does not exist. This is something of a sore point with the historian whose traditional territory the anthropologist muscles in on in this way. Let me try to make amends (and bolster my argument) by at least starting off with an historical example: the Packington Street Affair.

The Packington Estate in Islington in North London consisted of one long street of early Victorian terraced houses called Packington Street and a number of smaller streets of similar houses which included one side of a large garden square—Union Square. The local council decided that this estate should be compulsorily purchased, demolished, and replaced by a complex of modern council flats. As usual, the interval between decision and implementation was lengthy and the houses suffered deterioration through 'planners' blight'. Even so, their condition was sufficiently good for a (largely middle-class) pressure group to oppose the demolition. They claimed that the houses were structurally sound, needing only modernization, bathrooms in the rear extensions, and so on, and that they were architecturally and environmentally valuable. The controversy raged and eventually reached the Housing Minister, who at that time was Mr Richard Crossman. He decided in favour of demolition. In his speech announcing this decision he said: 'These rat-infested slums must be demolished. Old terraced houses may have a certain snob-appeal to members of the middle class but they are not suitable accommodation for working-class tenants.'

From this amazing statement (he was a cabinet minister in a Labour Government) we can extract the Crossman definition of a slum, which runs something like this: 'An old building which, occupied by members of the middle class, forms part of our glorious heritage, is, if occupied by members of the working class, a rat-infested slum.' So Mr Crossman would have agreed with my thesis that slums are socially determined and that such physical, physiological, and economic considerations as poor living standards, lack of services and amenities, poor health, dampness, inadequate light, inadequate cooking facilities, overcrowding, high fire risk, whilst real enough are essentially the by-products of a concealed social process. They are the effects, not the cause.

A common-sense view of the nature of housing would be that, when new, a house had a certain expected life-span and a certain, quite high, value. As time went by the expected life-span would decrease and so would its economic value. When it reached its allotted span its value would be virtually zero, it would be demolished, replaced by a new house, and the process would start again.

A concealed social process operates behind this commonsensical façade. If we say that those houses with a finite expected life-span and decreasing economic value are in the *transient* category and those with zero expected life-span and zero value (excluding site and scrap value) are in the *rubbish* category, then we can see that there is a third category, the *durable* category, the members of which, flying in the face of common sense, have an ideally infinite expected life-span and increase in value over time: what the estate agent terms 'period houses', the buildings that constitute 'our glorious heritage'. The euphemistic terminology of the estate agent confirms the cultural nature of these categories. The transient houses are described as 'new' or 'contemporary' or 'post-war' and, if they happen to be terraced, they will be described as 'town houses' to avoid any polluting confusion with the rubbish houses which are optimistically described as 'older-type terraced houses'.

Economists, alas, are also a party to the commonsensical view of housing:

Houses are one of the most durable forms of capital. . . . As far as mere physical life is concerned, houses may last for generations, given reasonable maintenance. Admittedly they fall in public esteem, i.e. become obsolescent, sooner than this but even obsolescence takes place quite slowly.[1]

(There is, unfortunately, some confusion of terminology here, for which I must carry the blame. In describing housing as 'one of the most durable forms of capital' the economist does not mean that houses are in the *durable* category as I have defined it. He means that the value of houses decreases more slowly than that of most other things: that their expected life-spans are longer. But the economist puts all houses into my *transient* category and in so doing accepts the common-sense view in which there are only two categories, *transient* and *rubbish*. As a house transfers from the *transient* to the *rubbish* category so it passes out of the economist's field of vision, becoming valueless and so no longer possessing any sense of scarcity.)

The economist's assumption here is that the long expected life-span of a house derives from its intrinsic physical properties: the lastingness of bricks and mortar, tiles and plaster, timber and glass; and that its career (its gradual physical and social decline) is the natural outcome of fair wear and tear, of continual use and the ravages of the weather. This 'natural' gradual decline, so the argu-

---

[1] R. C. O. Matthews, *The Trade Cycle* (Nisbet, Cambridge, 1959), p. 101.

ment runs, is accompanied by, and may be slightly modified by, a parallel fall in public esteem, deriving from the effects of obsolescence and the vagaries of fashion.

The whole process and its interpretation all appears so obvious, so self-evident, that it may seem rather pedantic to go to such lengths to set it out here, but the whole of this common-sense account is based on the physical properties of houses and these, I wish to argue, are the by-products, not the determinants, of the process. Consequently the explanation must be stood on its head. It is not that the intrinsic properties of consumer durables naturally give rise to this familiar pattern of decline, but that those commodities which display this pattern of decline we (or rather, the economists amongst us) assign to the category 'consumer durable'. Further, this lastingness is imposed not by intrinsic physical properties but by the social system. An adequate theory of the economics of housing must be able to account for this social process of imposition; both the mechanisms that make it possible and the dynamic forces that cause it to change. I do not mean to imply that the natural properties of objects have *nothing* to do with this social process. Obviously, it is much easier to impose durability on a solid granite-faced Edwardian bank than on a thatched wattle-and-daub cottage, yet we frequently choose the more difficult alternative. Equally obvious is the corollary that any natural explanation for such a manifestly unnatural choice is bound to be inadequate.

First, the natural process of decline becomes a little less natural when we realize that the fact that buildings last for generations is dependent upon their receiving 'reasonable maintenance'. The amount of maintenance that is deemed reasonable is not a quantity deriving naturally from the intrinsic physical properties of the house and its environment. The level of maintenance that is deemed reasonable for a building is a function of its expected life-span and its expected life-span is a function of the cultural category to which that building at any moment is assigned, and, if its category membership changes, so will its expected life-span and its reasonable level of maintenance. For example, it is obvious, in view of the recent appeal for money and the vigorous public response to it, that most of us believe that £2,000,000 is a reasonable sum to expend on the maintenance of St. Paul's Cathedral, this being the amount required to prevent it from collapsing under its own weight. On the other hand, to expend an equivalent sum on a badly-bulged block of Victorian working-class dwellings in Limehouse would plainly be considered unreasonable. This is because the expected, or ideal, or hoped-for, life-span of St. Paul's is immense (at least a further 500 years) and perhaps infinite, whilst that of the slum tenement is a few years at the most. We might say that the 'natural' life-span of St. Paul's is being artificially prolonged, that of the slum tenement artificially curtailed. Both in the first instance were built to last. St Paul's Cathedral and the East End Industrial Dwellings are evidently in very different cultural categories and their expected life-spans and reasonable levels of maintenance vary accordingly. So the economist's argument remains reasonable as long as the expected life-spans of buildings change only in response to the march of time. If we find that their expected life-spans change in response to other factors, such as the socially induced transfers between cultural categories, then the economist's argument becomes fundamentally unreasonable.

Second, the decline in public esteem which normally is seen as a peripheral social accompaniment to the 'natural' process of decline of the house, is in fact a complex and partially independent process. And it looks as though the process of physical decline is not really a 'natural' process anyway, but is closely tied up with cultural categories and in particular with the expected life-span that we attribute to a building. In other words, the initial separation of natural and social factors is not valid. This decline in public esteem—that is, obsolescence —is commonly held to precede the natural physical decline of houses, but nevertheless is considered to proceed quite slowly. But is the rate of obsolescence a constant for any particular building or is it an independent or partially independent variable? To answer this we must enquire into just what obsolescence is. Obsolescence derives from the interrelation of the form of the building, which is largely fixed at the time of construction, and two influences which do change through time. One of these is technology and the other fashion.

For example, in the mid-eighteenth century, the owner of a new house in the City of London would find that his property gradually became obsolete in two ways. On the one hand his plumbing system discharging into a cesspit in his rear basement room, whilst perfectly adequate when the house was new, would gradually appear less and less attractive after the invention in 1779 of Alexander Cummings's patent water closet and in 1778 of Joseph Bramah's water valve-closet. And the longer it remained there the less attractive it would become. No matter how long he held on to his property he would never find it becoming more attractive, because it possessed such crude sanitation rather than a low-level bathroom suite with his-and-her bidets. That is, the march of technological evolution is irreversible and linear. By contrast he would find, to begin with, that the style of newer houses was in some ways rather different from that of his house and slowly these differences would become greater and greater. He would find public opinion swinging away from his style of house and rating the newer houses as altogether more fashionable. But, provided he and his heirs held on to their house (and assuming they staved off all attempts at compulsory purchase), they would eventually find that, rather than becoming less and less desirable, it was becoming more and more desirable—the style of his house had become fashionable once more. Thus the progress of fashion, whilst irreversible, is clearly not linear but cyclical.

The relative contributions to obsolescence of technological evolution and fashion may vary considerably; sometimes one is dominant, sometimes the other. But this balance is not reflected in the weight given to the two influences in scholarly commentary. The role of technological innovation features in every textbook on economics, but what of fashion? Well, that is best left to women's magazines. Fashion, being seen as frivolous, ephemeral, transient, and irrational, is not a fit subject for scholarly attention where what is prized is the serious, the persistent, the durable, and the rational.[2]

Serious thought has long been biased towards the utilitarian (for instance, the satisfaction of physiological and social needs in response to such universals as inclement weather and the threat of attack) and away from the question of fashion (for instance, the seemingly whim-like particularistic oscillations that elevate first one need then another, as shortlived as they are unpredictable, but essentially trivial in that they are seen as contained within the universal and eternal frame). Economics is no exception to this general rule; indeed it has produced one of the most explicit and persuasive formulations of it. What an awesome pit opens up in the hitherto firm

---

[2] Such a largely unquestioned assumption underlies the refusal, in the sixties, to grant the course in fashion at the Royal College of Art the degree status which was extended to all other courses.

terrain of understanding if we admit that perhaps all these years we have had things the wrong way round and that really, instead of examining the eternal and unchanging, we should have been studying the erratic flutterings of the butterfly of taste!

With this possibility in mind, let us take a garden square in an inner suburb of North London. The square is real enough but, to protect my sources, must remain unnamed. The date is 1965 and the square, though it still exists, is not now as it was then. All things are in flux, and when describing specifics one must always attach a time and place label. The generalities of the process, though, have a time-less and universal quality: there are other Innominate Squares in cities all the world over. When the houses in this square were new, they stood on the outskirts of the City, there were green fields visible from the rear windows and the majestic plane trees, for whose protection residents' associations are now organized, were tiny saplings. The square was part of a late Georgian and early Victorian suburb built by speculators in modest imitation of the earlier grand estates in central London such as Bedford Square and Belgravia. Sir John Summerson notes a certain decline in taste and competence about this period and that it was most marked in the 'remoter regions of Paddington, Chelsea, and Islington where a less prosperous class of tenant was anticipated'.[3] So these houses when new were moder-ately desirable, moderately expensive, designed for and occupied by moderately prosperous middle-class families: those in modest middle-management in the City or comfortable bureaucracy in Westminster, or perhaps fairly successful men of commerce, merchants, and large shopkeepers.

Over the next hundred or so years the houses in this square followed a career so familiar, not only in housing but throughout the entire range of what economists call consumer durables, that we accept it as part of the natural order of things. The houses declined, both in physi-cal terms and with reference to the social standing of their inhabitants to whom, over the years, they had been communicated. Consequently, it is rather difficult to imagine what a house in this square must have been like, both in physical and social terms, in 1840 when it was brand new and on the market for the first time. Obviously the structure, the paintwork, and so on would have been in excellent order, as would

[3] John Summerson, *Georgian London* (1945; Pelican edition 1962), p. 290.

the communal garden in the centre of the square. In social terms the house would probably have been seen then in much the same way as we now see a new 4/5-bedroomed Wates-built town house in a tasteful little development in Barnet, Chislehurst, or Carshalton Beeches. Over the next sixty years or so the house declined surprisingly rapidly. This was the heyday of the Industrial Revolution and the rate of technological change was extremely high. Yet it could well be argued that fashion played a more important role than technological change in bringing about this rapid decline. Islington had barely established itself as a desirable bourgeois suburb when the railways, main-line and suburban, totally invalidated the logic underlying its development. Admittedly, Barnsbury, Highbury, and Canonbury were served by the North London Line from Richmond to Broad Street, but the massive radiating network of lines that developed between 1838, when Euston was opened, and 1877, when the Holborn Viaduct was completed, meant that for the first time the moderately prosperous could work in London and live in the country (not that it remained country for long!). A spectacular change in fashion gave impetus to this migration: the rapid collapse of the classical tradition and its replacement by the various brands of Gothic, Elizabethan, and Venetian that characterized the Victorian era.

Almost overnight the Georgian house in Islington became unfashionable. The inhabitants fled, not so much because technological change had rendered inadequate the amenities of the houses, but in order to join their equals or betters in the optimistic new Victorian suburbs. Into the vacuum moved those on the next rung down the economic ladder. In these early years of decline Islington, along with Chelsea and St. John's Wood, exhibited a tarnished gentility and provided a favourite place for prosperous Victorian gentlemen to install their mistresses in pretty, but small and modestly priced, houses. But by the end of the nineties the area had descended past the naughty to the straightforward seedy and, eventually, the downright sordid.

And so the decline continued. In the period between the wars our Georgian house in a garden square, along with most houses in Islington, had become a multi-occupation tenement, each floor let as a single unit and, with luck, a cold tap and small lead-lined corner sink on each half-landing, and a single W.C. in the rear extension on the ground floor. Rents seldom exceeded five shillings per week per floor and the legislation provided by the various Rent Acts merely exacerbated the existing situation and trend. Landlords either could not afford, or saw no point in, maintaining their properties and this attitude was reflected and justified by the market value of the houses, which was extraordinarily low. One of the most spectacular examples concerns a four-storey house occupied by a winkle-stall-holder and her husband. Just after the Second World War they were offered their house, free, by the landlord. They refused to accept it. The house still stands and has changed hands several times since (but not for nothing). Evidently the life-span expected of the houses both by landlords and tenants was very short. Many of these houses did indeed attain their allotted span and were demolished and replaced by remarkably well-built blocks of workers' flats in a monolithic Queen Anne style, but the turn of events—the war and its subsequent years of austerity—imposed a long-protracted senility on the remainder, with the result that many, including the houses in our square, are still there today.

Externally they show most of the signs of long-term neglect: bulged brickwork due to failure to repoint, peeling or non-existent paintwork, decayed stucco, which in some cases has been removed (and not replaced) in response to a Dangerous Structures Order, cracked front steps, window sashes propped with short lengths of timber after the sash-cords have broken, slates cracked and missing, and, frequently, roofs waterproofed with hessian and bitumen—a cheap alternative to reslating. The railings around the basement area are rusty, often the elegant cast iron pineapples surmounting the corner posts have disappeared, the top-rail has rusted away from the post and is only held in place by a few turns of wire or insulating tape, and some of the uprights, having worked loose, have been appropriated as spears for long-forgotten gang-fights and replaced by odd lengths of redundant gas pipe. The front doors are often unpainted with a clear long triangular gap at the head—the result of distortion of the opening during settlement. But sometimes the tenant has modernized his front door by flushing it with hardboard in which case it displays a rusty chromium-plated letter-plate-cum-knocker made of pressed steel and a collection of assorted plastic bell pushes. The front area is usually decorated with a large number of dustbins (one for each occupation unit), and scooters and mopeds under waterproof covers. The door number is often simply crudely painted on in large figures and an end-of-terrace house will usually have its return elevation decorated with graffiti.

But, what is this! Here in the middle of all these uniformly dilapidated houses is one, immaculately painted, Thames Green with orange front door complete with six fielded panels, brass dolphin knocker and huge brass letter-plate to match. The leaded fanlight has been painstakingly repaired and, affixed to the brickwork at the side of the door, is a blue-and-white enamel number plate: a little touch of provincial France proclaiming that the owner drinks Hirondelle Vin Ordinaire with his Quiche Lorraine for his dinner and not Light Ale with his ham-and-egg pie for his tea. The cast iron balconies to the first floor windows are gay with geraniums and painted shiny black. Likewise the front railing, through which is visible, thanks to the enormously enlarged basement window (which has, not closed white net curtains, but a fully-retracted navy blue blind), the basement kitchen. Directly under the window is a two-bowl twin-drainer stainless steel sink with mixer taps and waste disposal unit. On each side it is flanked by formica-topped Wrighton units and the walls are clad with similar cupboards and clear-polyurethane-sealed knotty-pine matching. We catch a glimpse of a stuffed pike in a bow-fronted glass case fixed to the chimney breast, and below this, the space left by the now obsolete fire-place opening has been cunningly utilized as a mini wine cellar and is filled by a metal and beechwood bottle-rack. The dividing wall has been knocked through, an RSJ (Rolled Steel Joist, known in the trade as 'Irish Jays') inserted and clad in the ubiquitous knotty-pine, and so the heather-brown hexagonal quarry-tile floor extends in one unbroken sweep from the kitchen sink, through the rear dining area to the hardwood sill of the large french windows which open to the patio, paved with Staffordshire blue bricks, and the garden beyond. We cannot help but notice the pine farmhouse table from Heal's, the bright red bentwood chairs from Habitat, some large gilt letters in a bold type salvaged from a Victorian grocer's shop front, and a row of large blue jars with ground glass tops, similarly salvaged from an archaic chemist's and bearing in gold lettering the abbreviated names of assorted poisons. And so I could go on: every feature, every lick of paint, once one has learned the language, a clear statement proclaiming the presence of a frontier middle class.

This decoding of the environment, as well as providing a malicious parlour game, is now the orthodox concern of structural anthropology. When applied to housing it is particularly rewarding, for people cram an awful lot of carefully encoded information into their houses and its patterning reveals quite clearly that houses, like other communicable things such as motor cars, Stevengraphs, and ashtrays, are assigned to one or other of the cultural categories: transient, rubbish, and durable.

No great sociological insights are involved in pointing out that houses in the transient category tend to be inhabited by a sector of our society that is much concerned with respectability. From the viewpoint of those who do not live in them, the inhabitants of transient houses are the dull and plodding members of the lower middle class or upper working class. Houses in the durable category would seem to be the preserve of the more exalted middle class and of the remnants of the upper class: professional men, captains of industry, large landowners and the like. The rubbish houses tend to be inhabited by what is left: the lower end of the working class, perhaps criminal, shifting, or immigrant; and then those who exist on the margins of society: the non-coping families, the mentally ill and so on.

A neat self-perpetuating system we might think: the cultural categorization of the houses exactly matching the socio-economic divisions within the society. But to propose such a self-perpetuating system, though intellectually seductive, is to ignore the empirical data and to avoid asking the one really interesting question, which is: how can such a seemingly self-perpetuating system ever change itself? For houses sometimes transfer from one cultural category to another, and people sometimes move up or down the socio-economic ladder. Worse still, cultural categories sometimes cease to exist, and the socio-economic ladder sometimes extends itself or retracts itself as if it belonged to a fire brigade. In the later nineteen-sixties the inner suburbs of North London provided a ready-made laboratory for the study of this question, for these transfers virtually filled the social and physical arenas: there was hardly any self-perpetuation left in the system; almost all was change.

The interesting feature of this category system is that membership is not fixed for all time but is to some greater or lesser extent flexible. A member of the transient category can, and usually does, gradually transfer to the rubbish category and a member of the rubbish category can, under certain conditions, transfer to the durable category. The other transfers that would complete the diagram do not happen. So, dynamically:

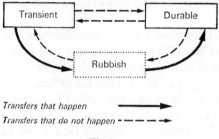

Fig.5

This then is the dynamic system of cognitive categories, and the problem now is to enquire how this cultural system can be related to the social order in such a way as to recognize that they are closely tied to one another yet, at the same time, are not in general mutually reinforcing and self-perpetuating. The arrows on the diagram, indicating those transfers that happen and those that do not, provide an obvious clue to the identity of the third and missing element between cultural and social order: control.

No great or revolutionary insights are involved in the realization that those who own and control durable objects enjoy more power and prestige than those who live entirely in a world of transience or, worse still, a world of rubbish. Similarly, when we look at examples of successful transfers of objects from rubbish to durability we see that, at the same time, their ownership is transferred from the rag-and-bone man to the knowledgeable collector, from the junk-shop window to the Bond Street showroom, from Steptoe and Son to Bevis Hillier *et al.* (ownership, of course, is just one kind of control).

The degree of control over the transfers between categories can vary widely and rapidly. Not even Mr Crossman could stem the innovative tide of the early sixties that transformed many square miles of inner London from rat-infested slum into glorious heritage—the phenomenon now known as 'gentrification'. In many ways 'gentrification' is an unfortunate term; for those young couples—actors, graphic designers, architects, art-school teachers, and television executives—who formed the vanguard of the frontier middle class were, we can now see with the benefit of hindsight, forceful and successful social climbers who competed (on very unequal terms) with the indigenous inhabitants of those run-down areas who, alas, had no access to durability. Something no gentleman would do (or need to do!).

Those much-satirized trendies, crashing through social barriers with the same insensitive arrogance that they knocked through the dividing walls of their terraced Georgian houses, believed themselves to be the harbingers of that egalitarian millennium where we would all end up like David Frost—classless and close-cropped, successful and suited by Cecil Gee. In the grey economic light of the nineteen-seventies, we see them consolidating their social gains with Volvo estate cars, the country life, and private schools.

At the risk of being accused of upper-class English romanticism of the worst kind, of preaching cultural separatism, and of advocating a return to Edwardian social distinctions, I will simply state that in the mid-sixties Innominate Square, Islington, was unstably inhabited by two groups so distinct in culture, in attitudes, in behaviour, and in world view as to constitute two separate tribes. This is not to say that they would always remain separate: that there would be no inter-marriage, no trade-offs between the groups as they readjusted their values in the light of their inevitable interactions. 'Interaction'—that optimistically egalitarian catchword of the ideologically committed sociologist—is ill-suited to describe the sort of social intercourse between these tribes who, living in different cognitive worlds, had to share the same cramped physical one. 'Head-on collision' would be more appropriate. And trade-offs there indeed have been. One now cannot predict, by decoding the exterior of a house, the social identity of the occupants with anything like the accuracy that was possible only ten years ago. Distinguished baroque harpsichordists and first-generation Turkish kebab-house owners now live behind identical and adjoining façades. And old terraced houses—carefully restored on the outside and thoroughly rehabilitated inside—are now, *pace* Mr Crossman, regarded as suitable accommodation for members of both the middle *and* working classes.

The two tribes are 'the Knockers-Through' and 'the Ron-and-Cliffs'. The Knockers-Through, immortalized by Alan Bennett, are often considered to be synonymous with the frontier middle class.

This is not quite correct. The Knockers-Through constitute only a part of the frontier middle class and there are many others, such as those who engage in meticulous but low-key restoration. However, there can be no doubt that the Knockers-Through, in their strident patronizing of their indigenous neighbours (if there are any left) and their crushing insensitivity to the cognitive boundary fences of those who still persist in distinguishing between public and private, personal and impersonal, are by far the most prominent members of their class. What is more, they are surprisingly long-lived and even in the mid-seventies the diligent anthropologist could still occasionally experience the thrill of overhearing the classic remarks: 'We're knocking-through, you know' and 'Yes, we were the first people to come and live here.'

But one can be too hard on these courageous and creative pioneers. Only ten or fifteen years after the event, architectural students to whom I teach Urban Sociology will tell me that the Knockers-Through did it for the money. This is not so: they did it for love, and from a Dr Johnson-like commitment to London; and they did it against considerable odds. This tiny band who, with little money and much faith, began restoring rubbish houses in the late fifties and early sixties were ridiculed by the staid and established members of the middle class who regarded Hampstead, Highgate, and Golders Green as the only habitable atolls in the North London Sea of Plebs. Their attitude was reflected by bank managers, estate agents, mortgage-brokers, building societies and borough architects (not surprisingly, since they are one and the same!), and so, as anyone who has ever attempted to buy a house will appreciate, a massive economic barricade was erected to keep the rubbish out: out of the durable category, that is.

Their indigenous working-class neighbours were equally unsympathetic, but for different reasons. Their response was that, in buying and doing up a rubbish house, the frontiersman was throwing good money after bad: 'They're all coming down, them houses' was their endless refrain. These are the Ron-and-Cliffs: proud, competitive, working class, frequently self-employed, villainous, anti-union, racially-prejudiced, Conservative-voting inhabitants of rubbish or near-rubbish houses.

The origin of this not very scientific nomenclature is almost lost in the mists of unrecorded time—but not quite. The originators were two printer friends of mine who in the mid-sixties had a factory near Euston Station. The derivation is rooted in interminable archetypal conversations in the local pub, between young men with razor-cut hair dressed in Fred Perry shirts, fawn cable-knit cardigans with leather buttons, and large boots, which were always of the following type:

'Hey Ron! What you doing tonight?'
'Well Cliff, I thought I'd go down the boozer/do an oil change on the Consul/take the bird out down the West End.'
(aside) 'I'm sorry mate, did I spill your beer?'
'Sorry Ron. What was you saying?'
'Well Cliff . . .'

The Knockers-Through and the staid established members of the middle class are united by a world view that clearly includes, and places a high value upon, the durable category, and are divided only as to what shall be included in that category. The Knocker-Through wants to get his rubbish house in: the bank manager wants to keep it out. The Ron-and-Cliff has no access to durability: he is committed to a world in which there is only transience and rubbish. In consequence he can see no future except demolition for the house he has to live in.

This is a profound cultural difference which, once recognized, allows us to make sense both of the divergent behaviour of the Knocker-Through and the Ron-and-Cliff when faced with the same situation, and of the contradictory encodings that they make of their environment. And nowhere is this contradictory encoding more marked than in the Knocker-Through's and the Ron-and-Cliff's treatments of the front door—that secular icon of urban life.

The Knocker-Through makes his early Victorian house older by fitting a six-panelled Georgian front door with exact reproduction brass door furniture from Beardmore's and painting it either a classic dull colour such as Adam Gold or Thames Green or, better still, black or white. His Ron-and-Cliff neighbour makes his house younger by flushing the original four-panelled door with hardboard, fitting pressed steel or brushed aluminium door furniture such as one would find on a modern private estate and in the local hardware shop, and painting it in a contemporary bright colour such as Canary Yellow or Capri Blue. The Knocker-Through, having access to durability, is trying, successfully as it turns out, to push his house from the rubbish to the durable category. His neighbour, living in a world of transience, is trying, rather unsuccessfully, to prevent his house from sliding further down the slippery slope from the transient to the rubbish category.

The egalitarianism of a world bereft of durables can be, and in this case is, spectacularly competitive. Along with the flushed front doors go plastic flowers, nylon net curtains, highly polished motors, and the whole well-scrubbed, sharply-dressed, cigar-smoking, fiver-waving, round-buyer bravado of the Saturday night 'dahn the boozer'. The whole business of 'putting on the style'—the devotion to sport, often expensive sports like power-boat racing, duck-shooting, or trout or shark-fishing; the gambling; the leather coats, Silver-Cross prams and elaborate hair-dos of their wives; the conspicuous consumption of drink, tobacco, sea-foods, and mohair suitings beloved by street-traders, crash-repair specialists, offset lithographers, asphalters, and self-employed central-heating engineers, carpenters, and ornamental plasterers—all serves to define an aristocracy of transience, piratically scornful of those who put their trust in durables, and viciously exclusive of social rubbish. Their motto is 'easy come easy go', for in the Land of Transience, the man with the highest turnover rules, OK? The Ron-and-Cliff stands in the same relationship to our society as the Bedouin of the Euphrates Delta does to the rest of Iran. 'The Bedouin should gain his living by the sword. All his values are those of a warrior society, in which the two dominant themes are courage and generosity. By displaying courage in war and so obtaining plunder he gains his livelihood. Through generosity he disposes of what he owns. To be mean implies a want of confidence in one's ability to gain more plunder.'[4]

The secondhand car dealer whose ageing Ford Consuls filled the front garden of a rubbish house I once considered buying was pessimistic: 'All coming down, you know. All Darkies and Bubbles in them houses. Diabolical state. Cook chickens with the insides still in them. The way some people live—fucking disgusting.'

The Knocker-Through and the Ron-and-Cliff, though their behaviour is widely divergent, are both perfectly rational in terms of their differing relations to the transient to rubbish to durable transfers.

---

[4] S. M. Salim, *Marsh-dwellers of the Euphrates Delta* (London, 1962), p. 140.

That is, the category system furnishes each of them with a different set of rules. But what about the despised social rubbish—the Darkies and the Bubbles (rhyming slang—bubble and squeak: Greek)? They don't seem to know about the rules at all. The Greek Cypriots, in particular, are much addicted to metal-frame windows and to brick façades painted pink with all the mortar laboriously picked out in pale blue. As the transfers to durability gain momentum so Conservation Areas are designated and legislation is now contemplated forcibly to prevent the Bubble from going to this enormous trouble to knock thousands of pounds off the market value of his house. This would seem to be the thin end of a very nasty wedge. For the thick end of this attack on rubbish is the gas-oven and the elimination of those who have no place within the system. If there is one thing worse than someone painting the front of his Regency villa pink and blue, it is stopping him from painting it pink and blue.

I would claim that the foregoing treatment of housing in general and of the problem of slums in particular has taken us a long way from the more familiar position set out within the collective conventional wisdom of urban planners, educationists, and anti-poverty campaigners. But whither has it taken us? And, in view of the present vexed, intractable, and serious problems that are involved, what are the implications of this shift of position? Like all journeys, it is easier to tell how far one has travelled than to discover where exactly one has ended up. The distance can be measured in three ways.

First, the conventional approach assumes that objects have the qualities that they have as a result of their inherent physical properties—that these qualities are, as it were, a 'given': a part of nature. The present approach avoids this assumption, and, whilst not denying that there *are* certain natural limits, replaces it with the notion of the social malleability of objects—the idea that objects have the qualities that they have as the result of a social process of endowment. It follows that the same forces that confer these qualities may, in changed social circumstances, withdraw them. Society giveth and society taketh away; and, in the act of giving and taking away, society is itself changed.

Second, the conventional approach, like most serious thought, does not pay much heed to rubbish. The attitude is that rubbish housing unfortunately exists, that this is a bad thing, that something should be done about it, that it constitutes a problem to be solved. Just as household rubbish presents a problem that is solved by refuse collection and disposal, so the first solution that comes to mind is slum clearance—a once-and-for-all round by the housing ash-cart, that becomes instead a permanent and expensive social service. Having (by treating the symptoms and not the cause) failed to cure the disease, these urban doctors conclude that the disease is incurable and that it can only be arrested by regular and massive injections of cash. The present approach sees rubbish housing not in the first instance as a public health problem but as a crucial integral part of the system. Slums are social in origin but physical in manifestation. As the social nexus varies so does the physical manifestation: sometimes almost vestigial, sometimes so widespread as to become a 'problem'. And this is the trouble with the conventional wisdom relating to the slum: it suffers from the narrowness of all problem-oriented research. The great landscape gardener, Lancelot Brown, when confronted with a client's estate, did not say 'what is your problem?', he asked 'what are the capabilities of this piece of land?' Optimism, generality, and scope flowed where otherwise all would have been pessimism, specificity, and narrowness. That is what is wrong with the conventional wisdom: not enough Capability Browns and too many Problematical Toms, Dicks, and Harrys.

Third, since the conventional approach ignores the social malleability of objects, it is led away from the sort of investigations that would confirm and illuminate this malleability. The present approach places great emphasis on cognitive frameworks and in particular on *discontinuities* between cognitive frameworks. This means that where there are cultural boundaries within a society, their existence is recognized and taken into account. The conventional approach tends to ignore cultural boundaries; this approach is focused upon them.

For example, Gillian Tindall[5] has shown how the way the inhabitants of a street in Kentish Town see that street varies spectacularly with the social context of the inhabitants. The indigenous working-class inhabitants see it as on the way down because immigrants have moved in and the Knockers-Through sit with their curtains open and wash their dirty dishes at the front window. The Knockers-Through, on the other hand, committed to their restored frontages

[5] Gillian Tindall, 'A Street in London', *New Society*, No. 433, 1971.

and leafy patios, see it as on the up-and-up. Significantly, she does not notice that she fails to describe how the immigrants see the street.

Now these different street-views may coexist peacefully enough in the back garden but they are inevitably in conflict in the market place. There is only one market, and either it will confirm the view that the street is on the way down (in which case houses in the street will sell for less and less money as time goes by) or it will confirm the view that the street is on the up-and-up (in which case houses will sell for more and more money as time goes by). So, in the market place, one street-view will win and the others will lose. Why is it that, in this case, the Knockers-Through win and the Ron-and-Cliffs, the Bubbles, and the Darkies lose? What sort of control mechanism lies behind this real-life Midas touch: the power to make things durable?

The different world views of the Knockers-Through, the Ron-and-Cliffs, and the Darkies and Bubbles correlate to widely differing patterns of investment and of sociability, which in turn reveal striking differences in control over time and space. These differences are so marked as to define three largely autonomous cultures: a middle-class culture based upon durability which secures an extensive control over time and space, a culture of transience with a proportionally higher investment in social relationships but with much less extensive control over time and space, and a culture of poverty with a pathetic portfolio of investments and very little control over either time or space.

For instance, what very different world views and what very different, yet equally realistic, expectations of events in time and space are embodied in the Curzon family motto: 'Curzon hold what Curzon held', and in the ever-present fear of those struggling to leave the lower orders: 'clogs to clogs in three generations'. In other words, what I am suggesting is that the power to make things durable is a function of the relative extents of this control over time and space, and that control over time and space is secured by gaining control over knowledge. That is, it is not just physical objects but also ideas, historical facts, and systems of knowledge that are subject to social malleability. Stevengraphs and houses are only the physical tip of a huge conceptual iceberg.

An anecdote may help to clarify this point. The Ron-and-Cliff, like the Euphrates Bedouin, not only maximizes turnover but must be seen to maximize turnover by constantly reaffirming his relationships through generosity. Pay night (we were always paid in the pub) was a veritable potlatch of round-buying (often £5 and in recent years as much as £15 for a single round). What is more, one could not just quietly slip the money to the barmaid and ask her to give everyone a drink, it had to be the highly ritualized performance befitting an urban warrior: first empty one's own glass whilst everyone else's is still half-full, then shout for the ex-boxing champion landlord and, with him in attendance, address all one's friends and acquaintances one by one, even if they are in the other bar ('Hey, Alf! What you drinking? Light Ale! Have a scotch.')

Another example of turnover maximization was a 'foreigner', which two of us undertook and which involved installing a mid-Victorian cast-iron grate and marble surround in the drawing-room of a Regency house belonging to an executive of a large company. The grate and surround were, in fact, from my own house (where they had been removed to make room for a kitchen) but we spun an elaborate and convincing tale about having had to buy them out of a Regency house that was being converted and so had to pass on what at the time we thought was an exorbitant price. The fireplace was quickly, but neatly, installed and we retired to the pub with our £30, well pleased with our Ron-and-Cliff piracy and at having exploited the Knocker-Through owner by convincing him that a mid-Victorian fireplace was really a Regency one.

A few weeks later, while we were doing some more work in the same house, the owner proudly showed the drawing-room to a friend who exclaimed: 'Oh, isn't that splendid. Whatever you do you *must* keep that marvellous fireplace.' At that moment I realized that we were the exploited ones. The fact that we knew that the fireplace had just been installed and was of the wrong period was irrelevant, for all that matters is that those who exert the widest overall control over time and space believe it to be original. Already the value of the house had risen by very much more than £30. Credibility, not truth, is the name of this game.

It is tempting but unwise to rush ahead and try to discover what practical implications flow from this acknowledgement of cultural boundaries and of their role in shaping our urban environment. For instance, take the dynamic phenomena of class apartheid and ghetto formation. The interaction of the rules derived from the

c

category system and the fixity of houses (the fact that domestic buildings, Mongolian yurts and some timber-frame houses apart, are indissolubly linked to the ground on which they stand) gives rise to the curious process, running counter to the second law of thermodynamics, whereby a completely random, disordered, mixed-up residential arrangement gradually moves towards a structured, orderly, crystallized arrangement of rich and poor ghettos. If we accept the present fairly widely held view that class apartheid is a bad thing and that something should be done about it, then the first thing to do is to stop all local authority projects which are virtually uniclass—for example, many new towns, huge council estates, and high-rise blocks. Further, local authorities could take a positive approach to the probem of class apartheid by using their powers to mix up continually the crystallizing process—I suggest moving Pentonville Jail to Belgravia; a fruit and veg, secondhand clothes, and junk street market in Bond Street; a transport café and lorry park in place of the proposed new hotels in the Cromwell Road; and the moving of the Bank of England to the Isle of Dogs. The ludicrous nature of these proposals indicates that these extreme procedures are probably impossible. That is, they would be trying vainly to impose flexibility upon buildings and areas that currently form part of the region of fixed assumptions. The problems of class apartheid would be nothing compared to the social problems of a world with no fixed assumptions. It is rather like suggesting beheading as a cure for migraine. Even so, more modest proposals along the same lines should prove quite feasible and, indeed, are now happening, though more from economic necessity than from free choice. We would be well advised to make a virtue of necessity and to welcome the British Museum Library in the Somers Town coal depot and the council-renovated house in the owner-occupied Georgian terrace.

Another warning against leaping too eagerly to practical conclusions, as a result of the recognition that slumminess is imposed by the social system, is contained in the extreme and contradictory policies that can result. On the one hand, the argument can run like this: that slums are socially determined; that slumminess is in the eye of the beholder; that the social system imposes slumminess on certain areas of the urban and social environment in order to maintain the *status quo*. On this argument, the slum is an instrument of oppression and the slum-dweller who accepts the judgement of non-slum-dwellers and shares *their* disgust with *his* living conditions is possessed of false consciousness and is actively conniving at his own exploitation. Rubbish theory thus provides the starting point for a revolutionary course of consciousness-raising: 'you have nothing to lose but your slums'.

On the other hand, one can argue like this: rubbish is an integral and extremely important part of the category system, and in particular the existence of the rubbish category, together with the possibility of the transfer from rubbish to durable, permits the social mobility which relates our social system to changing technology and other macro-forces. This means that we cannot get rid of slums within the framework of our present social system since our present social system is the cause of the slums. So, if we wish to keep the present social system (more or less) we must accept slums (in one form or another), must realize that they will always be there and that they are a functional component of the system. So this approach supports the argument which claims that every city should have its Skid Row, its East End, its Soho, in so far as it demonstrates that we cannot get rid of this rubbish without a revolutionary change in society.

There is clearly something too simplistic about a model that ends up uniting the conservatives and the radicals (who agree on the cultural boundaries and their location within society and disagree only as to whether they are a good or a bad thing) against the liberals (who try to pretend that the boundaries are not there).[6]

This simplistic model depicts nothing other than the invalid self-perpetuating system which represents the three largely autonomous cultures of the Knockers-Through, the Ron-and-Cliffs, and the Darkies and the Bubbles as persisting unchanged in their essentials (their relative control over time and space). Instead of rushing to wild problem-oriented conclusions, it would be more sensible for those who make decisions (supposedly) on our behalf to try to find

[6] Post-mortems on the poverty programmes in the United States during the sixties chronicle in detail the problems that await any social programme based solely upon the middle-class world view and a complete disregard for the boundaries between sub-cultures (particularly scathing is Daniel P. Moynihan, *Maximum Feasible Misunderstanding*). The programmes in the seventies that emphasize bi-culturalism and minority rights will probably reveal the different problems that arise from having too much regard for the same boundaries.

out why, in general, these cultures do not persist unchanged. They should enquire how these boundaries may shift one way or another, become more pronounced or more blurred. They should try to understand how the transactions across these boundaries, which are inevitable given that the bearers of the different cultures are members of the same society and inhabit the same physical universe, may sometimes bring about the convergence of the world views that they separate, and may sometimes add fuel to their divergence.

To enable them to do this we must look at the social control of knowledge: we must generalize the argument from Stevengraphs and houses to ideas. In doing this we come up against the great philosophical divide between idealists and dialectical materialists. I will argue that what holds for objects also holds for ideas. Ideas, I agree, are ideally free and unconstrained but in reality they must always be generated within a social context and so will inevitably be constrained by control mechanisms. To those idealists who criticize Marx for unjustifiably putting economics, that is things, before ideas, I would reply that Marx should not be saying that things are prior to ideas but that ideas are things.

4 From things to ideas

I just love history: it's . . . it's so old.' *American lady tourist.*

We all know that our beliefs and the way we see and understand the world influence our actions. We do something because we believe it to be right and we do not do something else because we believe it to be wrong. In other circumstances, we do something because we expect that the results will be to our advantage and we refrain from doing something else because we expect that the results will be to our disadvantage.

So we can say that, inside our heads, in our thoughts, and in our language, we carry a more or less coherent model of the world—a world view—a way of making sense of our environment, social and physical. We also have a more or less coherent set of moral injunctions: our idea, not of how the world is, but of how it should be. But, as well as believing, we also act. When we act we are part of the world and, indeed, are actually changing the world: so we have a world view within our minds whilst our bodies form a small part of that world. We can speak of world view and of action and we can enquire how, if at all, they relate one to the other.

This is clearly a most fundamental distinction and within sociology and social anthropology it receives recognition in a variety of contrasts: for example, those between category and action, between values and behaviour, between culture and society. Consequently, it may surprise the person who is neither a sociologist nor a social anthropologist to learn that the question as to the nature of the relationship between world view and action remains unresolved, and it may even shock him to learn that most practitioners of these disciplines are either unaware of this fact, unconcerned about it, or erroneously believe it to be already resolved.

The trouble is that these various distinctions, by the form in which they are drawn, prejudge the issue. The basic assumption is either that one's world view determines one's actions or that one's actions determine one's world view; and the analyses and theoretic elabora-

tions must start from one or other of these positions. The choice between these alternative viewpoints is determined, sometimes by the
nature of the problem to be investigated, more often by personal
temperament and inclination, and as a result the protagonists of
these two views find themselves forced either into acrimonious conflict or into a studied ignorance of one another's existence. But
sometimes, especially in the area referred to as 'grand theory'
wherein these questions are dealt with in a more formal and explicit
way, there occurs the more sophisticated response that *both* of these
viewpoints are valid, that world view can be analysed on its own and
that social action can be analysed on its own. Now if world view and
action were, in fact, entirely independent of one another this would
be the end of the matter. But they are not independent of one
another, they are related, and to the extent that they are related they
are not independent. To the extent that they are related these two
viewpoints are contradictory: one maintains that world view is prior
to action, the other that the reverse is true.

The presumptions implicit in the views of category theorists, of
action theorists, and of grand theorists, that world view is prior to
action or *vice versa* and that these views are either contradictory or
complementary, rule out of court any questions of degree: about
the extent to which they are complementary and the extent to which
they are contradictory; about the regions within which one is valid
and the regions within which the other is valid. More important, these
prescriptions rule out of court any chance of talking about the
shifts, both gradual and sudden, that may, and in fact do, occur
between these regions.

The comforting and deeply-ingrained habit of thought, based on
the clear initial separation of the concepts of category and of action,
is our inheritance in the philosophical line established by Descartes.
The heirs to this tradition, like landed gentry, feel both a great
honour and a great responsibility. They ask for nothing more than
the privilege of cherishing this vast estate and the satisfaction of
passing on the land to the next generation in even better heart than
when they themselves received it: what more *could* one ask for? But,
of course, philosophical traditions, like great country houses, can
become white elephants and this, despite its great achievements in the
past, would seem to be the present status of cartesianism.

Within grand theory this cartesian habit of thought gives rise to a pair of mutually contradictory answers to the question: 'How is society possible?' One of the answers states that within any particular society there is general agreement among the members as to the valuations that are placed on things, people, and ideas: that is, there is *consensus* as to what is relevant and what is irrelevant and there is general agreement as to the evaluations to be placed upon that which is held to be relevant. In those areas where, for some reason or other, consensus is lacking or poorly developed, the process of social life is envisaged as operating in such a way as to minimize contradiction and confusion, thereby working towards consensus. The other answer states that the essential condition for the functioning of society is the *lack of consensus* and the continual and widespread disagreement both as to what is relevant and what is irrelevant and as to the evaluations to be placed upon whatever it is that the members variously consider to be relevant.

The first answer leads to the concept of culture as a sort of rule book common to all the members of the society, a collection of shared habits everywhere and always constraining and channelling their actions, their behaviour. The second answer leads to the discarding of culture as a useful concept by a sort of *reductio ad absurdum* that insists that the only level at which it could apply is that of the individual; that there are, as it were, as many cultures in relation to any society as there are members of that society.

The consensus answer results in the isolation of culture as a very powerful concept—the limiting framework within which the actions of the members of the society, as individuals or as groups, must be contained. In this sense, the assumption of consensus makes the cognitive categories of individuals prior to their actions. In contrast, the assumption of a lack of consensus entails the rejection of this priority. Beliefs and actions are still related but there is no basis for deciding which are prior. Each may be seen as the reflection of the other, but, whilst the cognitive categories are assigned to the hermetic level of mind, the behaviour which they reflect is seen as occurring in the real world and as subject to all the natural constraints that characterize it. On this view, mental structures are anchored only to one another whilst actions are firmly rooted in reality. For all practical purposes, action becomes prior to category.

Once any specific analysis is under weigh this clear distinction between category and action is soon obscured by fieldwork data and detailed exposition and it is often difficult (both for writer and reader) to discover which answer is being given. The same convenient obscurity allows the supposedly eclectic answer that both points of view are valid. On this argument society is possible only if consensus is both present and absent; a common theoretical position that is wholly invalidated by the fact that, since the two answers are contradictory in every respect, they cannot both be true.

The examples of the Stevengraphs and of North London houses are remarkable in so far as they reject both these answers and the possibility of their combination. For instance, if the first answer was correct there could be no transfer between the cultural categories 'transient' and 'durable'. If the second answer was correct there could be no areas of fixed assumptions since the region of flexibility would have to extend to the entire system. If the combination of these answers was correct the transfers would be possible but the categories non-existent whilst at the same time the categories would exist but the transfers between them would be impossible.

Perhaps the most impressive piece of cartesian estate improvement this century has been the massive formalization and rigorous elaboration of category theory to form what is virtually a complete new discipline: semiology.

In the classic theory of information the process whereby information is transmitted is divided into five sequential stages. First there is a source, then there is an encoder which processes the source into a form suitable for transmission through, for example, the telephone wires which constitute the third stage. The last two stages simply reverse the first two stages and when they are completed the information will have been transferred.

Information theory provides a method for optimizing the encoding of the source. For example, if we take a very simple source producing, let us say:

ABBABABBABABBB . . .

this can be encoded by simply using two 'bits', one for A and the other for B. But, looking more closely at the source, we see that A is never followed by another A and so we can make a considerable economy by allowing one bit to encode not just A but AB. Clearly, as the source becomes more complex so the optimization that information theory can make will become more valuable.

Semiology from this point of view would appear to be a way of obtaining a very much more accurate and detailed model of what is, in terms of information theory, an extremely complex source— natural language or culture. In general a model of the source can be built up in two ways. First, if the source is fully determined, as for example in the case of artificial languages (such as those used in computer science and artificial intelligence) or the arrangement of DNA molecules, then we can state the constraints which define it. That is, we can model the source with foresight. Second, if the source is not fully determined we can only model it by reference to its own history. That is, we can model the source only in hindsight. For example, if the source producing ABBABABBABABBB . . . is fully determined we can say that A will never be followed by A, and we can point to the deterministic mechanism which ensures this. But if the source is not fully determined then all we can say is that *up till now* an A has not been followed by another A.

Now culture is without doubt a source of this second type. It is demonstrably never fully determined and it is therefore a source that can be modelled only in hindsight. A consequence of such modelling of the source is that it is impossible to distinguish something which can *never* happen from something which has not happened *yet*.

If we take the case of the source producing ABBABABBABABBB . . . , which has been efficiently encoded via semiology so that one bit encodes AB, then what happens when, for the first time in history, A *is* followed by A? This enormously significant piece of information is discarded as 'noise'. That is, semiology cannot distinguish change from noise.

At this point, of course, the semiologist will say: 'Quite so, but we never said it could!' Indeed, it is often cited as the great distinguishing feature of structuralism that it rejects causation and diachrony and embraces interrelation and synchrony.[1] For instance, this separation of time and space, the one going to history the other to anthropology, is an explicit assumption in Lévi-Strauss's structuralism: 'One of them unfurls the range of human society in time, the other in space.'[2]

---

[1] I should apologize for using these disgracefully trendy (but useful) words. Synchrony just means all at once, diachrony one thing after another.

[2] Claude Lévi-Strauss, *The Savage Mind* (Weidenfeld & Nicolson, London, 1966), p. 256.

What I wish to argue is that the objection I have raised, that semiology provides a static model of a source which is never static, is not trivial and that the conventional response of the semiologist, that he is not concerned with such changes in the rules but simply with the rules, implies that he is not concerned with anything at all, for the class of phenomena with which semiology cannot cope includes all those phenomena to which it addresses itself.[3]

That said, I wait anxiously for the heavens to open and for the impact of the thunderbolt that will strike me dead. It does not happen; so perhaps a worse fate awaits me: the blackballing, for committing a social gaffe beside which the ordering of grouse out of season pales into insignificance, of my application to join the anthropological club. For it would appear that I have asked the question which all the members of the club have tacitly agreed should never be asked: I have questioned the good lie on which the club is founded. But, in mitigation, I would plead that this good lie has not always been the common bond uniting the members of this club, and that, not too many years ago, some members did indeed ask this question. What is more, this questioning did not take place in some dark corner but in the clear daylight illuminating that classic area of anthropological enquiry concerning societies that use as their main organizing principle an institution known as the segmentary lineage.[4]

The direction of social anthropology over the last forty or so years and, in particular, the development of structuralism have been largely determined by the continuing efforts to resolve the problems raised by these societies which, as a consequence of this curious organizational principle, are sometimes classified as 'acephalous societies', that is, tribes without rulers. These were, in part, practical problems concerning administration in the colonial context since, for instance, it is difficult to implement the policy of indirect rule if one cannot find any chiefs or headmen through whom to rule indirectly. However, the fieldwork and the resultant ethnographies and theore-

---

[3] This is something of an over-simplification. Structuralists do concern themselves with certain sorts of (rule-bound) change. For a more complete treatment of the reasons for rejecting structuralism, see Chapter 7.

[4] Inevitably, within the space of a single chapter, I can give only the sketchiest illustration. My present aim is not a full delineation (which would be a massive undertaking) but merely an outline sufficient to allow the argument to proceed.

tical writings, though financed and supported by colonial considerations, far transcend the ephemeral conditions within which they developed. Britain may have lost her empire but anthropology still has its lineage theory.

There are two definitive characteristics of segmentary lineage systems. First, descent is reckoned through one parent at each generational level. Generally it is the male line that is chosen but there is no reason why it cannot be the female or various combinations, such as male but with the occasional convenient female being regarded as a male. The essential feature is that at each level descent is reckoned through only one parent. This mode of reckoning results in a framework which is really a taxonomy in reverse. The great complexity of the living population is rendered orderly by apportioning them to pigeon-holes labelled with the names of their unique ancestor-at-one-remove and these are then ordered according to the unique ancestor-at-two-removes, and so on, until finally a single apical ancestor is reached. The height and span of this framework will depend upon the size of the population and the average number of children per ancestor.

The logical priority of the bottom of this pyramid over its point must be emphasized, since many factors combine to predispose us to see it the other way around. For instance, the direction of the biological process whereby parents produce children who in turn produce grandchildren runs from the top downwards and the chronological sequence from top to bottom further induces the misconception that the tip is causally prior to the base. Such a lineage framework, whilst it undoubtedly contains some history and may well be believed by those whom it embraces to be their history, is not so much a history as an element in a world view concerned with imposing order upon and making manageable the vast chaotic diversity of human distribution (the framework generally relates to geographical as well as sociological space). Such orderliness and manageability can only be achieved at considerable historical cost: the consigning to oblivion of all those ancestors through whom descent is not reckoned.

This distinction between (unattainable) total history and (attainable) world-view history has been emphasized by Lévi-Strauss.

... the historian and the agent of history choose, sever and carve them [historical facts] up, for a truly total history would confront them with chaos. .... Insofar as history aspires to meaning, it is doomed to select regions, periods, groups of men and individuals in these groups and to make them stand out as discontinuous figures, against a continuity barely good enough to be used as a backdrop. A truly total history would cancel itself out—its product would be nought. .... History is therefore never history, but history-for.[5]

But having made the distinction Lévi-Strauss uses it for the wrong purpose—to depose the special prestige which he holds philosophers accord to history, 'as if diachrony were to establish a kind of intelligibility not merely superior to that provided by synchrony, but above all, more specifically human'.[6] In its place he proposes a symmetry and complementarity between history and anthropology: one unfurling the range of human societies in time, the other in space. But this carve-up between time and space, the one going to history, the other to anthropology, though it provides the justification for Lévi-Strauss's structuralism does not in any way follow from his distinction between 'history' and 'history-for'.

'History-for' is the only sort of history we can have and, since histories and the agents of history must select, sever, and carve-up, we should go on to enquire why some histories should be led to select, sever, and carve-up in one way and others in another way, and then we should go on to enquire into how sometimes one and sometimes another of these 'histories-for' gains credibility. That is, the creation of 'history-for' is a political activity, it is one particular form of knowledge that is shaped by the social forces that influence acceptance and rejection.

These social forces are brought into play by the second defining characteristic of segmentary lineage systems: what is called 'segmental opposition and balance'. If, for example, two men become involved in a dispute, each will mobilize his supporters by reference to the lineage framework, first of all his close relatives, then those connected to him via more remote ancestors, until he comes at last to those whose linkage to him is marginally longer than their linkage to his opponent. In this way two segments are mobilized, their size being a function of the genealogical distance between the two disputants: if they are closely related the two segments will be small

[5] Lévi-Strauss, op. cit. p. 257.
[6] Ibid. p. 256.

family groups; if they are very distantly related the whole population may split in two; if one is from another tribe altogether the entire people will be mobilized. Once the dispute is resolved the two segments are demobilized and dissolve back into the whole. For this kind of arrangement for resolving disputes to retain general support it is essential that the mobilized segments are fairly evenly matched. There is little point in mobilizing segments if they are so unbalanced that the result is a foregone conclusion.

A system conforming to these two requirements, reckoning descent through a unique ancestor at each generational level and maintaining the segmental balance and opposition, appears logically to be impossible. First, the framework would grow ever larger as the generations progressed, becoming increasingly unwieldy. Second, the inevitable fortunes and misfortunes, ecological and social, will continually upset the balance between the segments. Consequently, demographic changes, changes in settlement pattern, conflict with neighbouring peoples, epidemics and the like, will in aggregate cause some segments to grow enormously whilst others atrophy, and so, whilst they may still be opposed, they will no longer be balanced.

In practice, however, this does not happen. The framework remains of fairly constant length (for example, about 15 generations for the Tiv, 12 for the Kuma in New Guinea, 9 for the Nuer[7]) and the segments remain balanced. This happens in the following way.

First of all, in non-literate societies it is difficult to remember much history. There are no written records to consult and so plenty of opportunity for argument as to just which ancestor is where. If a body of historical data, such as a lineage framework, is continually increasing in size then it will ultimately attain a maximal size where the rate of input equals the rate of output: that is, when the rate of remembering equals the rate of forgetting. When written records are introduced, as for instance in Southern China,[8] the equilibrium will be upset and the body of data will continue to grow, segments will be less easily balanced and the functional significance of the lineage

---

[7] Laura Bohannan, 'A Genealogical Charter', *Africa*, Vol. 22, No. 1, 1952; Laura and Paul Bohannan, *The Tiv of Central Nigeria* (1969); Marie Reay, *The Kuma: Freedom and Conformity in the New Guinea Highlands* (Melbourne University Press, 1959); E. E. Evans-Pritchard, *The Nuer* (Oxford, 1940).

[8] M. Freedman, *Lineage Organization in South-eastern China* (Monographs on Social Anthropology, No. 18. Athlone Press, London, 1958).

system is likely to decline. On the other hand the size of the body of data may be stabilized long before this limit is reached by the intervention of other institutions. For example, in Bali the institution of teknonymy (the practice of naming parents after their children, e.g. 'William's Daddy') makes it practically impossible to extend the lineage framework beyond the range of the living (and so permits the operation of village councils which otherwise would have to operate in conflict with lineage loyalties).[9]

Secondly, all members of the society will produce a lineage framework to describe their society and their own place within it but no two such frameworks will exactly match. People will tend to remember only that part of the framework which seems relevant to themselves and thus these individually constructed genealogies will usually contain considerable lacunae. When they are compared with one another there will be some mis-matches both in the detail of the remembered parts and in the distribution of the lacunae.

Thirdly, the manipulation of this uncertainty and disagreement constitutes the politics of such a society and this continual process restructures the framework so as always to re-establish the balance of opposing segments. (Presumably this is because, out of the various possible restructurings, the one that comes closest to balancing the segments that it has the potential to mobilize is the one that is likely to gain the support of the greatest number of 'voters'.)

But not all of the framework can be restructured; not all of it lies within the political realm. Taking, as an example, a society where the lineage framework is uncomplicated by written records or the presence of modifying institutions (the Tiv or the Kuma are admirable in this respect), the system can be conveniently represented in diagrammatic form (see Fig. 6 opposite).

Since new generations are continually being added at the base of the pyramid whilst its depth remains fairly constant, telescoping must be happening somewhere. There are certain regions of the framework, however, where telescoping cannot happen. The Tiv themselves say, 'a man has three fathers', by which they mean three ancestors of whom they have personal remembrance. (Every Tiv man must have, in total, the fifteen fathers through whom he traces his descent

[9] Hildred and Clifford Geertz, 'Teknonymy in Bali: Parenthood, age-grading and genealogical amnesia', *Journal of the Royal Anthropological Institute*, Vol. 94, Part II, 1964.

from Tiv himself. This natural limiting of human memory, incidentally, is of much the same time-span as must elapse before literature
and the historical record become fit subjects for university study
and before an artefact becomes an antique.) Clearly, telescoping is
impossible, or at least very difficult, within this region of the lineage
framework.

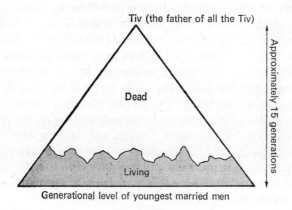

Tiv (the father of all the Tiv)

Dead

Living

Approximately 15 generations

Generational level of youngest married men

Fig.6

Similarly those ancestors at and near the top of the framework
must be immutable (unless there were a massive upheaval within the
society) for, whilst the Tiv man's three fathers constitute his 'real'
history, Tiv, his sons and his grandsons constitute the mythical
history of the entire people, and their positions and relations to one
another are unambiguously defined in the myths and general oral
literature of the society. Thus it is in the mid-ground between these
two regions that the 'bulge' occurs and ancestors begin to pile up
just at the moment when the living population's memory of their
exact position is beginning to become rather hazy. It is here that Tiv
politics are located as those with the requisite knowledge and rhetoric
are able to restructure the framework so that it may more closely
accord with the situation they are trying to bring about, and in the
process many a son becomes a brother to his father and many more,
since they happen not to form the focus of any segment within the
living population, are propelled into oblivion.

A neat example of this political arranging and rearranging of ancestors can be seen in the current fluid state of the history of the English landscape garden, and this example also serves to demonstrate how historians, unlike anthropologists, do try to investigate the social forces that shape and reshape knowledge. The generally accepted ancestry was authoritatively stated at the time by Horace Walpole as running in a direct continuous professional line, from Capability Brown to Humphry Repton to William Kent, representing a steady progression towards the picturesque. Recently a garden historian, George Clarke,[10] has questioned this orthodoxy. He points out that Walpole, being a Whig, was particularly disposed to see history as a smooth and steady progression and, in support of this contention, he quotes Butterfield: 'It is part and parcel of the Whig interpretation of history that it studies the past with reference to the present. . . . Historical personages can easily and irresistibly be classed into the men who furthered progress and the men who tried to hinder it.' Clarke, taking presumably a Tory view of history, convincingly argues for a more discontinuous, largely amateur, sequence involving Hoare and Cobden (the professionals' clients) that plays havoc with the idea of progress.

That is, historians, like Tiv orators, rearrange ancestors for political ends and, what is more, they are well aware that this is what they are doing and that this is what history is about. As the history of gardening crystallizes, which of these disputable ancestors will become indisputable and which will be expelled into oblivion or, at the most, receive a passing mention in a footnote?

This telescoping is sometimes referred to as 'structural amnesia'[11] and we can visualize it as a process in which a curtain of amnesia continually falls to remain in line with the fathers' fathers' fathers of the youngest married men. If the equilibrium is broken by the introduction of written records, then the curtain gradually recedes until clearly remembered or unambiguously recorded history invades myth itself. If the equilibrium is broken by the intervention of other

---

[10] George Clarke, 'William Kent, Heresy in Stowe's Elysium' in Peter Willis (ed.), *Furor Hortensis: Essays on the History of the English Landscape Garden in Memory of H. F. Clarke* (Elysium Press Ltd., Edinburgh, 1974).

[11] J. A. Barnes, *Politics in a Changing Society: A Political History of the Fort Jameson Nguni* (Manchester, 1967).

institutions, then the curtain may descend, as for instance in Bali where it falls almost to the present day.

Thus politics—the art of the possible—are confined to the mid-ground and, whilst they continually restructure the framework, their restructurings are themselves contained between the tip and base of the framework where no such restructurings are possible. So ancestors in this mid-ground are equivocal whilst ancestors at either extremity are unequivocal. Yet these regions are quite fortuitously balanced, the boundaries between them are not permanently fixed. Ancestors may, and usually do, get transferred across them and certain changes such as the advent of writing or of teknonymy may, by their effect on these transfers, drastically alter the positions, or even the existence, of these boundaries. Expressed diagrammatically, the system looks like this:

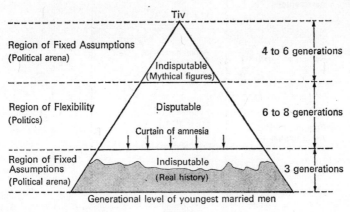

Fig.7

The argument from things to ideas may be conveniently and economically summarized by setting this diagram beside the earlier one appropriate to physical objects (see Fig. 8 on page 70).

This parallel between ancestors and Stevengraphs, between ideas and things, is drawn at a rather abstract level. The parallel is located not in the detailed mechanisms to which they are subject, for these inevitably vary considerably, but in the common pattern that results from these different mechanisms: the regions of flexibility and of fixed assumptions and, more important, the relation between these regions.

One common cartesian approach is to identify these regions and then, having clearly separated them by using the notion of frame and framed, develop the appropriate specialist analyses in terms of such distinctions as 'arena' and 'politics', 'field' and 'political process', or simply 'macro' and 'micro'. Such an approach, since it takes as its starting point the conceptual separation of the regions of flexibility and fixed assumptions, can say nothing about the extent to which they are not separate, that is, about the transmissions between one region and the other and about changes in the position and clarity of the boundary between these regions that result from such transmissions. Such an approach may be termed 'static'.

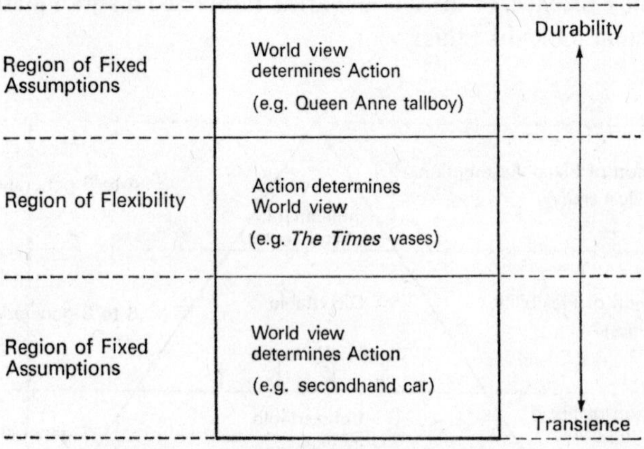

Region of Fixed Assumptions	World view determines Action (e.g. Queen Anne tallboy)	Durability ↑
Region of Flexibility	Action determines World view (e.g. *The Times* vases)	
Region of Fixed Assumptions	World view determines Action (e.g. secondhand car)	Transience ↓

Fig.8

For example, in a recent book subtitled *A social anthropology of politics* Bailey[12] says: 'No statesman is effective unless he knows the rules of attack and defence in the political ring.' Thus frame and framed (the Queensberry rules of politics and the practice of the noble art of politics) are identified and clearly separated, and the method of analysis follows automatically: 'Only after we understand the rules can we start evaluating the behaviour', and 'our business . . . is to distinguish between effective and ineffective tactics.' Such an approach would be fine if the rules of the game were never changed

[12] F. G. Bailey, *Stratagems and Spoils: A social anthropology of politics* (Blackwell, Oxford, 1969).

by being broken, but of course they sometimes are. And Bailey, unable to cope with this, will be led to evaluate as 'ineffective' (since it broke the rules) Ellis's tactic of picking up the ball which, since it founded the game of Rugby Football, was probably *the* most effective tactic ever adopted on the football field.

By contrast, the approach advocated here, whilst it accepts the distinction between the regions of flexibility and fixed assumptions, does not assume that they are completely separate. Indeed, it particularly focuses on the relation between these regions, on the manner in which transmissions are effected, and on the resultant boundary shifts, blurrings, and sharpenings. Ultimately it is concerned with the limits of such boundary changes, that is, with how such systems may come into and pass out of existence. Let us call this approach 'dynamic'.

If we take a particular small-scale dispute involving two segments, the relationship between which is, however, not *entirely* certain, then the mediating ancestor will be very close to the curtain of amnesia. If it turns out that, in the interests of segmental balance, this ancestor should become the brother of his father (views as to the relationship between these two being contradictory and uncertain anyway) then the dispute will be resolved by doing this (that is, by redefining the relationship between the segments). When the dispute has been resolved the segments are demobilized and dissolve back into the whole, but, at the same time, this whole will have been slightly but definitely changed as a result of the political process that occurred within its framework, for the mediating ancestor is now quite definitely on the other side of the boundary between the region of fixed assumptions and the region of flexibility; and that which hitherto was impossible is now possible. (That is, an ancestor's status has moved from the political arena into the politics that it contains and both in consequence are slightly but definitely altered.)

Within this continual process such segments do not have a permanent existence but emerge only in response to some event. The relationship between 'real' tangible segment (substance) and 'unreal' intangible lineage framework (structure) poses a nice philosophical problem which, in its general form, had been dealt with by Whitehead long before acephalous societies ever came to the attention of anthropologists. The segmentary lineage framework (the world view) would be in Whitehead's terminology an 'eternal object' in that it constitutes a 'possibility for an actuality'. The mobilized segments are that actuality. Thus, in response to certain stimuli, segments are formed, interact, and then dissolve, and as such constitute ephemeral actualities, but the lineage framework itself goes on seemingly for ever. It constitutes, as it were, the rule book which specifies the entire range of possible actualities. But this is not the end of the matter. Rule-book and possible moves, eternal object and actuality, are not entirely insulated from one another, nor are they mutually irreducible in the manner of the programme and the throughput of a computer. The two are related by what Whitehead calls the eternal objects' 'mode of ingression' into the actuality (as for example can be seen in the resolution of the dispute between segments just described).

Whitehead's 'mode of ingression' is the crucial linking concept between his 'eternal object' and his 'actuality'. If it were absent and we had just the eternal object and the actuality then we would be back at the cartesian position:

Eternal objects are . . . in their nature abstract. By 'abstract' I mean what an eternal object is in itself—that is to say, its essence—is comprehensible without reference to some one particular experience. To be abstract is to transcend the particular occasion of actual happening. But to transcend an actual occasion does not mean being disconnected from it. On the contrary, I hold that each eternal object has its own proper connection with each such occasion which I term its mode of ingression into that occasion.

Thus the metaphysical status of an eternal object is that of a possibility for an actuality. Every actual occasion is defined as to its character by how those possibilities are actualised for that occasion.[13]

Whitehead's philosophy in terms of the eternal object, the actuality, and the mode of ingression of the former into the latter, was developed in relation to physics and mathematics, but should be of general validity. Unfortunately, it is not easily grasped. Even Bertrand Russell, who had worked with Whitehead, confessed that he is 'often very obscure and difficult to read' though he hastens to add that 'to say that a book is difficult is not in itself a criticism'.[14] He goes on to summarize Whitehead's metaphysics in the following way:

[13] Alfred N. Whitehead, *Science and the Modern World* (Macmillan, New York, 1926), pp. 228 ff.

[14] Bertrand Russell, *The Wisdom of the West* (Macdonald, London, 1959), p. 297.

... to grasp the world we must not follow the tradition of Galileo and Descartes, which divides the real into primary and secondary qualities. On this path we merely reach a picture distorted by rationalist categories. The world much rather consists of an infinite collection of full-blooded events, each of which seems to be somewhat reminiscent of a Leibnizian monad. However, unlike monads, events are momentary and die away to give rise to new events. These events somehow happen to objects. Sets of events might be thought of as a Heraclitean flux, and objects as Parmenidean Spheres. Separately they are, of course, abstractions; in actual processes both are inseparably connected.[15]

It is worth pausing, whilst at this high level of generality, to survey the now clearly visible wood before descending again into the specific empirical trees that normally obscure it from view. Three features need to be discerned: the eternal object, the actuality, and the mode of ingression of the former into the latter. Most curiously, contemporary thought appears to assume that there are only two features in the wood: the eternal object and the actuality. For instance, the anthropologist's static notions of 'category' and 'action', the former denoting the possibilities for behaviour, the latter the behaviour itself, is of this type and we will search in vain for the third feature, the mode of ingression of category into action, for the slavish devotion to cartesian dualism ensures that it is always assigned to one side or other of the dichotomy and its existence continually denied.

If its existence is admitted, and if the wood is seen as composed not of two features but of three, the consequences for cartesian sociology are certainly profound and probably fatal. There can be no peaceful co-existence between the two-feature view and the three-feature view since the development of the latter requires us to focus attention upon the mode of ingression, that is, upon the very feature the denial of which is a necessary condition for cartesian vision.

In relation to the segmentary lineage system, it is possible to see the eternal object, the lineage framework, as the rule-book, and the actualities, the mobilizing and demobilizing of opposed segments, as the moves in the game. Alternatively, the eternal object constitutes the political arena and the actualities the politics themselves. If the reality of the mode of ingression is recognized then it is clear that eternal object and actuality are not always fully insulated and mutually

[15] Ibid. p. 297.

irreducible and that in the course of the ingression the two must become, to a greater or lesser extent, merged and indistinguishable. Thus it is possible (but not certain) that there will be some interchange between the two: that certain actualities that hitherto were impossible will become possible (for instance, a pair of hitherto inflexible *Times* vases may become flexible or an unequivocal Tiv ancestor may become equivocal) and that other actualities that previously were possible will cease to be possible (for instance, a pair of hitherto flexible *Times* vases may become inflexible or an equivocal Tiv ancestor may become unequivocal). That is, the boundary enclosing the region within which *The Times*' advice—'it's not what you say, it's the way that you say it'— is valid, is not fixed. Nor can we assume a balance between input and output with the loss of some possibilities being balanced by the acquisition of new ones so that the eternal object, whilst still eternal, is continually transformed. We must expect that in certain circumstances possibilities may continually increase (the erosion of frame by framed) and that in other circumstances possibilities may continually be eliminated (the extension of frame at the expense of framed). The former will lead to politics with no arena, the latter to an arena with no politics. The cartesian viewpoint would still remain valid, however, if these possible changes in the eternal object due to its mode of ingression into the actuality did not in fact occur, but it is an easy task to show that they do: a task that I feel has already been adequately performed by reference to Stevengraphs, houses, and ancestors.

There are consequences also for Whitehead's terminology and his 'eternal object' turns out to be something of a misnomer. By focusing on the mode of ingression we are able to consider how the entire wood may come into existence, change, and go out of existence. In talking about politics with no arena and arenas with no politics we are talking, paradoxically, about the birth and death of eternal objects.

This in turn begins to blur the pristine distinction between the eternal object and the actuality. We cannot rule out the possibility that an eternal object may be *truly* eternal (what is sometimes called a 'cultural universal') but to know that some at least are born and eventually die leads us to enquire into their life-spans. This in turn leads to the realization that eternal objects may be ranged along a scale from those with immensely long life-spans involving the possibility for an astronomical number of actualities to those with quite short life-spans encompassing the possibility for only a very few actualities. At the limit there is an eternal object so short-lived that it contains the possibility of only two actualities and beyond that comes the eternal object containing the possibility of only one actuality, which, of course, is not an eternal object at all but simply an actuality or else nothing at all, depending upon whether the possibility happens or not.

The grinding poverty of cartesianism is now clear. Surrounded by all this richness involving the birth and death of systems, the immense variations of their life-spans, and the scale which relates the eternal object and the actuality, it can cope only with the one special case, the 'truly eternal object', where the life-span happens to be infinite: a special case, moreover, which quite possibly does not even occur.

Unfortunately, those of little faith may, in view of the evident mortality of the eternal object, be feeling that the same is true of Whitehead's metaphysics. This, I feel, is not the case. The objections indicate, not that Whitehead's philosophy has broken down, but that it has not been developed far enough.

When I asked a colleague to read an early version of this chapter it returned with the pencilled comment: 'Too Sybilline, Talmudic— Buddhist even'. This I took to be an unlooked-for compliment: a hint that I was on the right lines after all. To a generation weaned on Hermann Hesse's story *Siddharta* with its central image of The Great River, the prospect of a rigorous elaboration of Heraclitus' statement, 'we step and do not step into the same river: we are and are not', is powerfully attractive. Turning to Russell's miniature exegesis of Whitehead I found that: 'As for genuine contact with the real this seems to require a knowing from within, a conflation of the knower and his object into a single entity.'[16] Whitehead, when in later life he transferred his professional focus from mathematics to philosophy, may have moved bodily westwards from England to America, but spiritually he appears to have travelled in the opposite direction.

Whitehead's ideas were taken up by two men who were contemporaries at Oxford: the anthropologist Evans-Pritchard and the philosopher and historian Collingwood. Evans-Pritchard's classic

[16] Ibid.

monograph *The Nuer* is the first application of these ideas in socio-logy, and is now recognized as one of the original sources of the structuralist approach; but for many years its significance was obscured by a resurgence of the empiricism that is never far from the surface of British intellectual life.

At the same time, Collingwood[17] was isolated and neglected as the tide of interest turned towards Wittgenstein and the elaboration of 'Oxford philosophy'. In this way an enormously attractive and promising line of enquiry was lost and is only now, thirty or more years later, being painfully rediscovered.

Collingwood takes Whitehead's position and shows that it must be contained within an historical frame: '. . . natural science as a form of thought exists and always has existed in a context of history, and depends on historical thought for its existence . . . no one can understand natural science unless he understands history: and no one can answer the question what nature is unless he knows what history is. This is a question which . . . Whitehead [has] not asked.'[18]

Similarly, Evans-Pritchard[19] maintained that anthropology must ultimately be contained by history. This can be seen as simply the restatement of Whitehead as modified by Collingwood: that specific case relevant to anthropology of a general philosophical position.

But is this the end of the matter? What about the other possibility: what if history is contained by sociology? Can we not also argue that historical thought must always take place within a social frame? If we accept this then no one can answer the question what is history unless he knows what society is. This is the question Collingwood has not asked! This is the question I am asking and it leads to an enquiry, not into social phenomena, but into the possibility of social phenomena. Such a framework contains history, for history consists of that subset of possible phenomena that have actually happened.

[17] See the rather bitter R. G. Collingwood, *An Autobiography* (Penguin, 1944).
[18] R. G. Collingwood, *The Idea of Nature* (Clarendon Press, Oxford, 1945), p. 177.
[19] E. E. Evans-Pritchard, *Anthropology and History* (Manchester, 1961).

5 A dynamic theory of rubbish

The general form of the argument can now be given quite precise expression. The basic idea is that physical objects have certain important properties imposed on them as a result of the processes of human social life, and, conversely, that if these properties were not conferred upon them then human social life itself would not be possible. Since people are physical objects, they too are subject to the same process. Nor does it stop here. Ideas, since they must always be generated and communicated in a social context, are also constrained so as to become, to a somewhat variable extent, thing-like. I will now use the word 'object' to refer, not just to physical objects (including people), but to ideas as well.

The fact that objects are socially processed in this way means that, once we ourselves have become socialized, we can no longer see objects in their raw and unprocessed state. This human faculty of perceiving not the raw but the socially processed object is called 'cognition': seeing plus knowing. Since all knowledge must involve knowing, any argument that claims access to raw objects must be suspect. The term 'cosmic exile'[1] has been coined to describe a person who makes such a claim. The fact that objects are processed in a systematic way means that they must become ordered in some way. This means that we can speak not just of cognition (the consequence of the social processing of objects) but of a 'cognitive framework' (the consequence of a systematic component in that process). Rubbish theory is concerned to say something about the relationship between the 'raw', whatever that might be, and the various kinds of 'processed'.

In the examples of Stevengraphs, of houses, and of ancestors, the

[1] W. V. O. Quine, *Word and Object* (MIT, Cambridge, Mass., 1960), p. 275. When people do play the cosmic exile, and claim to have access to raw objects, they are simply insisting that their socially processed objects are better than other people's: that their cognition is true and that of others is false.

systematic component in the social processing orders objects in such a way that they fall either into a region of fixed assumptions or into a region of flexibility. Objects in a region of fixed assumptions are unequivocal, those in a region of flexibility are equivocal. This state of affairs can be represented diagrammatically like this:

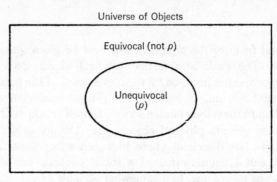

Fig.9

Since it can be shown that some objects which were once equivocal are now unequivocal and that others which were once unequivocal are now equivocal, the boundary between these two areas cannot be closed. That is, the system is not static. There must be some possible transfers and some mechanisms by means of which these transfers are effected. In, for example, the case of the durable and transient categories these mechanisms develop in the unseen region between the raw and the processed: between the universe of objects and the cognitive framework that results from our systematic processing of that universe—the durable and transient categories. In the Venn diagram (Fig. 9) above, p and not-p exhaust the universe of objects. That is, there is nothing that is neither p nor not-p. Because, not being cosmic exiles, we must always operate within a cognitive framework, we tend mistakenly to assume that the same is true of the transient and durable categories. In fact, the appropriate diagram must involve a further class of objects that are neither p nor not-p. The full picture requires three areas: two representing the cognitive framework and the third that which the cognitive framework holds does not exist. The outline of this full picture may be represented diagrammatically like this:

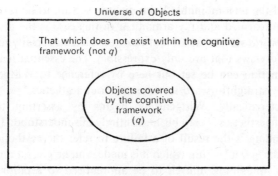

Fig.10

Now the cognitive framework q is simply the first Venn diagram (Fig. 9) and it would seem that the full picture will be obtained by combining Fig. 9 and Fig. 10. Such a combination is impossible, and I would suggest that it is the fundamental contradiction involved in making this combination that makes society possible. This contradiction may be expressed in its most generalized and abstract form as a set of irreducible equations expressing the combination of these two Venn diagrams:

p + not p = unity   (Fig. 9)
q + not q = unity   (Fig. 10)
p + not p = q < unity   (Fig. 9 + Fig. 10)

From this position it is now possible to revise the tentative and inadequate definition of rubbish advanced in the initial hypothesis. The task of defining rubbish is beset with hideous pitfalls. The problem can be put like this:

If rubbish resides in the gap between any cognitive framework of the universe and the universe, how, since we must always operate within a cognitive framework, can we ever see it?

Alternatively, if we can see it, it must be within our cognitive framework, in which case it cannot be outside it which is where it is supposed to be if it is rubbish.

This is the all-too-common fallacy of the earth-bound observer playing the cosmic exile by falsely claiming to have taken up a position outside of any cognitive scheme—claiming, in other words, to have combined the uncombinable Venn diagrams. Still, to be forewarned is to be forearmed and my armament in this case is the distinction between world views that are both expressible and socially realizable and world views that are only expressible. The essential features of this distinction can be set out here by reference to Wittgenstein's admirably straightforward statements about aesthetics.[2]

Characteristically, Wittgenstein begins by asserting that the subject of aesthetics is very big and entirely misunderstood. This misunderstanding is the result of a failure to refer the aesthetic judgement to the 'game' within which it is made, and he gives a number of examples. Imagining himself to be apprenticed to a tailor, he describes the way in which he is drilled into the rules. He talks of developing a feeling for the rules, of interpreting the rules, of rejecting anything that is not right—that is, is not according to the rules. Here aesthetic judgements—whether something is right or wrong—are determined by the rules, and if he hadn't learnt the rules he wouldn't be able to make the aesthetic judgements. He then contrasts the tailor's aesthetic game with the 'tremendous' things in art. The tailor's game is still appropriate in certain styles of architecture where, for example, you appreciate the 'correctness' of a door. 'But in the case of a Gothic cathedral, what we do is not at all to find it correct. Here there is no question of *degree*. The entire *game* is different.'[3] He then moves outside the confines of European culture and puts himself in the position of someone studying a foreign tribe and trying to learn not just their aesthetics, but their language as well. To find out their words that correspond to 'good', 'fine' and so on, he has to look at their behaviour, watching for smiles and gestures, discovering what they eat and don't eat, seeing the children's toys and the way they play with them.

Wittgenstein's lecture now really warms up and he moves outside the confines of his planet to speculate upon Martian aesthetics.

If you went to Mars and men were spheres with sticks coming out, you wouldn't know what to look for. Or if you went to a tribe where noises

---

[2] These are, to be precise, not what he said, but what his students say he said. The only record of his lectures on aesthetics (and other subjects) at Cambridge during 1938 is compiled from the notes of some of his students. L. Wittgenstein, *Lectures and Conversations on Aesthetics, Psychology and Religious Belief*, ed. Cyril Barrett (Blackwell, Oxford, 1966).

[3] Ibid. p. 8.

made with the mouth were just breathing or making music, and language was made with the ears. Cf. 'When you see the trees swaying about they are talking to one another.' You compare the branches with arms. . . . How far this takes us from normal aesthetics. We don't start from certain words but from certain occasions or activities.[4]

At this point in Wittgenstein's exposition the anthropologist can scarce forbear to cheer. But, in his laudable insistence on the social embeddedness of aesthetics, he has overdone the separation of the various games. For what Wittgenstein is saying is that there is no comparison between games (or, to use another terminology, between world views). In other words, he is taking up a position of extreme cultural relativity.

He rightly insists that to describe fully a set of aesthetic rules you have to describe the social context within which they are valid. 'To describe what you mean by a cultural taste you have to describe a culture. . . . What belongs to a language game is a whole culture.'[5] He argues that what we now call a cultured taste perhaps did not exist in the Middle Ages, but in his very next sentence the 'perhaps' disappears: 'An entirely different game is played in different ages.'[6] He is very insistent upon this complete separation between games and goes on to emphasize it by asking his students to suppose that one of them, Lewy, does in fact have what is called a cultured taste in painting. 'This is something entirely different to what was called a cultured taste in the fifteenth century. An entirely different game was played. He does something entirely different with it to what a man did then.'[7] Lewy, encouraged by this doctrine of cultural relativity which Wittgenstein has built up by considering either the same society at different periods in history or different societies at the same moment in time, takes the next step of considering different individuals *in the same society at the same moment in time*, and puts to Wittgenstein the proposition:

If my landlady says a picture is lovely and I say it is hideous we don't contradict one another.[8]

[4] Ibid. pp. 2–3.
[5] Ibid. p. 8.
[6] Ibid.
[7] Ibid. p. 9.
[8] Ibid. p. 11.

Wittgenstein's reply is hardly satisfactory. He avoids the problems posed by Lewy and resorts instead to blustering.

In a sense you do contradict one another. She dusts it carefully, looks at it often, etc. You want to throw it in the fire. This is just the sort of stupid example which is given in philosophy, as if things like 'this is hideous', 'this is lovely', were the only kinds of things ever said. But it is only one thing amongst a vast realm of other things—one special case. Suppose the landlady says: 'This is hideous' and you say: 'This is lovely'—all right, that's that.[9]

Now this simply will not do. The game which Lewy is playing and the game his landlady is playing (whatever they are) are clearly not one and the same but are they entirely different? The aesthetic judgements, 'this is hideous' and 'this is lovely', are mutually contradictory and can only both be valid if they relate to entirely different games. This separation would seem to be confirmed by the accompanying actions and gestures: the landlady dusting it carefully and looking at it often, Lewy trying not to look at it and wanting to throw it in the fire when he does. But, the landlady wants to dust the picture and does, whilst Lewy wants to throw it on the fire and does not (at least, not if he wishes to continue to enjoy his comfortable relationship with his landlady). So, if we follow Wittgenstein's exhortation to consider not only the spoken value judgements but all the other gestures and actions—'a whole situation and a culture'[10]—we find that the landlady's game and Lewy's game are, in some respects, separate and in other respects mutually accommodating. To the extent that they are separate they are played in different spheres and are non-contradictory; to the extent that they are mutually accommodating they are played in the same sphere and are contradictory. The accommodation which the players make permits the relationship between them. Mr Lewy pays his rent and accommodates the picture, and in return the landlady accommodates Mr Lewy. To imagine that the landlady/lodger relationship is entirely defined by the financial agreements into which they each enter, and to act accordingly, is to invite disaster. We are left with the unhappy conclusion that the games of Lewy and his landlady are both contradictory and non-contradictory.

[9] Ibid.
[10] Ibid.

Again, if the landlady were to die unexpectedly and her effects were auctioned, it is most probable that her painting would be thrown on the fire as unsaleable. Her untimely death would have severed the landlady/lodger relationship, Lewy would not need to (indeed, could no longer) accommodate her game, and the operation of the market, the macro-system which sustained their relationship, would perform the action which Lewy always wished to take yet never could. The landlady placed a high aesthetic value on the painting; Lewy an extremely low one. If there is no comparison between their respective games these valuations are non-contradictory. The market, in a most brutal fashion, does make this comparison. It says, quite unequivocally: 'The landlady is wrong and Lewy is right.'

So, if Wittgenstein's line of argument is to remain viable, all consideration of market forces must be eliminated. And what better way to ensure that such vulgar matters are never discussed than to form a league of gentlemen? (Gellner,[11] observing that 'ordinary language philosophy' was essentially the elaboration of the gentlemanly culture of North Oxford, was behaving like an *arriviste* Toad of Toad Hall amongst the Woodstock Willows, and the creatures of the river-bank, realizing that, unlike the real Toad, they could not bring him into line, closed their ranks.) Clearly, value (aesthetic value) and price (economic value) are related, yet, equally clearly, they are not one and the same. Nor is it justifiable to assume that this relationship is fixed. When Wilde wrote of a cynic as being 'a man who knows the price of everything and the value of nothing' he was accepting that the two were related and that, alas, the relationship was not fixed. Wittgenstein, flying in the face of evidence (by choosing as his examples games inevitably separated by time or place, or both time and place), is insisting that they cannot be related to one another. Small wonder he is such a popular philosopher among painters. His argument deflects the reality of the invasion of aesthetic value by economic value (the gallery system, the saleroom and the dealer) by simply denying its possibility, and thus the artist can sustain the belief that his calling is quite pure and enjoys the high status of an activity untarnished by any tawdry intrusions from the politico-economic domain. So, if we accept Wittgenstein's argument,

---

[11] Ernest Gellner, *Words and Things* (Gollancz, London, 1959).

we are left with the unhappy conclusion that there can be no comparison between games but that social life can only go on if there is.

This unhappy conclusion derives from the unjustified assumption that, because some games are entirely different, all games must be entirely different. Wittgenstein has to insist on seeing the games of Lewy and his landlady like this:

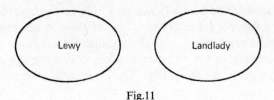

Fig.11

But, in fact, they are like this:

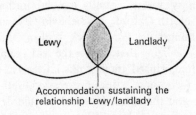

Accommodation sustaining the
relationship Lewy/landlady

Fig.12

There is not one game for Lewy and one game for the landlady but one complex game within which each plays his or her part. Who, we might then ask, plays this complex all-embracing game? The answer is 'no one' or 'everyone'.[12]

Lewy plays his part according to his rules, that is, his world view. The landlady plays her part according to her rules, that is, her world view. In so far as these rules are contradictory their world views are in conflict and, if they wish to retain their relationship, one, other, or both must modify his, her, or their actions. These modifications, in

[12] The nonsensical and contradictory nature of this reply does not invalidate the present argument but, rather, indicates that analogies with gaming are of limited utility in the explanation of social and cultural phenomena.

turn, may or may not modify one, other, or both of their world views but this is beside the present point. The point I wish to make is that Lewy has a world view which he both expresses and, by and large, realizes. He says, 'this is hideous', and he tries not to look at it and, in the main, succeeds in his negative endeavour. The landlady has a different, but not entirely different, world view which she both expresses and, by and large, realizes. She says, 'this is lovely', wants to look at it often and does, wants to dust it and does. Yet each of these world views by itself is inadequate to describe what is going on. To do this we must have both expressible and realizable world views and the relationship between them: the extent to which they overlap and the extent to which, in this area of overlap, they are modified (so as to reduce the points of contradiction) and become mutually accommodating.

Now this combined picture too is a world view. It is expressible but, unlike its two simple components, it is not socially realizable. That is, whilst it fully accounts for what is going on, I could not myself use it as a basis for action since, for example, it would require me simultaneously to dust the picture and throw it in the fire, all the time looking at it whilst avoiding seeing it. Alternatively, one could say that this world view is socially realizable (since it is a description of what is going on) but that there is no vantage point within that world which will afford the observer that view of the world.

To insist that all games are entirely different is to deny the possibility of any internally generated changes in the rules of the games: of mutual interaction between games. The existence of the rules must be ascribed to some external imposition and changes in the rules, if they occur, can be brought about only by external intervention. For Wittgenstein, the rules are simply given, and to enquire how they are given and by whom is to be ruled out of court for asking meaningless questions.

It is just a fact that people laid down such and such rules. . . . The rules of harmony expressed the way people wanted chords to follow—their wishes crystallised in those rules. . . . Although we have talked of 'wishes' here the fact is just that these rules were laid down. . . . All the greatest composers wrote in accordance with them.[13]

[13] Wittgenstein, op. cit., p. 6.

D

In reply to an objection by a student at this point to the effect that great composers do change the rules and get away with it and that this is a mark of their greatness, Wittgenstein replies: 'You can say that every composer changed the rules but the variation was very slight; not all the rules were changed. The music was still good by a great many of the old rules.'[14]

When we try to fit this disgraceful piece of special pleading to the repeated one hundred and eighty degree reversals of the rules in the examples of Stevengraphs, houses, and ancestors, Wittgenstein's game is up.

It is perfectly feasible to take two or more different (but not entirely different) world views which are both expressible and realizable and to relate them to one another in an all-embracing world view which is unrealizable. This can be done both by the intruding anthropologist with his technique of participant observation and by the native who is a participant by definition. This is not to argue that all natives are partially detached observers reflecting dispassionately on the nature of their social condition but, in a certain limited sense, this must be so. The process of social life continually confronts world view with world view and inevitably these are sometimes different or, at least, not quite the same. An example of such a confrontation is that between Lewy and his landlady. Here Lewy is forced to consider the possibility of something (the beauty of his landlady's picture) which until then he either was unaware of or deliberately ignored. If he is a field-working anthropologist, whose stock-in-trade is dispassion, he will think, 'how very interesting', and immediately start to construct his (unrealizable) anthropologist's model. If he is a passionate aesthete, for whom such a possibility is an impossibility, he will either run screaming from the house or throw the offending picture in the fire. If, like most of us, he lies somewhere between these poles of passion and dispassion he will restrain these impulses, resign himself to the presence of the picture by trying not to look at it (that is, he will try quite successfully most of the time to ignore the unattractive possibility), and later turn the whole unpleasant business to his advantage in the context of a university seminar. The possible responses may be summarized as: 'That is most interesting' or 'That is rubbish' or 'That is rubbish (but

14 Ibid.

most interesting)' / 'That is most interesting (but rubbish, of course)'.

In relation to this unrealizable world view that embraces the realizable world views of both Lewy and his landlady, the first response permits, indeed ensures, its construction. What is more, it would seem inevitably to involve the displacement of Lewy's earlier world view. This is generally a fairly rare response but when it occurs, that is, when rubbish disappears entirely and a realizable world view is replaced by one that is unrealizable, conditions of instability must prevail and rapid change is inevitable.

The second response nips this unrealizable world view in the bud, and it preserves Lewy's realizable world view intact whilst wholly denying the possibility of the landlady's world view. Such a response imposes a 'p and not-p' template upon social interaction—'If you are not with us you are against us.'

The third response permits the development of the all-embracing unrealizable world view but, at the same time, blocks the tendency for this one to replace the realizable world view. Lewy is able both to reflect on the unrealizable world view and to suspend this reflection in order to act on his realizable world view.

An understanding of the nature of rubbish is clearly essential if we are to analyse this dynamic that relates tolerance, intolerance, and the contradiction of the Venn diagrams depicting the universe of objects, to the stability and instability of social systems. It is now possible to define rubbish without stumbling into any unseen pitfalls. There is no longer any problem of looking at something which by definition must be invisible. The visibility of rubbish is generated by the process of social life that, continually confronting realizable world view with realizable world view, inevitably causes the at least partial construction of an all-embracing world view that subsumes the confrontation but at the same time is likely to be unrealizable. Of course, the variation between world views is made possible by the social malleability of objects, and I must be careful not to fall into the trap of imagining that there are no natural limits to this malleability. This means that rubbish may also become visible, not as the result of a confrontation between world views, but as a result of a confrontation between a world view and one or more of these natural limits.

The pitfalls have not been filled in: they have been mapped. In relation to rubbish we can distinguish two forms of blindness: there are those things or areas which we cannot see (though those with an entirely different 'game' may be able to see them), and there are those things or areas which we conspire not to see. When these latter intrude, and we cannot help but see them, we banish them from view (or, alternatively, neutralize their visibility) by assigning them to a unique cross-cutting cultural category which may be labelled 'rubbish'.

Seen in this way, rubbish is a universal feature, not necessarily of the human mind, nor of language, nor of social interaction, but of socio-cultural systems.[15] Rubbish is a consequence of the impossibility of ever fully specifying the relationship between a process and its cognition from a position which must always be contained by such a relationship. Yet it is a most curious sort of universal feature since it can (temporarily) disappear completely, and its defineability coexists with the recognition of the indefineability of that which we cannot see. There are transmissions across this boundary between that which we conspire not to see and that which we cannot see: it is not a fixed boundary. The problem is to devise a methodological framework for dealing with transmissions across a boundary which we can only ever know from one side. Cultural Relativity (such as that advocated by Wittgenstein) ignores the existence of these transmissions. Cultural Universality ignores the existence of the boundary. The one claims that there are innumerable incomparable games each played in isolation on its own cultural village green; the other, that there is just one big game which willy-nilly we all must play.

The attraction of rubbish theory is that it does not require us to take up either of these contradictory viewpoints. Instead, it focuses our attention upon this boundary and in so doing makes clear the fallacy that is common to both the relativist and the universalist positions. Rubbish theory is general and dynamic in that it pictures both the boundary and the various possible transmissions across it. It therefore contains the relativist and universalist positions as static special cases. The relativist position corresponds to those moments

---

[15] It would, for example, be an essential ingredient for a truly cultural artificial intelligence—a very distant goal in the discipline called 'artificial intelligence' which is at present struggling with the computer simulation of hand and eye.

when, for some reason or other, there happen not to be any transmissions across the boundary. The universalist position corresponds to the extreme situations where, as a result of unilateral transmissions across it, the boundary is pushed completely to one side or the other. In the absence of rubbish theory there is no option but to treat the specific in place of the general and the static in place of the dynamic, and to speak always in one or other of these extreme and contradictory languages.

This is the cartesian solution. Although it excludes almost everything of interest in social phenomena, it remains extraordinarily prevalent. This is because of the contradiction between concepts, which are always static, and processes, which are never static. When we start to talk about some process, the concepts we use have an inbuilt tendency to migrate towards the static extremes and to ignore what lies between them. This tendency is not restricted to the social sciences and an atomic physicist, Louis de Broglie, has provided us with a nice description of it.

... The individuality of the elementary particles is more attenuated the more they are engaged in interaction. As, on the one hand, there is no completely isolated particle and as, on the other hand, the bonding of the particles into a system is practically never sufficiently complete for something of their individuality not to remain, it can be seen that reality seems in general to lie somewhere between the concept of autonomous individuality and the concept of a completely fused system.[16]

The same is true of Lewy and his landlady, the fusion or separation of their games. If the reality never touches, even momentarily, either of these polar concepts but must always lie somewhere between, then we can never grasp, even fleetingly, from either one of these conceptual positions the dynamic situation which we seek to describe. This unapproachability is confirmed when we attempt the synthesis that would provide access to the reality as it fluctuates between, but never reaches, these poles. Any such synthesis is precluded by the contradiction of the concepts—a completely fused system denies autonomous individuality and *vice versa*. Thus the reality is totally unapproachable from either conceptual pole and the synthesis of these poles is impossible. Any approach will have to distort the reality

[16] Louis de Broglie, *Continu et Discontinu en Physique Moderne* (Paris, 1941).

into a shape which it can never attain, at the same time eliminating any means of measuring, and thus compensating for, the extent of the distortion. Neither concept by itself can resolve the problem and the synthesis of the two is impossible.

Is the problem insoluble? Must we always do such violence to the phenomena we wish to study? Are we doomed for ever to speak one or other of these contradictory languages? Well, one possible solution might be to use pictures rather than words. After all, the problem is insoluble only in terms of the two polar concepts; it does not even exist within the social reality—the phenomena that always recede beyond the concepts' grasp. If we avoid these concepts then there is nothing to prevent us from positioning ourselves, not at one or other of the polar vantage points, but in the mid-ground where the games are neither one and the same nor entirely different.

To take up this position we need a theory of rubbish. Social interaction continually contrasts world view with world view and so continually throws into sharp relief the very elements that differentiate and render socially unrealizable the combination of these world views; an example is the social interaction of Lewy and his landlady that forces Lewy to consider the possibility of the beauty of his landlady's picture—a possibility which is not permitted by the rules of his game, his world view. This is not to say that *all* elements thrown into relief by social interaction preclude the modification of world views. For instance, if, as seems quite likely, his landlady's game places a high gastronomic value on tripe and onions, a dish that lies outside Lewy's gustatory framework, then Lewy, overcoming, in the interests of his good relations with his landlady, his initial unease about something that is not covered by his world view, may eat the dish, find it quite palatable, and so come to place upon it a similar valuation to that which it enjoys in his landlady's game. No such accommodation is possible in the case of his landlady's picture for its incorporation into his world view would require him to perform contradictory and irreconcilable actions. The survival of a world view can be ensured only by eliminating, rejecting, or ignoring these intrusive and dangerous elements that preclude the continued coexistence of differing world views. These elements that elicit such responses constitute the cultural category 'rubbish'.

This definition of rubbish is at a high level of abstraction and provides the validating framework for the more readily comprehensible idea of rubbish that is implicit in the structural approach to pollution.[17] The advantages of this lower-level approach are offset by its rather intuitive basis which means that its acceptability rests ultimately not on reasoned argument but on temperamental and doctrinal persuasion. The intuitive element in this approach springs from the distinction it is forced to make between culture and nature: a distinction that presupposes that we can know what nature (as opposed to the idea of nature) is. It is one of the explicit assumptions of the higher-level argument that this is an unjustified assumption, that our idea of nature is to some extent socially determined, and that the extent to which it is socially determined is unknowable, except in its negative aspect, in the form of certain limits beyond which it cannot be manipulated. As, for instance, in one of Buckminster Fuller's aphorisms: 'If you can do it it's natural. If it's unnatural, you can't do it anyway.'

The argument for the lower-level approach to rubbish may be summarized like this: Nature is essentially chaotic and continuous; culture is orderly and discrete. Thus nature continually threatens to break down the water-tight compartments which culture seeks to impose on it. Since natural compartments seldom, if ever, occur, it is likely that there will be some natural elements which are on the borderline between two cultural categories, no matter where that borderline is drawn. These borderline cases (if they are 'visible') threaten to destroy the precarious order established by culture and so must be accorded special treatment by the culture-bearers. Taboo behaviour and pollution avoidances cluster about these borderline cases in all cultures and so, by looking for the anomalies, the taboos, and the avoidances, we can obliquely approach the cultural categories themselves.

But how are we to understand why some anomalous elements remain 'invisible'? Nature is not only chaotic and continuous, it is also so immense as to be unhandleable. We also impose order upon nature by whittling it down to manageable proportions. We make things important by making other things unimportant. That which we discard, shun, abhor, wash our hands of, or flush away, we are consigning to the rubbish category. Yet this is not quite correct. We

[17] See Mary Douglas, *Purity and Danger* (Routledge, London, 1966).

only notice rubbish when it is in the wrong place. Something which has been discarded, but never threatens to intrude, does not worry us at all. For instance, we are aware of the refuse in our dustbins and the mucus in our handkerchiefs but we do not make a great song and dance about them. These negatively valued things are in the right place and we can, by and large, ignore them. Not so the dewdrop on the end of a friend's nose or the dog faeces on the drawing-room carpet. This is rubbish in the wrong place: emphatically visible and extremely embarrassing.

The discarded but still visible, because it still intrudes, forms a genuine cultural category of a special type—a rubbish category. That which is discarded but not visible, because it does not intrude, is not a cultural category at all, it is simply *residual* to the entire category system.

Another difficulty with this lower-level definition of rubbish can be put like this: if something is seen to be intrusive then it may be, not so much put in its right place, as put from its wrong place by means of the response: 'this is rubbish'. The confusion arises from the use of the expression, 'in the wrong place', which implies that there is, somewhere or other, a right place. This may or may not be so. In some cases there is a right place. For instance, the right place for household rubbish is in the rubbish bin and the right place for a dewdrop is either back inside the nostril (provided this can be done surreptitiously by means of an inaudible and invisible sniff) or in a handkerchief. Such rubbish in the right place serves to define another sort of boundary, that between public and private or between social and personal. Each of us individually can see the contents of our dustbins and our handkerchiefs, yet collectively we suppress the sight.

The housewife, alone in her kitchen or backyard, may examine the contents of her dustbin quite closely, yet when we see people doing just this in a crowded street, be they tramps rummaging for tasty morsels or garbologists sifting Bob Dylan's detritus for tell-tale evidence to substantiate their Ph.D. theses, we are embarrassed, perhaps compassionate, perhaps indignant, but never unmoved, and we seek to repair this gaping hole in the boundary between private and public by averting our eyes. Similarly, it is certain that some people (and, for all I know, it may be true of everyone) when they are alone gleefully scrutinize the contents of their handkerchiefs after a really good nose-blow. Yet most people would never dream of doing this in public and some people are so conscious of this public/private boundary that they will leave the room every time they have to blow their noses. Conversely, to initiate successfully a dinner-table conversation on comparative nose-picking means spectacularly reducing the degree of formality and transforming the gathering from a social occasion to a very intimate piece of social interaction. Under such conditions the wider reaches of social life are suspended, since the necessary conditions for their existence are incompatible with such intrusive bodily processes. No man is a hero to his valet, and, if we wish to preserve heroism, we must somehow conspire not to see the soiled linen and the soggy handkerchiefs.

Again, the sociological implications of rubbish are apparent, for only with its help can we make this connection between the micro and macro levels of social life. An understanding of rubbish is essential if we are to uncover the mechanics of this sliding scale that relates private and public, informality and formality, expediency and principle. Without this key, we must inevitably focus either on the valet or on the hero and never on the relation between them.

In contrast to these things which, put from the wrong place by the rubbish response, end up in the right place, there are those things that have no place at all. For instance, within a wide range of British society, Gypsies are seen as social rubbish and they have only to tow their caravans on to the suburban verge to provoke the ferocious rubbish response of the sedentary residents. Inevitably, the local authorities and the police are called in to keep the Gypsies on the move in order, paradoxically, to keep them in their place. The paradox disappears (to be replaced by a fresh one) once one realizes that their place is 'nowhere'.[18]

Such homelessness arises when boundaries are drawn so clearly and so all-embracingly that they are of the 'p and not-p' type, and their control extends so absolutely and so far that that which happens to be neither 'p' nor 'not-p' can never find a squalid overlooked corner to make its own. Such slums have all been demolished. To be able to see the connectedness of everything is a very mixed blessing, and the politicization that results from ecological concern

---

[18] For evidence that this is, in fact, the prevalent response to the gypsy, see Nicolas Swingler, 'Move on Gypsy', *New Society*, No. 352, 1969.

and holistic vision, regardless of any explicit intent, must carry totalitarian overtones.

It is a philosophical commonplace that we are surrounded by things of whose identity we are quite certain yet which we would have great difficulty in defining. A classic example is Burke's characterization of the British Constitution as capable of being perceived yet defying definition. Another favourite example among philosophers is a dog. We all know a dog when we see one, yet few of us could give a definition that did not let in all sorts of animals that clearly are not dogs (like cats) and did not exclude all sorts of animals that clearly are dogs (such as those breeds that are hairless or barkless). Is it not possible that the same is true of rubbish? Conversely, is it not possible that this is not true even of dogs?

One of the most striking features of rubbish is that we all instantly recognize it when we see it, hear it, read it, smell it or, horror of horrors, touch it. The pleonasmic vehemence of the typical response, 'That is complete and utter rubbish', would appear to confirm the all-or-nothing quality of rubbish. Just as dogs are undoubtedly dogs, so rubbish is undoubtedly rubbish. There are no questions of degree. An animal is either a dog or it is not a dog, and something is either rubbish or it is not rubbish. Yet in the one case there is (apparently) complete unanimity concerning which animals are dogs and which are not, whilst in the other case there is often complete disagreement as to what is rubbish and what is not. A pair of examples will serve to demonstrate this self-evident distinction.

It would appear that dogs, in a modest way, form part of our region of fixed assumptions. We are all agreed on what dogs are, and on what is a dog and what is not a dog. In this sense, the identity 'dog' lies outside the politico-economic domain. There are no votes to be gained or profits to be made by suggesting that dogs are not really dogs at all. In this sense, then, dogs constitute part of certainty, part of the innermost core of our world view, those beliefs which we all share without reservation, beliefs so deep-rooted that we are often unaware even of the fact that we hold them. They are self-evident.

The molecular biologist, Jacques Monod,[19] has pointed out that, although value is a necessary condition for society, science con-

[19] Jacques Monod, *Chance and Necessity* (Collins, London, 1972).

tinually outrages value. Monod's own work, he believes, threatens to erode the boundary between the area of fixed assumptions and the area of flexibility and to place the identity 'dog' in the political arena, by showing that we do not know what a dog is after all. A most important element in our certainty concerning dogs is the self-evident fact that they reproduce themselves. That is, dogs produce more dogs (and we conveniently thrust from our minds the problems raised by the evolutionary theories to which we also subscribe which require us to consider those far-away creatures without which there would have been no dogs yet whose dogginess is highly debatable). For Monod, even the reproduction of present-day dogs, far from being self-evident, becomes quite extraordinary. The ludicrous question, 'Why don't dogs give birth to camels?' is the very guiding principle of the twenty-five years of research which culminated in his Nobel Prize.

I use this colourful example because it is the one Monod himself used in defending his position against a formidable array of critics (including George Steiner and Stuart Hampshire) in the BBC Television production 'Controversy' in September 1972. As yet, however, the outrage which this scientific advance threatens has not really occurred. There remains a high level of cognitive insulation between molecular biology and the world at large. One assumes that Monod himself, once he stepped out of his laboratory, did not confuse dogs with camels. Such outrage will only occur if these shifts in the boundary between the regions of fixed assumptions and of flexibility in relation to the biologists' world view are fully and systematically worked through in the various world views within society generally: that is, if Monod gains the credibility not only of the scientific community but of the entire society that contains it. To speculate on what would happen if this socially imposed mosaic of insulators were to break down and be replaced by perfect conductors, is to jump the gun and run the risk of trying to say what would happen if something that could not happen happened. First we must enquire into the social forces that confer or withhold credibility, into the mechanisms which govern social acceptance and rejection and are quite possibly the conditions without which society would not be possible. A modest step in this direction and the main point of this example is to show that whilst the identity 'dog' is (currently in British and French society) quite unambiguous, this unambiguity does not derive from any intrinsic properties of dogs. Quite the reverse: such certainty is achieved only through the suppression of uncertainty.

My second example is chosen to show the converse of this situation. During the early seventies there was much controversy concerning the proposed demolition of Grange Park—an enormous and appallingly dilapidated neo-classical mansion in Hampshire. Set out below, side-by-side in order that they may be more readily compared, are the views of two experts regarding the status of this building.

'. . . the interior can now only justify detailed recording and (anyway) it was disappointing as it bears no formal relationship with the great portico and façade that Wilkins wrapped around the seventeenth-century house in 1809.'

'It is the craftmanship inside the house that is superb . . .'

'Externally the Greek transformation is even more breathtaking than contemporary views would have one believe. It is virtually impossible for drawings or photographs to convey the spatial feeling of moving around a building, and therefore the loss of the shell of the Grange is irreplaceable.'

'There is nothing awe-inspiring or pleasurable about the Grange. On the contrary, it can best be described as a neo-classical horror, a phoney! The whole of the exterior of the building is fake stone including the massive columns.'

'It is the building's relationship to its landscape that needs to be saved. The house sits high on its terraces dramatically running out along a promontory into a valley.'

'The Grange is hopelessly out of keeping, poised like a multilegged prehistoric monster on a hilltop surrounded by some of the most beautiful countryside in Hampshire.'

'It is the combination of the Regency landscape and the Greek temple that makes Grange Park the epitome of the English marriage of Neo-Classicism and Romanticism.'

'Having known the Grange for over a quarter of a century, it conjures in my mind the most monstrous eyesore witnessed in all my 35 years as a designer and restorer of English country houses.'

(From a letter by Mr Peter
Inskip of the Department of
Architecture, Cambridge
University, to *The Times*,
9 September 1972)

(From a letter by Mr Michael
Toone to the *Sunday Times*,
10 September 1972)

The fact that these letters must have been in the post simultaneously rules out the possibility that one is by way of a rejoinder to the
other and makes the purity of their diametrical opposition all the
more remarkable. The forthright style of both Mr Inskip and Mr
Toone, and the fact that they both felt sufficiently strongly about the
Grange to write to the newspapers about it, suggest that for each of
them the identity of the Grange is unequivocal. For the first it is a
sadly misused durable, for the second an obnoxious and persistent
pile of rubbish—a transient that has overstayed its welcome. Each
in this case at least, can identify rubbish and durability as surely as
they can identify dogs. Indeed, they both resort to animal imagery.
Mr Toone sees it as a horrendous multilegged prehistoric monster
which, as if this were not enough, is not even a *genuine* monster but a
fake, a phoney. For Mr Inskip there is no chance of fakery. The
noble beast's pedigree is impeccable and indisputable: it is the
thoroughbred foal Epitome by Neo-Classicism out of Romanticism.
Within this sociological perspective architectural history (and art
history) is perhaps best viewed as an aesthetic Kennel Club.

It is clear that one man's rubbish can be another man's desirable
object; that rubbish, like beauty, is in the eye of the beholder. Yet it
would be wrong to explain away this distinction between the non-
contradiction of dogs and the contradiction of rubbish in terms of
the distinction between matters of fact and matters of opinion, since
on both sides there would seem to be exactly the same certainty that
characterizes matters of fact. To say that one man's meat is another
man's poison is not to explain anything, but simply to pose the next
question, which is: what determines which man gets poisoned?

In September 1972 the controversy still raged and Grange Park
still stood. (It is, I hope, apparent by now that each example that is
given to illustrate the argument must have a time and place label
attached to it specifying the situation wherein it is valid. Grange
Parks, Stevengraphs, and ancestors are continually on the move.
In this sense, all things are in flux. Thus in focusing on the movement

of any specific thing we must specify the particular time and place where that movement took place. However, these specific movements, in aggregate, themselves result in the shifting and modification of the boundary between the region of flexibility and the region of fixed assumptions. And so, if we shift our focus from things to the boundaries between things, we go from the specific and time-bounded to the general and eternal.) If the permission to demolish Grange Park was revoked and its preservation, either as a restored building or as a romantic ruin, assured, then its durability would be affirmed and Mr Toone would have to take the draught of hemlock. If, on the other hand, Mr Baring (the owner) was permitted to proceed with the demolition, the pendulum would swing in favour of transience, since 'out of sight is out of mind'. But the final outcome would still be in the balance. It is possible, but difficult, to create a negative durability, akin to the gap left by one extraction in an otherwise perfect mouthful of teeth, in relation to which the demolition is seen to be the near-criminal act of Philistines resulting in an irreplaceable loss to the community. The Doric propylaeum at Euston Station attained this negative durability after it had been demolished, thanks mainly to the efforts of the Smithsons (the eminent architects who have written a detailed and passionate book recording every step in this disgraceful affair)[20] and British Rail has been indelibly stamped with the mark of the Vandal.

The decision on Grange Park had to go one way or the other, there was no in-between. One or other of the protagonists would have to swallow the poison; yet there is nothing intrinsic to the Grange itself which can determine this decision. Admittedly, Grange Park is a large part of neo-classicism and the fact that in 1972 there were several important exhibitions devoted to neo-classicism and that various authoritative books on neo-classicism had either recently left, or were about to leave, the presses would indicate that durability was the most likely outcome. But this is simply to replace a specific problem by its generalization and there is still nothing intrinsic to neo-classicism to ensure its durability.

One should not overlook the fact that neo-classicism was the only major theme in the arts of Europe during the eighteenth and nine-

---

[20] Alison and Peter Smithson, *The Euston Arch and the Growth of London, Midland and Scottish Railway* (Thames & Hudson, London, 1968).

teenth centuries that had not received the doubtful privilege of exhaustive art-historical reappraisal and that, like an equivocal Tiv ancestor, it was pre-eminently suitable as the vehicle whereby Britain's historic entry into the European Community could be effected. (The exhibitions were associated with various other manifestations of the cultural ballyhoo entitled 'Fanfare for Europe'.) At the same time we can see why this seemingly overdue reappraisal of neo-classicism had not occurred earlier. To treat neo-classicism as a whole one must take a pan-European approach—a lineage with Napoleon for its eponymous ancestor, but this was precluded by the prior divergence of a Little Englander sub-lineage with Wellington as its founder. The Fanfare for Europe, one might say, was the mode of ingression of the eternal object history into the actuality of geopolitics, and in the course of the ingression, both were altered. It is not just the acephalous Tiv who manipulate their genealogies.

It is worth digressing from neo-classicism to Victoriana at this point in order to block, once and for all, this favourite bolt-hole whereby the problems presented by the Stevengraph are so frequently avoided. A common response is to ascribe the spectacular change in value of the Stevengraph to a general awakening of interest in things Victorian. The sixties saw the emergence of Industrial Archaeology; the publication of scholarly books on the great engineers and builders of the Victorian period—Brunel, Telford, Cubitt, Butterfield; the aesthetic reassessment of the Pre-Raphaelites and of Art Nouveau; the salvage from the Falkland Islands of Brunel's SS *Great Britain* (and its subsequent inspection by the Queen in Bristol in the summer of 1973); the conservation of the Kennet and Avon Canal; and the opening of Sotheby's Belgravia Auction Rooms devoted entirely to Victoriana. McLuhan[21] has observed this process and expressed its generalized form in a sort of natural law. According to McLuhan, as we emerge from one age into another (for example, from the Industrial Revolution into the Electric Revolution) so the earlier age becomes (in his terminology) an art-form.

Yet this formula, whilst excellent in furnishing a description of the general context of the process, provides no explanation of it. First of all, it begs the question of what criteria define an age by assuming a simple technological determinism. Secondly, the problems presented

---

[21] Marshall McLuhan, *The Gutenberg Galaxy* (Routledge, London, 1962).

by the Stevengraph, we are told, are to be understood as simply one element within the historical reassessment of the Victorian period. But, if we go on to ask just what form this historical reassessment takes, we find that it is nothing other than the sum of the numerous particular elements, one of which is the Stevengraph. McLuhan is trapped in a natural-order-of-things circularity, hence his quasi-natural law.

Grange Park still stands. It is now (1979) completely gutted and the shell is in the care of the Department of the Environment, whose intention it is to preserve it as a romantic ruin. The durability of Wilkins's façade, at least, would seem to be assured. The final outcome of the controversy was not the result of natural forces, but of a political struggle within which money was only one of the weapons. The owner, Mr Baring, was a merchant banker and so, not surprisingly, his argument was economic. The house, he asserted, was so dilapidated that restoration of any kind was not economically feasible and so he had reluctantly to face up to the fact that demolition was the only course open to him. The same canny instinct guided his decisions once he had obtained the necessary permission to demolish.

... demolition must start before further depredations on such items of value as still remained in the house could occur and a publicly advertised sale of everything that my advisors considered saleable, and that I did not wish to keep, took place a month or two ago. (From a letter by Mr John Baring to *The Times*, 9 September 1972.)

When this statement is set beside that of Mr Toone to the effect that 'it is the craftmanship inside the house that is superb and all this Mr Baring has saved', Mr Toone's impartiality as an expert becomes questionable and his role looks suspiciously like that of playing the architectural fiddle while an upper-class totter calls the tune ('Music To Asset-strip To', perhaps). However, this may only be an unfortunate coincidence and it is perfectly clear that, even if such economic forces do influence the composition of knowledge and the inferences drawn therefrom, they do not entirely control them. Thus Mr Inskip, his sole armament his expertise as an architect and the authority attendant upon his profound grasp of the historical context and significance of the Grange, can enter the lists from the other side, with a very good chance of success.

From all this it is apparent that, whilst the knowledge of the expert is neither the cause nor the object of the struggle, it is not independent of it. It is one of the weapons used in the fight and, as such, is subject to all the forces that ever hone its cutting edge. (It is also possible that, at the height of its development, it may be superseded, just as the horse had to give way to the tank.) It is no reflection on the integrity of Mr Inskip or Mr Toone to point out that whichever one were to find himself to be on the winning side would find that the system of knowledge which provided his orientation would gain that little bit more acceptance and that the institution within which it was propounded would gain that little bit more prestige, those few more post-graduate students, and that crucial increment in funds.

This political involvement of knowledge is now well recognized. It was first pointed out by the physicist Max Planck who saw through the accepted view of scientific progress which insisted that, once the shortcomings of an existing theory had been revealed and a new theory that could account for them was advanced, then scientists in response to their professional ethic automatically abandoned the old theory and embraced the new. The truth was much less ethical, much less tidy, and much more human. All that happened was that those who subscribed to the old theory eventually died. Once this is accepted, scientific progress becomes more like scientific meandering, and the idea that a science has only reached maturity when it can afford to ignore its history has to be stood on its head. Only by suppressing its history can a science present the appearance of maturity.

Kuhn's[22] theory of scientific revolutions is the logical development of the sociology of science that must follow from Planck's insight. Successive theories become exemplified by particular important pieces of work or experiments which Kuhn calls 'paradigms'. Most scientific endeavour is devoted to the elaboration of the unquestioned current paradigm—an activity labelled 'normal science'. When, for a variety of possible reasons, there is some loss of faith in the established paradigm, various conflicting alternatives may be proposed and there ensues an exciting and turbulent period of 'paradigm confusion', resulting, thanks to Planck's biological mechanism, in the eventual establishment of a new paradigm and a new period of normal science. An important point is that, though much energy may be

[22] T. S. Kuhn, *The Structure of Scientific Revolutions* (University of Chicago Press, 1970).

devoted to trying to demonstrate the reverse, there is no gradual transition within the theory from one paradigm to the next, but a total discontinuity—an epistemological break.

Anthropologists familiar with the neglected old Fulani herdsman who although still alive has been succeeded by his son, would introduce a sociological rather than biological definition of death.[23] This results in the potential speeding-up of the process. For instance, academic retirement often precedes death itself, and disregard often precedes even retirement. By these means the process of alternating periods of normal science and scientific revolutions, whilst still subservient to biological factors, is largely detached from them and becomes increasingly socially determined.

The possession of knowledge confers upon the holder the possibility of a wider and stronger control over time and space than that available to those without such knowledge. It is significant that the views of those who could not tell a neo-classical mansion from a Gothic Revival rectory are irrelevant to this struggle (unless they also happen to be the owner, aspiring buyer, or prospective demolisher). It is a battle between epistemological giants and the winner is able to rearrange the spatial configuration of the present that it may confirm the spatio-temporal requirements of his particular system of knowledge (as in the restructuring of lineage frameworks). This is not to say that there are no limits to where the boundary between the transient and the durable can be pushed, but only that such movements as occur are neither arbitrary, nor natural, nor homoeostatic. They are the outcome of social forces mediated by knowledge, and as such may be seen as the bending of reality to fit the dominant theory.

This may seem, in many ways, a dismal picture of the knowledge industry; especially for those who are committed to the belief that the pursuit of knowledge represents a fearless quest for the truth—the idea that, though one may never actually get there, at least one gets nearer. But at least it is realistic, and, if it requires us to adopt a Heraclitean sociology wherein all is strife, conflict, and no neutrality, and to abandon a cartesian sociology that pretends otherwise, then this is surely not too high a price to pay for the advancement of self-knowledge.

[23] D. J. Stenning, *Savannah Nomads* (OUP, London, for International African Institute, 1959).

6 Art and the ends of economic activity

The explanatory framework in terms of the three categories, transient, rubbish, and durable, and of the permitted transfers between these categories, is all very pretty but it does leave some unanswered questions. What happens to the durable item in the long run, when, still increasing in value, it disappears off the top right-hand corner of the graph (Ch. 2)? What happens when a supposedly impossible transfer occurs? For example, when something durable becomes transient or rubbish; when moth or rust corrupt or when thieves break through and steal; when an old master painting is slashed to ribbons, a Venetian glass goblet dropped and smashed into a thousand pieces, or a Georgian silver teapot overwarmed on the hot-plate and melted into a glistening lump? What about the situations where a new item suddenly appears out of the blue, or where an existing one suddenly disappears in an equally mystifying fashion? That is, how does this dynamic category system relate to the processes of production and consumption?

Ideally, durables last for ever and increase in value over time. In such a system items continually enter the durable category yet never leave it, and the fact that they all must increase in value simply exacerbates an already expansive or even explosive trend. We must ask whether this is what actually happens or whether in the long run other factors intervene to provide an upper ceiling or at least some retardation of what must otherwise be a runaway situation. Does the system carry within it the seeds of its own destruction?

One limit which durables undoubtedly approach, and which some classes of durable items actually attain, is total removal from circulation. This represents a perfect solution to this runaway problem, since the removal from circulation retards the expansion without in any way imposing on the durable items properties that would be incompatible with their membership of the durable category. The complete transfer of a class of items to museums and public collections is consonant with a general belief that, if only those items were in circulation, they would be increasing in value. In other words, they are so durable they are priceless.

The almost inevitable occasional destruction of durable items also helps to bring about this total removal from circulation, but it is in this case that the category system is in fact threatened. Of course, we all know that no physical object can last for ever and in consequence the durable category must logically be a class with no members. In practice, this seemingly insurmountable obstacle is easily overcome. Objects in the durable category do not have to last for ever, just long enough. As long as the majority of the items in the durable category survive the lifetime of the individual culture-bearers, and, more important, as long as during this time people act towards those objects *as if* they were going to last for ever, then the category boundary is unthreatened. In everyday human, rather than cosmic, terms the infinite life-span of durables is translated into the familiar sacred stewardship. Like bathrooms, we should pass on our durables to the next generation in the condition in which we should like to find them. We have to take our durables, like most things in life, where we can find them. Even so, the limits imposed by nature occasionally impinge and threaten to destroy the precarious order which the category system has made possible. In spite of all our attempts to make durables last long enough, they do occasionally and embarrassingly cease to exist, and when this happens we make an emphatic response in terms of sorrow, outrage, letters to the newspapers, and contributions to charitable funds to prevent the same sort of thing from happening again.

For example, a tremendous sense of shock was caused some years ago by the Florence floods. Both the shock and the response were on a scale quite out of proportion to the loss to life and limb, the criterion by which we tend to measure disasters in foreign parts (as in the apocryphal story of the winning entry in the competition for the most boring newspaper headline: 'Small Earthquake in Peru, Not Many Dead'). Appeal funds were set up, eminent persons' letters were published in *The Times*, and a charitable Florentine evening was held at Annabel's nightclub, the costs being borne by the management and the décor being provided free by an eminent designer and his assistants. This extreme response relates to the appalling jolt delivered to our conceptual categories by the news that some of the supremely durable objects of the Western world (the art treasures of the Renaissance) had overnight been rendered supremely transient.

This extreme response, whenever a durable ceases to exist, is comparable to taboo behaviour or pollution avoidance. It is a ritual form, a symbolic process, which heals the gash that chaotic nature has inflicted on the delicate cultural membrane separating the transient from the durable. In effect, this response erases the offending transfer, thereby modifying what actually happens so that it conforms to what is ideally possible.

A similar threat to this boundary is presented by objects which, rather than suddenly and unexpectedly leaping from durability to transience or even rubbish, simply exhibit a persistent backsliding tendency as a result of their physical properties. (A quality referred to by those who deal and speculate in commodities as 'inherent vice'. Copper for instance does not suffer from it but tinned salmon does. Virginity, too, is an asset that suffers from inherent vice:

> 'The grave's a fine and private place
> But none, I think, do there embrace.')

Art works, particularly paintings, with their flimsy canvas, worm-eaten stretchers, and fading pigments, are often at risk and a whole industry of conservation has been called into existence to counter this tendency by forcing these objects to exhibit the physical properties appropriate to the category in which they find themselves. These conservationists, hidden away in the basements of our museums and galleries, are the conceptual equivalents of those lonely jackaroos on Australian sheep stations whose entire working life is spent in repairing the fences that keep the sheep in and the rabbits out.

This upper ceiling, compounded from the removal from circulation of some durables and the regrettable disappearance of others, undoubtedly exists but it is not sufficient, at present, to bring about steady-state conditions within the durable category. This is because the rate at which items enter the durable category is consistently much greater than the rate at which they are removed from circulation, despite the fact that there has been an exceptional growth in the size and number of public collections. The long-run trend is undeniable but, whilst it is quite possible that such an expanding system will ultimately reach some insuperable limit, it would be most unwise to assume that such a crisis situation is either inevitable or imminent. The danger that ultimately the proliferation of museums will make us all homeless and that we shall all be employed as cognitive fence-repairers with nobody left for productive work, is not very real. The come-uppances which apocalyptic prophets claim as the inevitable outcome of our Gadarene behaviour presupposes that there is a bottom to the cliff to interrupt our headlong dash. The image of the man jumping off an infinitely high skyscraper and muttering as he passes each story, 'So far so good, so far so good', may be more appropriate to socio-cultural systems than the topographic setting of those foolish mythical pigs.

The rubbish to transient transfer is, theoretically, impossible for the following reason. Both the value and expected life-span of an item in the rubbish category are zero. In the transient category they are positive and decreasing. The transfer of rubbish to transience would involve a change from zero to a positive quantity which inevitably entails an increase (the criterion for membership of the durable category), and in consequence would exclude the item from the transient category. But do such theoretically impossible transfers occur in practice? They do occur to a limited degree, which does not seriously threaten the boundary maintenance, in the business affairs of the dealer. The successful dealer operates by manipulating the value and expected life-span of an item: by depressing them in one transaction and elevating them in the subsequent transaction. The secondhand car dealer is successful to the extent that he is able to delay the transfer of an item from the transient to the rubbish category; the antique dealer is successful to the extent that he is able to emphasize the durability of an item. The transfer of rubbish to transience occurs in the limiting case which exists in the context of the totter, the rag-and-bone man, the Gypsy and the scrap-dealer. It is implicit in the slogans, 'we want what you don't' and 'houses cleared free of charge'.

It is significant that the antique dealer, whose activities are consonant with the ideal properties of the category system, should traditionally be regarded as reputable and scholarly—the last refuge, some claim, of the gentleman—whilst the totter, rag-and-bone man, Gypsy, scrap-dealer, and secondhand car salesman, whose activities run counter to the ideal properties of the system, should be pooled with 'company directors of no fixed address' to form a criminal reservoir that, unless the dyke is maintained, will engulf our present social order.

The theoretically impossible transfers of transient to durable and durable to transient can be considered together. They correspond to the seemingly impossible market situation where some people are expecting to pay less and less for a particular item whilst others are expecting to pay more and more. Such a situation, should it exist, would be inherently unstable and would alter until the market wholly excluded those who were expecting to pay less and less. Similarly, in a crisis such as the Wall Street crash we could envisage a hypothetical situation where the sudden loss of confidence meant that those people who expected to pay more and more for, say, antique silver rapidly became fewer and fewer, with the result that those people who expected to pay less and less, and who presumably wanted the silver for brewing tea in and eating with, could enter and take over the entire market. It is evident that the long-term survival of the category system and the existence of transient to durable and durable to transient transfers are incompatible. Such transfers are an automatic threat to boundary maintenance and their appearance would seem to signal the imminent collapse of the durable category—as happened, for instance, with the destruction of the middle classes in Weimar Germany or the wartime privations that caused the (regretted) exchange of old masters for tins of corned beef. People become aware that they live in troubled times, not just because of the real physical dangers, but because of the real conceptual dangers as well. It is very alarming when objects cease to conform to the properties expected of them. Of course, these properties expected of objects and of ideas constitute our values, our civilization, and it is because of perceived threats to these properties that wars are fought. There was said to be an Oxford don who, when some of his uniformed ex-undergraduates hinted that perhaps he should leave his ivory tower and contribute to the war effort, replied: 'I *am* what you are fighting for.'

But there is another possibility. We can imagine the establishing of a permanent cultural boundary between those who expect to pay more and more and those who expect to pay less and less whereby those who expect to pay more and more take over the market entirely, and those who expect to pay less and less accept their exclusion from the market by denying the relevance, for them, of durable items. Such a boundary effectively eradicates competition in terms of the items defining it: it would be the sort of boundary which exists between castes rather than classes. This is the sort of boundary that at first sight appears to separate the Knockers-Through from the Ron-and-Cliffs. But in this case it no longer eliminates competition because the Knockers-Through, instead of aspiring to the durable houses of Belgravia, are trying to impose durability on the transient/rubbish houses that until recently were the exclusive preserve of the Ron-and-Cliffs. In this competition, characterized by different rules for each side, the Knockers-Through stand to gain status and power (via the increased aesthetic and economic value of their houses). The Ron-and-Cliffs stand to gain from the increased opportunities for displaying courage and generosity (via the conversion of durability into turnover; for instance, by stealing and flogging the durable contents of the Knockers-Through's durable houses). As one crosses the boundary the criminality of the Ron-and-Cliffs changes from deviance to normality. Only the existence of this cultural boundary can account for the observed facts that a considerable proportion of British society consistently behave as though there were no such things as durables and that some, if not all, of them continue to behave like this, even though they are fully aware that durables do exist, for the very good reason that they are 'not for them'. This is not said in any detrimental or patronizing sense. Such a person may be very well aware that, within his social context, five pounds spent on drinks for old or potential friends and acquaintances is a much better investment than five pounds' worth of unit trusts.

Two building-trade anecdotes may illustrate this point. While we were putting the finishing touches to a newly-durable North London house, a gas-conversion engineer arrived. Having seen only the six-panelled front door and the William Morris-papered hall he exclaimed, 'upper middle class'. He himself, though born in Islington, now lived in an all-electric modern house on a private estate near Barnet. As his gaze took in the central heating, the shower, the bidet and the Brazilia bathroom suite, the sanded and sealed floor of the kitchen-dining-conservatory area, and the red gas-fired Aga, he made the pronouncement, 'It doesn't matter what you do to a house like this—as far as I'm concerned it will always be a slum.'

Similarly, a carpenter colleague (who later married the 'au-pair' from one of the houses we worked on) said that he had come to appreciate, on aesthetic grounds, the real leather chesterfields and Regency walnut dining tables of the durable houses. He then went on to explain that he could not furnish his own flat in that way since such items regrettably were not for him. To surround himself with durables and not to have to replace a plastic three-piece suite every few years would be the signal to his (socially and economically vital) friends and associates that he had abandoned their culture of transience.

Generalizing, we can say that this cultural boundary, when competition is eliminated, separates castes and, when competition persists, separates classes. And competition is made possible by the existence of the transfers from transient to rubbish to durable. It follows then that under conditions where the possibilities of these transfers are progressively reduced the social stratification will tend to change from class-based to caste-based. (It is not possible at this stage to say anything about whether this change is likely to be gradual and smooth or sudden and discontinuous. This question is dealt with in Chapter 8.) The explanation is quite simple: the transient/rubbish/durable category system permits the uneven distribution of power and status within our society and is the basis for the cultural differences between the classes that are ranged along that distribution. The permissible, but carefully controlled, transfers between these categories allow the degree of social mobility sufficient to modify these classes so that they accurately reflect the inevitably changing distribution of power within our society. That is, they permit the continuous realignment of power and status.

Now, you might say, 'But power and status always go together, so how can they need realigning?' Well, in the West this indeed has tended to be the case, thanks to the transfers between categories, but in India for instance there were virtually no transfers through rubbish and power and status varied quite independently. The meat-eating Prince, for example, sat firmly at the head of the power structure but he deferred to the vegetarian Brahmin within the hierarchy of caste. This is the difference between class and caste, and there is no reason why power and status should not begin to vary independently here in the West as well.

The degree of control needed to ensure this constant realignment of power and status without, at the same time, threatening to destroy the cultural boundaries between the classes is not easily achieved. If control is too tight then the distribution of power and the distribution of status will tend to drift apart since the transfers that would keep them aligned are not allowed to happen. In this way, power and status will increasingly vary independently of one another: those near the top of the prestige league concerning themselves less and less with objects as sources of power and more and more with the embracing of some objects, and with the rejection of others, as indicators of purity and of separation. Social stratification will change from class-based to caste-based. If control is too loose, power and status will remain aligned but the status differential will be eroded as too much is transferred too rapidly between the categories, and it will no longer be possible to maintain the emphatic differences between them. That is, stratification will decrease, the durable category will disappear, and the society will move towards the egalitarian pole, becoming increasingly organized around differences only of a universal kind such as age, sex, and physical characteristics.

We can now see that by pushing the argument for a dynamic sociology to its logical extreme and considering not only the possibilities

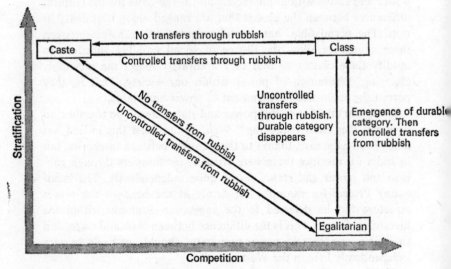

Fig.13 The Rubbish Triangle

of transfers between cultural categories but also the possibilities of the various permutations that result from the total elimination of some of these categories as a consequence of these transfers, we obtain a simple triangular range of transformations within which those supposedly fundamental social dimensions, stratification and competition, emerge as secondary abstractions (see Fig. 13).

The generalization does not have to stop at this stage. This 'rubbish triangle' provides, in outline, a description of all the ways in which the goods in circulation in any society may be conceptualized and of the manner in which these conceptualizations relate to the entire possible range of variations of the fundamental properties of social systems. In other words, it depicts the social laws that govern distribution and exchange. We can now ask how this model of all the socially realizable variations of the modes of distribution and exchange relates to the other two departments of economic activity, production and consumption, but first we should clarify the relationship between the 'rubbish triangle' and the model that has been used in the analysis of Stevengraphs and North London houses. This latter model is represented in Fig. 14 on page 112.

This model represents just one specific possibility within the total range of socially realizable possibilities given by the 'rubbish triangle'. It is, in fact, that possibility corresponding to the top right-hand corner of the triangle, the clearly defined class-based society characterized by high levels of stratification and competition. It is a description of one of the historic conditions of distribution and exchange. In contrast, the 'rubbish triangle' provides, in outline, a description of all such historic conditions, both those that have actually occurred and those that, although possible, may not have occurred yet. It is a description therefore of the universal qualities of distribution and exchange.

This distinction between universal and historic qualities is the starting point of Marx's social and economic theory and he accuses non-socialist economists of confusing the two and of assuming that the particular historic qualities that characterize the top right-hand corner of the 'rubbish triangle' are true for all time: that the capitalist system is a truly eternal object. Thus he sets out by casting his methodological net much wider than his opponents and, since I have done the same, I am justified in following his description of the universal nature of the processes of production and consumption.

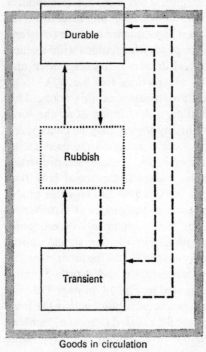

(i) Overt and covert components of the system are denoted by solid and dotted boxes respectively.

(ii) ⟶ possible transfers
‑ ‑ ‑ ‑→ impossible transfers

(iii) That part of the durable category outside the 'goods in circulation' boundary is composed of those durable items that have been totally removed from circulation

Goods in circulation

Fig.14

(It does not follow that in taking this step I am in any way committed to following Marx's views concerning the social laws that govern distribution and exchange.)

The universal (or natural) condition of these departments is, according to Marx, the identity of production and consumption but this identity is obscured by the interposition of the historic (or cultural) conditions of distribution and exchange which prevent us from perceiving it. This historic separation of production and consumption is contradicted by the existence of processes that can only occur if they are not separate, productive consumption (the use of a product in a new process of production) and consumptive production (the reproduction of human life). This state of affairs can be visualized as two contradictory forces, the historic condition separating production and consumption so that one becomes the beginning and the other becomes the end, the universal condition linking them together again to form a closed circle that makes nonsense of the idea of beginnings and ends. The manner in which the historic condition intervenes to obscure the universal unity can, with the help of this chicken-and-egg image, be represented like this:

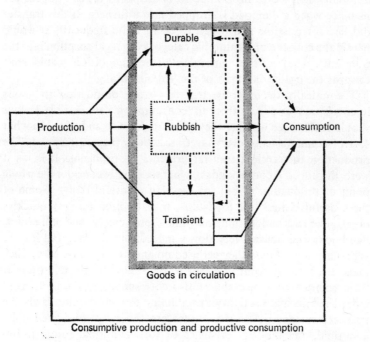

Consumptive production and productive consumption

Fig.15

Concerning the various possible and impossible transfers on the diagram, those within the 'goods in circulation' section have already been accounted for (as too have Marx's self-evident yet troublesome productive consumption and consumptive production) but we should now look more closely at those transfers crossing from 'production' to 'goods in circulation' and from 'goods in circulation' to 'consumption'.

Taking the impossible one first, that from durable to consumption, we can see that this is ideally impossible since durable objects ideally last for ever. They may be removed from circulation (as is represented by that area of the durable category which extends beyond the goods in circulation boundary) but they may not cease to exist, that is, be consumed. This transfer is simply a variation of the ideally impossible transfer from durable to rubbish which has already been dealt with. It corresponds to the destruction of a durable which leaves no residue to be disposed of, as happens for instance when a diamond is dropped into a furnace. If this transfer did become possible and began to occur quite frequently it would herald the collapse of the durable category (by its absorption into the transient). That is, this particular historic condition would shift towards the egalitarian apex of the 'rubbish triangle'.

Theoretically, the other five transfers (from 'production' to 'goods in circulation' and from there to 'consumption') are feasible and we should look to see whether they occur in practice and, if so, to what sort of common-sense everyday transactions they correspond. The production to transient transfer presents no problems. It is, as it were, the norm. It corresponds to what we usually consider the whole point of production to be: the creation of useful things. Some of these useful things, like foodstuffs, may be used up very quickly; others, like cars and washing machines, less quickly; and still others, like books and houses, very slowly indeed, but the essential feature is that as they get used they get used up and as they get used up they make the transfer from transient to consumption. So this transfer from transient to consumption also corresponds to the norm, and indeed the normal route from production to consumption is via the transient category. All other routes are generally considered quite abnormal, and the very existence of such abnormal routes is frequently ignored and sometimes even denied.

The production to rubbish transfer, at first sight, appears rather unlikely. After all, who would go to all that expense and trouble to produce rubbish. Of course, nobody would do this deliberately but inevitably the production of useful things often involves the production of rubbish as well, as an unwelcome but unavoidable by-product. So the transfer 'production to rubbish' corresponds to all that is produced that is persistent and useless. This is an aspect of production that is often disregarded and may even be denied. Currently, in certain quarters, however, it is the subject of much attention. The production to rubbish transfer corresponds to pollution.

The transfer 'rubbish to consumption' is quite common. It occurs whenever rubbish is got rid of, for example, refuse collection and incineration, sewage treatment, the reinstatement of waste land, the clearance of slums, the deportation of undesirable aliens and, at its most extreme, the gassing of Jews and Gypsies in Nazi Germany. Such consumption is generally seen as a social service: a necessary transfer, but one which nevertheless is a burden on the community. The real horror of Nazi Germany resides not in its collective madness but in the perfect reasonableness of the behaviour in terms of the particular category framework that constituted its historic condition.

The last transfer, that from production to durable, is extremely uncommon but does sometimes occur. It corresponds to the starving artist's dream come true. Certain categories of person operate with the intention that their products shall be assigned directly to the durable category, but this very seldom happens. A particularly well-established painter may achieve this, especially if his rate of production is low. Recent examples would be Bacon, Coldstream, or Hundertwasser. The same may sometimes happen with other hand-crafted objects such as Fabergé Easter eggs, Tiffany lamps, and Lutyens mansions, but those objects that go straight from production to the durable category represent a minuscule proportion of all the objects being produced. Objects which make this transfer are clearly distinct from those involved in the other transfers that have just been described; they are art. (All objects which make the direct transfer 'production to durable' are art but not all art objects make this particular transfer.)

Those persons who are particularly concerned with the manning of the controls on the transfers between categories—art critics, golf club secretaries, Oxford philosophers and colonels of cavalry regiments—operate almost entirely in terms of aesthetic values, refusing to countenance the vulgarities of economics, and directing all their energies towards the paramount duty of maintaining purity by identifying rubbish and preventing it from getting anywhere it does not belong. Examples might include T. S. Eliot's idea of the poet's role as 'purifying the language of the tribe', or Quine's idea of the philosopher's role as 'exposing and resolving paradoxes, smoothing kinks, lopping off vestigial growths, clearing ontological slums'.[1]

---

[1] W. V. O. Quine, *Word and Object* (MIT, Cambridge, Mass., 1960), p. 275.

Some art and literary critics (for example, Clement Greenberg[2] and Roy Fuller[3]) discern three levels of art, highbrow, middlebrow, and kitsch, and insist that all those art-works in the kitsch category are of no aesthetic value, those in the middlebrow are of limited value, whilst only those in the highbrow are worthy of really serious (i.e. their) attention. So, their argument runs, you must have nothing to do with kitsch, you may have a light-hearted interest in the middlebrow where you are free to form your own value-judgements, but, when it comes to the highbrow, it is so valued that you must not arrive at your own valuations but have them made for you by a high priesthood of professional critics.

It is tempting to suggest that the relationship between value (both economic and aesthetic) and rubbish is simple, namely that rubbish consists of that which has either no value or negative value. This indeed is the common-sense definition of rubbish, it is the rationale behind our daily ordering of the environment. Yet, at the same time, it is hopelessly inadequate. First, this definition can say nothing about, and indeed denies the possibility of, the transfer of an item from the transient to the rubbish category or from the rubbish to the durable category; that is, about the processes whereby value is destroyed and created. Second, something which *is* of value can be seen as rubbish if it is in the wrong place. There is Lord Chesterfield's definition of dirt as matter out of place. This definition assumes simply some orderly arrangement and a disruption of that order. On this argument a weed is simply a plant in the wrong place— a tomato among the gladioli or, conversely, a gladiolus among the tomatoes. Fuller directs his strongest abuse at the 'middlebrow masquerading as the highbrow': at the Beatles getting in among the Schuberts, or at the attention given by the critics to the televised version of *The Forsyte Saga*, 'though Galsworthy's pretensions as a serious novelist were discredited forty years ago'. But would he have reacted in the same way if it had been Schubert in among the Beatles or Dickens, say, bracketed with Galsworthy or Harold Robbins? I think not.

Lord Chesterfield's definition is inadequate for it says nothing

---

[2] Clement Greenberg, *Art and Culture* (Thames & Hudson, London, 1973).

[3] Roy Fuller, Inaugural lecture as Professor of Poetry at Oxford University (1969), *Times Literary Supplement*, 20 Feb. 1969.

about whether the orderly arrangement is hierarchical or not—about whether one object's right place is higher than another object's right place. Some, and perhaps all, orderly arrangements are hierarchical—not everything in the wrong place is rubbish, it depends on the displacement relative to the value gradient. The Old Master print in the junk shop window may be out of place but it is certainly not rubbish. Similarly, if a flower among the vegetables were really every bit as rubbishy as a vegetable among the flowers, then Gracie Fields would never have enjoyed much success with her song, 'I'm a lonely little petunia in the onion patch'.

Since the 'production to transient to consumption' sequence provides the norm, and since the rubbish category is also covert, there is a tendency to ignore, and even deliberately to deny, the existence of this consumption of rubbish. Consumption is normally assumed to mean the consumption of valuable things and, in consequence, a person's level of consumption provides an indication of his status and power. The overt inclusion of the transfer 'rubbish to consumption' would play havoc with keeping up with the Joneses. After all, the his-and-her-Jensen-Interceptor family is hardly likely to be outfaced by the ardent composters next door. But perhaps this is not so ridiculous as it sounds. If one accepts the consumption of rubbish as a part of consumption—that is, if one makes rubbish overt rather than covert—then the compost heap becomes a powerful status symbol. The growing concern with ecology, pollution, and conservation inevitably makes rubbish overt and allows the development of that most prestigious of all consumption activities, conspicuous non-consumption. Hence the compost heaps, the macrobiotic food, the little French cars, the dendrophilia, and the country cottages of those whose income and educational status are such that never for one moment could we confuse them with rude peasants so poor as to be unable to afford chemical fertilizers, fresh meat and Mother's Pride bread, chain saws, and proper vehicles.

Here, in a shift in world view, we have the first indications of a change in the historic condition. The overtness of rubbish, the willingness, among an intellectual and influential section of the middle class, to see the connectedness of everything, impedes and may even completely prevent the transfers from transient to rubbish to durable, a necessary condition for which is the unconnectedness of everything—the covertness of rubbish. Inevitably, status and power

E

diverge, the new castes proliferate, and the historic condition moves towards the caste apex of the 'rubbish triangle'.

The same sort of shift in world view may be discerned in recent developments in art. The first step is to discover the system of cultural categories concerning art consistent with the recent historic condition already described in terms of the rubbish, durable, and transient categories. Let us take a particularly simple example, an ideal system of only two categories, and let us label these 'art' and 'non-art'. Further, let us take the simplest case consistent with the recent historic condition of art, where candidates for membership of one or other category are material objects. The assignment of a candidate to one category or the other is determined by the criteria which define each category. Again, we take the simplest ideal case and assume that such criteria are explicit, unambiguous, and universally agreed upon so that each object can be unequivocally assigned to the correct category. This simple system gives rise to four logical possibilities. First, an art object placed in the art category; second, a non-art object placed in the non-art category; third, a non-art object placed in the art category; fourth, an art object placed in the non-art category. Simple real examples of these four logical possibilities might be: first, the Mona Lisa in an art gallery, described in art history books and so on; second, a bentwood hatrack in a surburban hall with hats, coats, and so on hanging on it; third, a bentwood hatrack (without hats or coats) standing in an art gallery, mentioned in the catalogue together with the name of the artist, price, title and so on; fourth, the Mona Lisa being used as an ironing-board in a suburban house together with electric iron, clothes, chair, housewife and so on. The third and fourth examples are anomalous in that they elicit (or elicited) the sort of outraged, amused, or disgusted responses that occur when a cultural membrane is pierced. By what might be called the anomaly technique, these two examples confirm the recent validity of our initial hypothetical assumption that a cultural boundary separates the art and non-art categories.

The next step is to discover whether this very simple orderly arrangement is hierarchical or not. If the two categories 'art' and 'non-art' are not hierarchical then they are of equal status. If this were so then the two anomalous examples would be equally likely and the two 'correct' examples would be equally likely. When we look at what actually happens we find that this is not so. The first possibility occurs with some difficulty and is stable. That is, objects that satisfy the stringent criteria for membership of the art category gain entry to it and, once this has happened, they tend to stay there. The second possibility occurs readily and is stable. That is, objects that satisfy the much less stringent criteria for membership of the non-art category gain entry to it and, once this has happened, they tend to stay there. The third possibility occurs with some considerable difficulty but is then stable. Classic examples of this are Duchamp's urinal signed F. Mutt and his ready-mades, including the famous bentwood hatrack. These are so stable that, at a retrospective exhibition of Duchamp's work, limited signed editions of these objects found a ready market at prices considerably higher than one would normally expect to pay at builders' merchants or furnishing emporia.

The fourth possibility is the odd one out. It hardly ever occurs and, when it does, it is always unstable. Degas is reputed to have used a Rodin sculpture as a clothes-horse but one assumes that when his effects were sold it reverted to the art category and fetched an appropriate price. Similarly, I know of a family that owns a very large Turner which they were considering having made into a dining table. I was disappointed to hear that, rather than eating straight off the oil-painted surface, they planned to protect it beneath a sealed glass frame and that they abandoned the whole project when they found that this could not be done in such a way as to guarantee that the painting survived unaltered—proof that one cannot have one's art-cake and eat off it.

It follows from these examples that the relationship between the two categories art and non-art is not symmetrical since members of the non-art category can, and sometimes do, transfer to the art category and remain there, whilst members of the art category cannot make the stable transfer to the non-art category. This relationship is comparable to that between officers and non-commissioned officers in the Brigade of Guards. An officer crystallized this relationship by explaining that he would expect to be invited to his Sergeant's wedding but that the Sergeant would not expect to be invited to his. The asymmetry here indicates that the status 'officer' is higher than the status 'NCO', and likewise the category 'art' is of higher status than the category 'non-art'.

Symmetrical orderly arrangements imply horizontal control: some objects this way, other objects that way. Hierarchical orderly arrangements imply vertical control: admission upwards, expulsion downwards. Art and non-art are subject to vertical control but many artists try to operate as if they were not. Such an approach can produce some very interesting art but it does not get rid of the vertical control, it just shifts it somewhere else. The hierarchical order pops up again in the distinction between the small group made up of the artist and his peers and the much larger group that makes up the art market. For the smaller group all the objects produced by the artist are, since they are made by an artist in an art context, in the art category. The larger, and dominant, group accepts this but considers it unimportant. The larger group distinguishes instead two categories of art object: 'good art' and 'rubbish art'. Rubbish art is of low status and to think otherwise is to be contaminated and run the risk of finding one's own status declining to the same level. Good art is of high status both in terms of the scholarly attention devoted to it and of the amount of money paid for it on the art market.

We have restricted ourselves to the simple case where candidates for membership of the two categories are material objects, and so all members of the categories 'rubbish art' and 'good art' are objects but not all objects are members of the rubbish art or good art categories. Thus the rubbish art and good art categories form a sub-system within the wider system relating to the classification of objects; that is, the system relating the transient, rubbish, and durable categories. The way in which these two systems relate is very simple. An artist producing an art object will find that, regardless of his intention, it is assigned either to the durable category, in which case it is also in the good art category, or to the rubbish category, in which case it is also in the rubbish art category. Of course, it may at some later time be discovered (the rubbish category being covert) and transferred to the durable category. The relationship can be represented as shown in Fig. 16.

Now to suggest that the best art is that which fetches the highest price in the saleroom is blasphemy indeed and, of course, art works are also assigned to the rubbish art and good art categories on the basis of another aesthetic derived entirely from the art context. The exact nature of this aesthetic would be extremely difficult to isolate but it is sufficient for the present purpose simply to acknow-

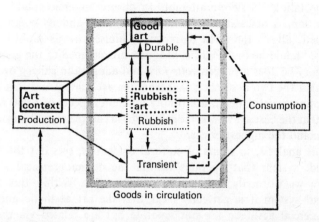

Fig.16 For clarity, only the possible art transfers are shown. Much rubbish art
is consumed but no good art. The non-art category is now redundant: it is in fact
the whole system less rubbish art and good art.

ledge that it exists. If the art sub-system were a closed system then
the assigning of an art object to the appropriate category would be
according to criteria derived entirely from this aesthetic. But the art
sub-system is not closed. It is, by virtue of the fact that art gives rise
to art objects, inevitably a sub-system of a much larger system relating to the communication of objects in general, and so is inevitably
subject to the criteria deriving from a commercial aesthetic. Whether
we like it or not the artist, simply by producing art objects, is both
accepting the commercial aesthetic and reinforcing the power
structure. This is a taboo area for the artist, and indeed for the
culturati:

The Times Sotheby Index 1968 represents the very height of vulgarity and
crass commercialism.

It is a sad reflection on the prevailing materialism in this country that
works of art are no longer valued for themselves but are merely considered
as another avenue for speculation.

One day, please God, the tide will turn. The air-conditioned vaults of
philistine businessmen will be broken open and the contents expropriated
and your wretched art journalists will be stoned to death with fake
Etruscan bronzes.

(From a letter by Mr F. J. Oliver to *The Times*, 22 October 1968)

The taboo behaviour attempts to obsure an unacceptable contradiction. A detestation of the gallery system and its commercial aesthetic allows the artist to reconcile himself to his rubbish products. Should he find that his products are assigned to the good art category he does a sudden *volte face* and adopts the gallery owner's line that the two aesthetics, that from the art context and that from the commercial context, are simply different aspects of some whole and that the best art works, judged by the art aesthetic, will inevitably command the highest prices.

This analysis, in terms of cultural categories, sets out the 'concealed' system that operates behind the commonsensical façade where we normally encounter the art object. Within this 'concealed' system it is perfectly clear that the art aesthetic and the commercial aesthetic are not separate but are related via the art object. What is more, the relationship is not symmetrical: the commercial aesthetic contains the art aesthetic because the art object is contained within the entire range of communicable things. Yet, when we look at the common-sense façade, this relationship is nowhere to be seen. Here the art aesthetic and the commercial aesthetic are clearly separate, each referring to separate systems which, ideally, have no connection one with the other. Hence the outrage when, as in the case of *The Times* Sotheby Index, this improper interpenetration is seen to occur. But, in a system which demands that its art shall come in the form of objects—possessable objects (and the fact that even earth artists and conceptual artists have found patrons shows that almost anything can be made possessable)—the commercial aesthetic and the art aesthetic can never be separate, yet they can only exist if we insist that they are.

We cannot assume that this taboo behaviour always has, and always will, obscure this contradiction. Art has not always come in the form of possessable objects and there is no reason for assuming that it will always continue to do so. As the dynamics of the category system vary so, under certain conditions, will the taboo behaviour effectively hide the contradiction and, under other conditions, will it tend increasingly to draw attention to the very thing it strives to conceal. It is these shifts between the concealment and the salience of the contradiction that, transforming world views, propel the historic condition hither and thither within the 'rubbish triangle'.

For instance, the very fact that I am able to put forward this analysis is evidence of some shift in my own world view and indicates that I have found myself operating under conditions where increasingly my attention has been focused upon this glaring contradiction. Nor can I claim any great originality since, by the time I had formulated the analysis,[4] it no longer fitted the facts, and many artists were similarly engrossed with the supposedly taboo contradiction. Their work took the form of the rejection, in various ways, either of the art object itself or of one or more of its defining criteria.

If we were to analyse what has been produced in art schools during the 1970s we should find that only a small proportion of the activity has been devoted to producing art objects, and often if an art object *is* produced it is in order to stress its unimportance. New directions in art which between themselves have little, if anything, in common can be seen as alternative responses to this change in world views: as attempts to transcend the now visible paradox relating to the commercial and art aesthetics.

Auto-destructive art is an explicitly revolutionary head-on clash with the established order which it simply aims to turn upside-down. The established order insists that its art must come in the form of objects and that these objects should be durable and possessable (or capable of being made to conform to these criteria). Auto-destructive art puts forward objects that cannot be durable since they destroy themselves. Often this is done by deliberate fabrication but sometimes in the form of putrefying *objets trouvés* such as the polythene bags filled with restaurant refuse piled on the Soho pavements late at night that have been proposed as art works by Gustav Metzger. Auto-destructive art also strives to eliminate the object by proposing in its place the event. 'Happenings', of course, also do this. Auto-destructive art is essentially a millenarian movement dedicated to reversing the positions of the class and egalitarian apices of the 'rubbish triangle': an engaging, if impotent, rubbish cargo cult.

Alternatively one can produce art that is supposedly unpossessable—earth art, wrapped-up coastlines or trenches filled with water, and process art; or mass-produced art (multiples) which operate within the established framework of art, producing durable objects, but which aim to destroy from within, to flood the market, to create a

---

[4] An early version of this argument appeared in *Art Language: the journal of conceptual art*, Vol. 1, No. 2, Feb. 1970.

chronic inflation, so that eventually those who believe that status and power derive from taking possession of art objects will be staggering around with suitcases full of worthless Old Masters like shoppers in Weimar Germany going to buy a loaf of bread with a wheelbarrow full of marks; or democratic art which seeks to produce not high art but art for all: human rights art. The squatters claim that housing is a basic human right; those optimistic and exuberant landmarks of the sixties, the Isle of Wight Pop Festival, the Stones in the Park, the Arts Laboratory and the Underground, claimed that art is a basic human right. This approach attacks the established order by trying to eliminate the scarcity of art. If there is no scarcity then art is removed from the sphere of economics and it is this, the involvement of art with the commercial system, that, inspiring the outrage so unbearable that action must be taken, is the common starting point of all these disparate movements in contemporary art. In general, these are movements away from the class apex of the 'rubbish triangle' and towards the egalitarian apex and in this respect they should be distinguished from conceptual art which would appear to be a movement towards the caste apex.

Art is always a high status activity since artists handle the symbols of society. Others, for example politicians and engineers, also handle symbols but only incidentally and implicitly. Artists deal entirely and explicitly in symbols. This distinction is graphically apparent in the diagram (Fig. 16), where vulgar commerce, being concerned essentially with the production and consumption of useful things, is routed primarily through the lower part of the 'goods in circulation' box. Art, being concerned essentially with the creation of durability, is routed through the upper part of the 'goods in circulation' box. The fact that the rubbish category is covert further serves to emphasize this separation by obscuring the area of overlap and encouraging the common-sense view that economics is concerned with transience and art with durability. This is a view that is thankfully accepted by most economists and artists.[5]

Conceptual art, in a thorough and elaborated manner, detaches

[5] Even by Keynes, whose life was spent alternating between the two: Bloomsbury art and Cambridge economics. The separation is apparent in his famous after-dinner speech (to economists) when he spoke of economists not as the guardians of civilization (art) but as the 'guardians of the possibility of civilization'.

art from the art object. True, objects are still produced but they are not important as objects. 'The importance of the non-importance of the art object' is possibly the central tenet of conceptual art, certainly it is the most important politically. For it is the art object that connects and aligns art with the power structure within our society and in so doing (art being always a high status activity) maintains the alignment of power and status. Conceptual art, in detaching art from the art object, is sloughing off the power structure; is severing the alignment of power and status; and in consequence is tending to move our historic condition towards the caste apex.

This is, in some ways, an astonishing conclusion. For instance, it does not accord in any way with what conceptual artists themselves claim to be doing. Conceptual artists tend to see their work as a kind of superior art theory: a neutral, logical, even austere, meta-art. Their minimalism is simply the imposition of a fastidious vegetarianism upon the intellectual diet; their disdain for the art object and the economic forces that it mediates reveals a concern for purity; their opaque and often pretentious language indicates an overriding urge for high status. Sheathed in their impenetrable linguistic armour, radiating purity, and loftily dismissing their despicable non-conceptual colleagues (whose diet even includes the disgusting strong meat of the emotions) as mere object-makers and easel-weasels, the conceptualists look like becoming the Brahmins of the art community.

Must we then conclude that all this puritanism is a clever pretence aimed at drawing our attention away from the political objectives that are conceptual artists' real concern? Must we understand conceptual art to be ideology disguised as theory? A more plausible explanation is that the conceptualists are simply reacting to their situation on the basis of an inadequate understanding of what that situation is. Rather than developing an understanding of the way in which the commercial aesthetic and the art aesthetic are connected, they start from a position which declares that such a connected state of affairs is unacceptable. Since they can do little about the commercial aesthetic, they have no option but to try to move art itself to a position of safety. Whatever has to happen to art in the process, and whatever the political consequences may be, are simply part of the price we must cheerfully pay for rectifying this intolerable situation. Instead of looking at the present state of the connection between the art and the commercial aesthetics, finding it unattractive, and asking what other possibilities there are and whether they are more attractive or even less attractive—that is, asking 'What are the capabilities of this connection?'—they see the connection as problematical, as something to be got rid of at any cost. Denied, by their initial intolerant stance, the opportunity of standing back from their immediate situation, they become incapable of distinguishing bad from worse.

If I am particularly hard upon conceptual art it is because I have, in a modest way, been involved with it and because I believe that, if only it can be persuaded to shift its focus from problems to capabilities, it can indeed create the meta-art to which it aspires. For, having described both the commercial system and the aesthetic system in terms of a single dynamic model, we are now in a position to reject the prevalent common-sense view that, insisting on their separation, sees economics as concerned with transience and art as concerned with durability. We can now draw the framework for a general theory which will subsume the two within a single formulation.

Referring back to the last diagram (Fig. 16), we should note that first, all items entering the transient category are eventually either consumed or transferred to the rubbish category, and second, that some, but not all, rubbish is either consumed by services (e.g. refuse disposal, sewage treatment) or transferred to the durable category. Some remains as rubbish. If we isolate from this diagram the various permitted sequences we obtain the following:

1. Production to transient to consumption.
2. Production to transient to rubbish to consumption.
3. Production to transient to rubbish to durable.
4. Production to rubbish to durable.
5. Production to durable.
6. Production to rubbish.
7. Production to transient to rubbish.
8. Production to rubbish to consumption.

Additionally, in the case of all those sequences that end with consumption, we must distinguish between those that really end with consumption and those which are simply artificial abstractions from what is really a cyclical sequence in which consumption is again linked to production via the processes of consumptive production and productive consumption. Rearranging these we find that, out of a total of eleven possible sequences, three are cyclical and eight are linear. Of these eight, three end in consumption, three end in durable, and two end in rubbish.

It follows that a view which holds that consumption is the only end and object of economic activity[6] is extraordinarily myopic, for it fails to perceive that much of economic activity, being cyclical in nature and so having no ends, cannot be described in terms of ends, and that, even within that part of economic activity that can be described in terms of ends, there are in general not one but three alternative ends: consumption, the creation of rubbish, and the creation of durability. We are everywhere surrounded by the consequences of this myopia. The more we insist on seeing the aesthetic and economic systems as clearly separate, the more we are forced to focus upon the connection between them. A pair of examples will serve to illustrate this point: the first showing our inability to act appropriately towards the classification scheme we have imposed upon the universe of objects, the second our inability to make objects conform to their classification even when we do act appropriately.

Value Added Tax is designed as a tax on consumption. In essence it was thought of, in Britain, as a rationalization of existing tax structures (notably Purchase Tax) that would help to bring the country into line with the rest of the Common Market. At no time was it suggested that it was a radical reform calculated to transform beyond recognition our present social order. If it is a tax on consumption then it should apply only to those goods following the routes numbered 1, 2, and 8—that is, those that end in consumption—and should exclude those that follow cyclical routes or end in durability or rubbish. If this were done then it would provide a powerful incentive to switch goods from consumption on to these exempted routes, thereby initiating a rapid change in the patterning of distribution and exchange and hence of the social order that it regulates. Of course, these

---

[6] For instance:
'Modern economics . . . considers consumption to be the sole end and purpose of all economic activity, taking the factors of production in land, labour and capital as the means.'
E. F. Schumacher, *Small is Beautiful*, chapter entitled 'Buddhist economics' (Blond & Briggs, London, 1973).

exceptions were not made for the simple reason that the existence of these alternative routes was not recognized. All routes were assumed to end in consumption and the fact that many do not meant that, even before Value Added Tax reached the statute book, zero-rated exception was piled upon zero-rated exception. Antiques and works of art, regardless of the problems of definition, are not zero-rated and so, by treating these durables as transient, Value Added Tax provides a strong incentive for the switching of goods from the durable to the transient category and is certainly a powerful disincentive to the transfers from transient to rubbish to durable. If we assume that our legislators are not all party to a conspiracy aimed at converting us into an egalitarian caste society, we must conclude that they have little understanding of what they are doing.

The second example concerns the garden as an art form. It is hardly surprising, in view of our present insistence on the durability of art, that art forms tend to be arranged hierarchically with, at the top, those that are readily preserved, recorded, and generally accessible to art historical study, such as painting, classical music, literature, sculpture, architecture, and now film, and, at the bottom, those that do not easily afford these facilities, such as cooking, firework displays, dancing, and gardening. Now it is often claimed that England's greatest contribution to the visual arts has been the landscape garden of the eighteenth century. If this is so then England, in order to take her rightful place in the art league of the Western world, must impose durability upon this unique heritage. Unfortunately, it turns out that these landscape gardens were pre-eminently works of conceptual art and that the special problems connected with their conservation are insurmountable. In fact, the art works are not there to be conserved.[7]

In general, a garden is an assemblage principally of vegetation kept in a preferred state of ecological arrest by the craft of gardening. It follows that if control is removed it ceases to be a garden.

---

[7] An argument that has been elegantly advanced by Fricker, to whom I am also indebted for the definition of the garden. L. J. Fricker, *Report on special problems connected with the conservation of gardens of historical interest in Great Britain*. Presented to the first symposium on problems relating to gardens of historical interest. Organized by the International Council of Monuments and Sites and the International Federation of Landscape Architects. Held at Fontainebleau, September 1971.

How does the English landscape garden of the eighteenth century relate to this definition of gardens in general? Horace Walpole provided the answer in his celebrated statement, '[William Kent] leaped the fence, and saw that all nature was a garden.'[8] But if this is the unique characteristic of Kent's landscapes it follows that they cannot be gardens. The contradiction can be set out as follows:

Gardens in general: Nature = no control ≠ garden

Kent's landscapes: Nature = garden

Alternatively, we could interrogate Walpole's ghost in the following way:

> *Us:* 'What fence did Kent jump?'
> *Walpole:* 'The garden fence.'
> *Us:* 'Out of the garden into what?'
> *Walpole:* 'Into nature, of course.'
> *Us:* 'But, as you say, all nature is a garden so he jumped out of the garden into the garden, so there can't have been a fence there in the first place.'
> *Walpole:* 'Well . . . er . . .'

There is no getting around it. The eighteenth-century landscape garden is an exquisite conceptual art work built upon this paradox. The insurmountable problems involved in our current attempts to render durable the art object (the physical form of the gardens) demonstrate paradoxically that only the art concept of the eighteenth-century garden is durable. If our commitment to durability increasingly requires us to impose upon things qualities that they can never accept then the continued existence of the durable category itself is threatened.

These two examples, Value Added Tax and the eighteenth-century English landscape garden, demonstrate that there is no neutrality: that the dynamics of the process that allocates people, things, and ideas to alternative cultural categories continually reacts upon the social system that provides its support, transforming it, the social contexts of its constituent members, and their various world views.

Going back to the example of the recent change in world views within the art community, evident in the shift away from the art object towards the art concept, we should attempt to describe the

---

[8] Horace Walpole, *Essay on Modern Gardening* (1784), p. 55.

dynamic that has caused it. Two possibilities exist. The first is the familiar argument that capitalism in its advanced form has extended its control to every human activity and that its intrusion into the art aesthetic is now so extensive that no conspiracy of blindness can conceal it. If this is the case, then the reaction is away from the class apex of the 'rubbish triangle' towards the egalitarian apex: an explanation that would fit quite well the phenomena of auto-destructive, multiple, and democratic art. The second possibility is less familiar and may be derived from certain autonomous changes within art education itself; changes which were occurring, in Britain at least, during the late 1960s and early 1970s. These may be described (as indeed they were) as a move from a hierarchical organizational structure towards a network structure. This shift would result in lateral connections being discovered between areas which hitherto were either unrelated or related only through the higher levels of the hierarchy which thereby could monitor and control any connections which might be made. It follows that it is much more difficult to conceal a conspiracy of blindness in a network system than it is in a hierarchical system. A reaction of this nature is not adequately described in terms of a shift from the class apex towards the egalitarian apex, for it also, and more significantly, involves a shift, at right angles to this, towards the caste apex. An adequate explanation of the phenomena of conceptual art must take account of this direction. A full description of reactions in general, and of the changes in world view that accompany them, must take account of both these directions and of the relation between them; that is, of all the possibilities contained within the rubbish triangle. (The class apex to caste apex is dealt with in Chapter 8, the class to egalitarian apex in Chapter 9.)

Such an account would provide the basis for a general predictive theory of the alternative allocation, via cultural categories, of people, things, and ideas between, in the first instance, cyclical routes and routes with ends, and in the second instance between consumption, rubbish, and durability. As such it would constitute a sort of meta-economics referring not only to the conventional subject matter of economics but to the entire range of social, cultural, and economic phenomena: a unified field theory of the social sciences.

7 Monster conservation

Rubbish theory, if it does nothing else, serves to draw our attention to the way in which objects are socially processed and to suggest that a description of this process should be included in the answer to the question 'How is society possible?' If I had to answer this portentous question in just one word it would be 'contradiction', and to me the charm of rubbish theory is that it seems always to lead straight into illogicality, anomaly, and paradox. Regrettably, there are many who find these qualities not so much charming as monstrous, and there are some who would go so far as to maintain that the proper aim and object of serious thought should be the systematic exclusion of such monsters. Monster exclusion is, at its worst, intolerant, puritanical, and repressive. At its best, it reveals a dubious prettifying intent that leads to the pretence that things are tidier than they really are.

Monster exclusion is a distinct, and often dominant, intellectual style. We have already seen one very clear example of this style in Mr Toone's bid to prevent the serious consideration of Grange Park as a part of our glorious heritage. Because the building transgresses all Mr Toone's aesthetic principles (such as harmony with nature, truth to materials, and consistency between inside and outside) it becomes, for him, an abomination, '. . . out of keeping . . . the most monstrous eyesore . . . phoney . . . a neo-classical horror . . . a multi-legged prehistoric monster'. Of course, aesthetics is a very argumentative business with all kinds of contradictory opinions being attacked and defended in this sort of way, but the same style is found even in science and in philosophy.

The monster exclusion that is entailed in Monod's definition of objectivity (for which he has a high regard) as the systematic denial of final causes puts him in a very different stylistic category to, say, Aristotle, who was happy to countenance all sorts of different causes. The same distinction is apparent between, on the one hand, those expansive philosophers who would like to consider not just things that they know do happen but also things that might happen, and, on the other hand, their tight-lipped colleagues who are aghast at the idea of expanding their universe so as to include all possible entities. Herbert Marcuse,[1] for instance, is anxious to include certain possible entities. He would like the concept of beauty to comprehend all the beauty not yet realized but, at the same time, he manages to ignore the fact that the realization of some possible beauty must involve the suppression, the non-realization, of some other possible beauty. Consequently, he is irritated when he comes up against another philosopher, Quine, who is actively involved in this process that Marcuse has ignored. Quine is not fond of possible entities; to him they are 'so-called possible entities' and he very definitely wants to keep them out: '. . . such an overpopulated universe is in many ways unlovely. It offends the aesthetic sense of us who have a taste for desert landscapes. But this is not the worst of it: [such a] slum of possibles is a breeding ground for disorderly elements.'[2] Of course, ostriches, too, have a taste for desert landscapes, and Quine wilfully refuses to countenance quite real possibilities. What so infuriates Marcuse is that the 'so-called possible entities' that Quine rejects happen to include all those most dear to him. Quine has rejected the possibility of the different social order that Marcuse has set his heart on. For Marcuse a 'possible entity' is something he would like to happen. For Quine a 'so-called possible entity' is something he would like not to happen. Both are monster excluders, it is just that Quine's monster happens to be Marcuse's sacred cow.

Could it be that the style is really the philosophy and that the content, all the talk about entities and their possibility, is just an irrelevant distraction? If the answer is 'yes', then an understanding of the rival styles, one based on keeping monsters out, the other on keeping them in, could lead to a synthesis (monster conservation) which would allow us to tolerate the monsters that undoubtedly exist in our world and, at the same time, would prevent us from ending up knee-deep in them.

The effects of monster exclusion are more far-reaching in the

---

[1] Herbert Marcuse, *One-Dimensional Man: The Ideology of Industrial Society* (Routledge, London, 1964).

[2] W. V. O. Quine, *From a Logical Point of View* (Cambridge, Mass., 1953), p. 4.

social sciences than they are in the natural and physical sciences. For instance, if the idea that the earth revolves around the sun is abominable in relation to a particular pattern of belief, the monster can be excluded. The earth still continues in its orbit, only the idea of its orbit is suppressed. In social matters, the exclusion of a monster can achieve the equivalent of stopping the earth and making the sun go round it instead. For instance, Mr Toone is not suggesting that we ignore Grange Park, he is arguing for its demolition. He would be delighted to see such monsters become extinct in his beautiful Hampshire countryside. The fact that social processes, unlike physical and natural ones, have this self-fulfilling capacity means that monster exclusion can all too easily become monster extermination. Monster extermination can result in the permanent removal of the exceptions to a social theory and, in consequence, monster exterminators are particularly prevalent in the social sciences. The result is that social processes that rely on contradictions for their very existence are almost invariably described by theoretical models of impeccable internal consistency. By contrast, a monster conserver should aim to produce models that take account of the contradictions. A step in this direction would be a monster-conserving model of the relationship between world view and action, and rubbish theory helps us to take this step. It serves the double purpose of revealing just how monster-excluding present models are, and of suggesting how one might set about constructing a less repressive version.

To make sense of the world in which we live we need a world view but, given the choice, which world view would we choose? Rubbish theory clearly demonstrates that all are restrictive in the sense that, once we have latched on to one way of seeing things, we are also latched on to not seeing things in other ways. Well, the irony is that we are not given the choice. We could only choose between alternatives if, first, we knew that they existed and, second, we had access to some means of evaluating them but, of course, if we have these necessary conditions we already have a world view in which case we are no longer in a position to choose one. Man, one might say, is born with 360° vision yet everywhere we see him in blinkers. The three big questions now are: 'How does he get his blinkers?', 'How many kinds of blinkers are there?', and 'What decides which kind of blinkers he gets?'

The classic model of the way people acquire their blinkers is provided by transaction theory.[3] Transaction theory, like rubbish theory, suggests that world views are not acquired simply by solitary introspection but through involvement with both people and objects. The idea is that an individual has, initially, a rag-bag of disparate values and that, on the basis of these values, he engages in transactions with other individuals over various valued objects. This rag-bag of evaluations constitutes his world view and provides him with some sort of basis for deciding what courses of action are open to him and for predicting their likely outcomes. Being an intelligent and thinking man, he follows the course of action that his world view suggests is likely to be most advantageous to him. In transacting over a valued object he will probably find that his rag-bag of values is differently constituted from that of the individual he is transacting with. In other words, it is very likely that there will be a mismatch between the expected and the actual results of his actions. In the light of this mismatch, he rearranges his values in the hope of doing rather better next time. The end result of this sort of behaviour in myriad and often overlapping transactions is that his rag-bag of values gradually becomes more systematized, more internally consistent, and more like those of the individuals with whom he has been transacting. In this way, world views become more orderly, more accurate in their prediction, and more shared.

The trouble with this model of the blinker-acquiring process is that it is too good. It results in all the transactors ending up with the same world view, and different world views can exist only between populations that don't transact with each other. In other words, transaction theory is too deterministic.

This over-determination results from the invalid assumption that everyone's rag-bag has got the same contents and that just the values attached to them are different. But the fact is that the universe of objects is so vast as to be unhandleable and, if we wish to handle it, we must first whittle it down to manageable proportions. Our world view must, willy nilly, be constructed only from those objects that we happen to have in our rag-bag in the first place. Inevitably we suffer a cognitive bias: the contents of our rag-bag furnish us

---

[3] See Frederick Barth, *Models of Social Organisation*. Occasional papers of the Royal Anthropological Institute, No. 23, 1966.

with a way of seeing and a way of seeing is also a way of not seeing.

When this requirement for cognitive bias is incorporated into the transaction model it results in one small but crucial change. A transacting individual now modifies his values, not on the basis of the results of his actions, but on the basis of the *perceived* results of his actions. If two transacting individuals happen to have rather different cognitive biases it is now, with this modification, quite possible that in the process their world views, whilst each becoming more systematized and more internally consistent, will at the same time become *less* shared. In other words, they will both still be acquiring blinkers but they will be different kinds of blinkers.

This small modification to transaction theory, the inclusion of the single word 'perceived', takes care of the objections that rubbish theory raises. Rubbish theory scotches the idea that, by looking at the process of social life, we can gain access to its concrete reality. Instead, it shows that all we ever have access to is socially processed reality in all its fluid variation. The way in which transaction theory excludes the monster that rubbish theory is so concerned to conserve can best be clarified by comparing the assumptions that each theory makes about the process of social life.

Transaction theory was originally conceived as a way of getting a closer and more realistic picture than that obtained by looking just at the relationships between people. People, it was pointed out, do not just interact: they interact over *something*. Transaction theory set out to improve the model by replacing the basic isolate, the interaction person–person, with the transaction person–object–person. Rubbish theory has no quarrel with this, but it does reject the next assumption of transaction theory which is that this basic isolate person–object–person is *natural*.

If we were able to look down upon some social system from a sufficiently high vantage point, we should see the process of social life spread out below us in a myriad of transactions in which people interacted over almost innumerable objects. Assuming that we could positively identify each individual and that we could label each object, rather in the way that an ornithologist affixes rings to the legs of birds to discover their migratory patterns, we might be able to make some sense of what was going on. The only isolable natural units in such a system would be two distinct types of chain.

First, there are those initiated by the entry into circulation of a particular object and terminated by its removal from circulation. Such a chain could be artificially decomposed into an initial transaction person–object, a variable number (m) transactions of the type person–object–person, and a terminal transaction object–person. Only in the special case where m equalled zero would this natural unit be of the form person–object–person. In all other cases the transaction person–object–person is an artificial abstraction from this natural unit.

Second, there are those chains initiated by the entry into social life of a particular individual and terminated by that individual's death (or removal from social life should that happen to precede his death). Such a chain could be artificially decomposed into an initial transaction object–person, a variable number (n) transactions of the type object–person–object, and a terminal transaction person–object.

These chains, then, and not the triad person–object–person, are the natural isolable units that make up the process of social life. This triad person–object–person does characterize one type of chain but transaction theory, by insisting that it is *the* natural unit, completely ignores the other type of chain that is characterized by the different triad object–person–object. Since these two types of chain are complementary, this piece of monster exclusion has some serious consequences.

The first kind of chain consists of the careers of particular objects as they traverse an environment of individuals and groups; the second consists of the careers of particular individuals or groups as they traverse an environment of objects. Nor, so far as the properties of the process of social life are concerned, is one inevitably prior to the other. In one situation it may be reasonable to assume that people are being manipulated by objects, in another we can assume that objects are being manipulated by people, and in a third that people are both manipulating objects and being manipulated by them. What is more, within this dynamic process, situations may be continuously transformed, with the manipulator becoming the manipulated and *vice versa*. This systemic view, which gives equal emphasis to both types of natural unit, is the starting point of the analytic approach which I took in examining the Stevengraph.

The property that maintains fluidity in the case of the Stevengraph is its social malleability. The varying social controls on the allocation of Stevengraphs to the transient, rubbish, and durable categories, and on the transfers between these categories, means that there is nothing natural about the length of the natural chains. Chains there will be, but the lengths of the chains (the values of m and n) are variables that are, to a considerable extent, socially determined. Transaction theory, by ignoring one kind of chain altogether and by insisting that in the case of the other kind of chain the value of m is always zero, excludes this fluid monster. Once this monster has been excluded the theorist can claim to be a 'cosmic exile' with direct access to the raw unprocessed 'natural units' that constitute 'concrete reality'.

The great advantage of conserving this fluid monster is that we avoid this 'cosmic exile' pitfall and instead are led towards the idea of mapping those areas in which people manipulate objects and those areas in which objects manipulate people. Our attention can then focus on the variations in the distribution of these areas of flexibility and of fixed assumptions, and we are then able to examine the manner in which the boundary between these areas may change. So rubbish theory, by allowing for cultural bias, conserves all the fluidity that is undoubtedly present within the process of social life. Transaction theory excludes it.

So this modification, the inclusion of cognitive bias, alters the answer to the second big question about how many different kinds of blinkers there are. Instead of 'one', the answer is now, 'more than one'. If there was only one, the Ron-and-Cliffs and the Knockers-Through would, as a result of their social involvement with objects, end up with the same view of the world. This they emphatically do not do. Thanks to their different cognitive biases (one towards transience, the other towards durability), the more they transact the clearer their divergent views of the world become.

This answer is likely to be very discouraging to social scientists and explains why it is that they should be so happy to go along with any monster-exterminating scheme that will give them the other answer. If they get the answer 'one' then they can get down to analysing concrete reality and really produce some results, but what if the answer is 'more than one'? If the reality they have to deal with is not concrete but fluid, what chance have they got? They might just as well pack up and go home.

This, in fact, was the conclusion that I first drew from rubbish theory, but is it really valid? After all,'more than one' is not quite the same as 'infinity', and only if socially processed reality was so fluid that it could be anything at all would I have been justified in concluding that social science was impossible. This might well have been the end of the whole affair had I not one day happened upon an article in the *Times Literary Supplement* about something called 'catastrophe theory'.[4] Catastrophe theory was invented in 1968 by a French mathematician, René Thom,[5] and its significance for social science is that it suggests that it is very likely that the range of different kinds of blinkers we can wear is really quite limited.

As far as rubbish theory is concerned, Thom's timely invention of catastrophe theory is a remarkable stroke of luck: it enables us to *do* something about rubbish theory's conclusions. The whole point of rubbish theory is to demonstrate the fallacy inherent in the 'concrete reality' picture of the process of social life, and to replace it with a fluid, socially processed, reality. Catastrophe theory provides the tools we need in order to be able to handle this fluid reality.

In fact, as often happens in applied mathematics, we only need for this purpose a very few items out of Thom's tool-bag. These specific tools can most readily be explained by means of worked examples (which are provided in the next two chapters), but what does need to be explained first is the underlying philosophy of catastrophe theory. Thom's style is very much that of monster conservation, and the parallel between what he has succeeded in doing in mathematics and what I have been blundering about trying to do with rubbish theory may help to explain just how it is that catastrophe theory provides us with the key to a monster-conserving social science.

My reason for hammering away at transaction theory is that, by uncovering the mistakes in its initial assumptions, we may be able to avoid repeating them. Transaction theory is explicitly designed to provide models of empirical social forms and to mirror observed social processes. That is, it is strictly limited to things that we happen to know happen, and it is not concerned with things that, though we don't know of them happening, might happen. It is this lack of interest in possible entities that is directly responsible for the mon-

[4] E. C. Zeeman, 'The Geometry of Catastrophe', *Times Literary Supplement*, 10 Dec. 1971.

[5] René Thom, 'Topological models in biology', *Topology*, Vol. 8, 1969; *Stabilité structurelle et morphogénèse* (Benjamin, Paris, 1972).

ster exclusion that so debilitates the theory. To avoid repeating the same mistakes we need some method that will allow us to shift the focus of attention from social phenomena to the possibility of social phenomena. Catastrophe theory gives us that method.

The way in which Thom is trying to widen the enquiry, by considering not phenomena but their possibility, can be made clearer by comparing his approach with that of Monod. Monod extrapolates from molecular biology, the genetic code, and the random occurrence of mutations, to the entire universe and concludes that chance is a basic law of nature. Extrapolating still further, from nature to society, he argues that man needs ultimate values but now, thanks to modern biology, knows that he can never have them. But is this kind of argument, from nature to human nature, valid? Rubbish theory shows that we do not have access to raw nature but only to its socially processed form. So, when Monod speaks of 'nature' he must be speaking of 'the idea of nature', and the idea of nature is a social product.

The anthropologist is interested in the rival and conflicting views of creation proposed by different specialists not in regard to their truth or falsity, which he is unqualified to judge anyway, but in terms of their persuasive rhetoric, their ability to attract new adherents and heightened respect. Thus, if Monod, in arguing from nature to human nature, is putting the cart before the horse, we should conclude not that he is naïve in the matter of transportation but that he is making a shrewd and skilful bid to raise the status and importance of molecular biology. To the extent that he proves successful we will be convinced that the cart should be before the horse and that, all these years, we have had them the wrong way round. Anthropology itself cannot, of course, claim exemption from this analysis, and in making it the anthropologist is simultaneously revealing and entering the arena within which different specialists compete for status and power, respect and adherents.

Where Monod starts from biology and expands to fill the universe, Thom by contrast starts from a theoretical position which in effect considers not only this universe but all possible universes. He then progressively narrows his focus on to modern biology. The article in which Thom first did this is highly technical and concerned with identifying and resolving a specific problem, that of morphogenesis, the origin and evolution of biological structures. But in his conclusion he momentarily steps back from his particular concern to look at what it is that he is doing. He is not proposing a scientific theory but a method and this method does not lead to specific techniques but to what he calls 'an art of models'. This art of models, be believes, satisfies a fundamental epistemological need. This need, I suggest, is the need for monster conservation and Thom's art of models is the style that will allow us to satisfy that need.

The monster-conserving style of Thom's art of models is made very clear when we examine the way it handles the question of whether physical processes are deterministic or indeterministic. Monster excluders tend to favour the deterministic hypothesis which holds that all external phenomena are rigidly determined and that, in those cases where we cannot specify what this deterministic mechanism is, the fault lies in the inadequacy of our techniques or our tools. For Thom, this insistence that the determinism must be there and that if we look hard enough we are sure to find it is a repressive article of faith to which he is anxious not to subscribe. Nor, on the other hand, does he want to become such a monster lover as to insist that nothing is determined. He simply points out that, since you can select phenomena to uphold the deterministic hypothesis and you can select phenomena to invalidate it, it is desirable to take an approach that does not have to exclude one or other of these sets of phenomena. Rather than taking examples of indeterminacy that occur in those mysterious regions that lie at the very limits of human observation, in cosmology, and in elementary particle physics, he chooses an everyday example of discomforting familiarity.

When we pull the plug out of the bath the water runs out, sometimes clockwise, sometimes anticlockwise. Thus a part of our world that we have no difficulty in observing exhibits a kind of very high instability. Under experimental conditions the bath is idealized, becoming perfectly cylindrical, filled with water perfectly at rest, and devoid of occupant. When the plug is removed the water begins to spin in a cyclonic movement the handedness of which is, in practice, indeterminate. Thus the final state exhibits less symmetry than the initial data, that is, a 'breaking of symmetry' occurs. Thom argues that any phenomenon exhibiting such a breaking of symmetry cannot be given a deterministic formalizable model. Of course, supporters of the deterministic hypothesis may say that the initial data were not perfectly symmetrical. They may make appeals to the residual motion of the water, to the movement of the air over its surface, or to the Coriolis effect due to the earth's rotation, but in doing so they are merely deflecting the objection. Since they have not yet been able to prove the deterministic link between one of these initially asymmetric sets of data and the way the water goes down the plughole, they really should entertain the possibility that no such deterministic link exists. (Contrary to popular belief, the bathwater does not go out one way in the Northern Hemisphere, the other way in the Southern Hemisphere, and straight down on the equator. It goes down either one way or the other in both Hemispheres and never goes straight down— not even on the equator.)

Turning to the phenomena which uphold the deterministic hypothesis, Thom points out that, in contrast to the highly unstable bathwater, there are many cases where the determined character of a process is experimentally obvious. This is often the case in morphogenetic processes such as, for instance, the high degree of determinism required to ensure that chickens produce eggs that produce chickens. When, in such a process, a given morphology remains stable with respect to small changes in the initial data the process can be said to be the support of what Thom calls a 'morphogenetic field'. Another word that is sometimes used is 'chreod' meaning 'necessary path'.[6] The whole point of going to all this trouble to define the deterministic component in this way is to ensure that, when you have succeeded in describing the morphogenetic fields or the chreods involved in a process, you do not fall into the deterministic hypothesis trap and believe you have finished the description.

For example, there are some (Samuel Butler, Marshall McLuhan, and many a schoolboy among them) who have attempted to resolve the problematical relationship between the chicken and the egg (as to which is prior) by bracketing away the linear sequence: chicken–egg–chicken–etc. as an irrelevancy. They are left with the simple relationship:

Fig.17

[6] See C. H. Waddington, *The Strategy of the Genes* (Allen & Unwin, London, 1958).

and the chicken becomes simply the transitional state between egg and egg, and the egg becomes simply the transitional state between chicken and chicken. Or, as the schoolboy usually puts it, 'the chicken is the egg's way of producing another egg'. This simple relationship constitutes the morphogenetic field or chreod; that is, the determinism entailed in the morphogenetic process described by the reproduction and evolution of the domestic fowl. But, of course, since it brackets away the linearity of the process, it cannot specify anything about the transitional sequence from primeval slime to chicken and from chicken to goodness-knows-what in the future. This process may or may not be sustained by other chreods or morphogenetic fields yet, even when these have been identified, the process is still not fully described. Indeed, the chreods define the boundary between what is describable and what is indescribable, and it is one of the major achievements of Thom's theory of structural stability that, for the first time, it allows us to identify this boundary and lets us make provision for that which cannot be described.

For any natural morphogenetic process, it is very important to isolate first those parts of the process which are the supports of morphogenetic fields, to find out the *chreods* of the process. They form kinds of islands of determinism separated by zones of instability or indeterminacy. That such a presentation is possible amounts to say [*sic*] that the morphology is more or less *describable*. In fact, almost any natural process exhibits some kind of local regularity in its morphology, which allows one to distinguish recurrent identifiable elements denominated by words. Otherwise, the process would be entirely chaotic and there would be nothing to talk about.[7]

Lest it might appear that this constitutes a claim for access to raw unprocessed nature, I should point out that, though these recurrent identifiable elements may exist in natural processes, they do not determine what we talk about; they determine the limits of what it is possible for us to talk about. In different social and cultural contexts the recurrent elements are differently identified. Culture, the denomination of recurrent identifiable elements, can take more than one form and, in consequence, one man's denominated recurrent element can easily be another man's innominate chaos.

[7] Thom (1969), p. 321.

It is interesting to note that the biologist's quest for chreods has been paralleled in anthropology by the development of structuralism. First, the Butler/McLuhan/schoolboy partial resolution of the problem presented by the chicken and the egg, with its moratorium on the linear, its convergence of past and future, its isolation of binary oppositions, and its emphasis on mediation, epitomizes the structuralist approach. Second, Thom's definition of a morphogenetic field bears a remarkable resemblance to Lévi-Strauss's[8] almost mystical appeal to structure through his renowned jigsaw analogy. Lévi-Strauss argues that in the case of a puzzle where the pieces have been arbitrarily cut there is no structure at all. But if (as usually happens) the pieces are cut into different shapes by a mechanical saw that has its movements controlled by rotating cams, the puzzle does have a structure. This structure does not exist at the empirical level, since there are many ways of recognizing the way the pieces fit together. Rather, the structure lies in the mathematical formulae expressing the shapes of the cams and in their relative speeds of rotation. Lévi-Strauss insists that, though this structure is something very remote from the puzzle as it appears to the person solving it, it is the one and only intelligible way of explaining it.

Thom's approach allows us to identify a crucial difference between the structuralist technique and structuralism. The structuralist technique allows us to discover the 'islands of determinism' within a process. Structuralism insists that these islands fully describe the process: that is, it denies the existence of their circumambient ocean of indeterminacy. So, Lévi-Strauss, having isolated his chreod, the mathematical formulae for the cams, falls into the deterministic trap of believing he has completed the description and explained the puzzle. In consequence, structuralism is paradoxically revealed to be aligned with the crude and oppressive positivism that it explicitly rejects: if it's indescribable, it isn't there. The structuralist technique says, 'This is the part of the process that is describable'. Structuralism says, 'This is the description of the process'. In transforming a technique into an 'ism', the anthropologist has embraced the deterministic hypothesis and abandoned monster conservation. It is because of the alarming ease with which this can happen that Thom

---

[8] Claude Lévi-Strauss, 'On Manipulated Sociological Models', *Bijdragen tot de taal-, land-, en volkenkunde*, No. 116, 1960, p. 52.

is at pains to emphasize the 'philosophically important fact' the recognition of which forms the basis for his entire approach: '... a deterministic system may exhibit in a "structurally stable way" a complete indeterminacy in the qualitative prediction of the final outcome of its evolution.'[9] The problem now is to work out how to depict the relationship between world view and action in such a way as to recognize this philosophically important fact.

The deterministic component, the chreod, in the example of the chicken and the egg can be represented as a closed system of just two states, egghood and chickenhood, linked by two irreversible processes, laying and hatching.

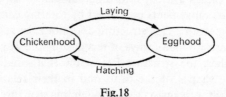

Fig.18

Such a closed system can never change itself, so this is an inadequate description in that it ignores the evolution of the system. The evolution occurs because at some point in the cycle new genetic possibilities enter from time to time, and at some other point in the cycle genetic possibilities are lost from time to time. This indeterministic

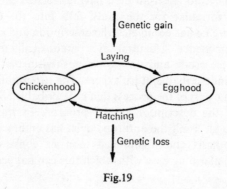

Fig.19

9 Thom (1969), p. 321.

component can be included in the representation by adding two processes that connect the closed deterministic system to the outside world. If we ignore for the moment just where in the cycle genetic possibilities are gained and lost, we obtain a picture as shown in Fig. 19 opposite.

For reasons that will become apparent once the 'feeds' are labelled, I choose to represent the relationship between world view and action like this:

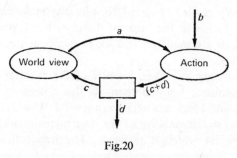

Fig.20

The indeterminate gain *b* enters the cycle in the action domain. It represents novel action—the exercising of choices that previously have not been exercised. The indeterminate loss *d* is depicted as occurring in the course of a process, and the box represents a monitor or filter which separates what shall be retained within the cycle *c* from what shall be lost *d*. We now need to give descriptive labels to the various processes and to explain just how they relate the two domains, world view and action, to each other and to whatever it is that lies outside them both.

The deterministic and monster-excluding chicken-and-egg model is, of course, already fully developed in transaction theory and we can draw upon this both to save time and effort and to help clarify what it is that I am trying to do, by emphasizing the points at which I diverge from existing representations.

Transaction theory commendably sets out to resolve the self-inflicted problem that has resulted from the separation of social and cultural abstractions. It aims to provide a theory of how cultural and social abstractions are connected. It accepts that values and behaviour, like the chicken and the egg, are cyclically connected and elects to start with values. Thus a person, before he acts, will have some values and these values enable him to discriminate between the various courses of action that are open to him. His values therefore furnish both the constraints and the incentives that enable him to choose a particular course of action. He then acts or rather, since he is going to be coming to terms with some other person over the attainment of some valued object, transacts. He is then able to re-assess his initial values in relation to the results. If his expectations are realized, then his initial values are confirmed. If they are confounded or only partially realized, then he may make certain adjustments to his values in the hope of doing rather better next time. Thus his values are modified and so, in consequence, are his subsequent actions.

We have already seen that, because of the monster exclusion it entails, this eminently commonsensical description of the connection between world view and action is not valid. What is more, it does not even possess the stability of the deterministic chicken-and-egg representation on which it is based. The transaction process is envisaged as doing two things. First, as people transact over a specific object their initially rather different evaluations move closer together. The aggregate effect is that people come to have more similar evaluations of specific objects. Second, just as objects do not exist in complete isolation from one another, neither do the valuations that are placed upon them. There are, in addition to specific values, 'canons of value' which relate to the patterning of valuations. The theory assumes that the transactional process acts always to systematize and integrate these canons, and it emphasizes the role of cultural integrator that is performed by those individuals, entrepreneurs, who make connections between hitherto unconnected value patterns and in so doing establish over-arching canons of value.

Such a system, in the absence of any gains or losses from outside, would move steadily in the direction of increasing order. Values and patterns of values would become more and more consistent, systematized and integrated, until at last they could go no further. They would then provide the best possible basis for making choices, and the results of actions based on these choices would no longer modify values since these values would have attained their optimum configuration and any change would actually make the results of choices less predictable. As this optimum point was approached and finally reached, alternatives (the possibility of choice) would diminish and finally disappear. In other words, the two connecting feeds would cease to exist. This means that transaction theory's common-sense model of the way in which values and behaviour are connected would, if it were valid, ultimately lead to a situation in which they could not be connected. This, I suspect, is not quite the resolution that it set out to provide.

The serious consequences of transaction theory's monster-excluding style are now obvious. The model has excluded the two feeds (the creation and the destruction of value) which, by acting in such a way as continually to mess up this ordering process, offer the only way of making the model work. We are now in a position to make the model work by focusing on these excluded feeds and considering the logical requirements for an adequate sociological theory of creativity (and its dark side, destructivity).

We have already seen, in the examples of Stevengraphs, ancestors, housing, and art objects, that that which is residual to the system of cultural categories has important sociological implications and that transaction theory makes no provision for, and so in effect denies, the existence of these processes. Further, we know that the category system furnishes us with a way of seeing, and that a way of seeing is also, most importantly, a way of not seeing. Thus, of the results of our actions we see a certain fraction and fail to see the remainder. This relevation/irrelevation process is represented in the diagram (Fig. 20) by the monitor. The contents of the world view domain determine the criteria which the monitor applies in discriminating between the feeds c and d, but the control exercised by the monitor can never be complete: it can never stabilize the situation in such a way that the world view can never be altered. Cognition—our way of seeing and our way of not seeing—may, in the area I have termed 'overt', be subject to perfect control, but in the 'covert' area control can never be perfect since our way of seeing denies the very existence of this area. It is not possible to legislate effectively against that which it is held does not exist.

The consequence of this inevitably imperfect control by the monitor is that, despite all its efforts, some unruly elements get through into the world view domain. The arrival of such new elements is likely to mess up the ordering process, in some cases giving rise to quite serious contradictions between hitherto integrated patterns of value. If the world view domain becomes changed in this way then the operation of the monitor will also change, with the result that some information, which previously would not have been selected, will be, and some information, which previously would have been selected, will be rejected. This new increment to the feed out of the cycle is the negative aspect of creativity. It comprises that which once was visible and is now invisible.

The description of the monitor and of the feeds into and out of it is now complete and all that remains is to describe the feeds into the action domain. Transaction theory's representation recognizes that there is often a marked discrepancy between the expected, or hoped for, results of our actions, and what actually happens; and its model simply depicts the manner in which we strive to minimize this discrepancy. So the feed from the world view to the action domain remains the same (the existing world view furnishing a set of constraints and incentives acting on choices). However, transaction theory is mistaken in assuming that this exhausts the universe of action. There is also the feed *b* which is shown as connecting the cyclical deterministic system with the external realm of 'possible entities'.

Despite the assumptions of transaction theory, we know that not all actions result from choices made on the basis of established values. We must consider the possibility that some acts are deliberately irrational: the result either of impulse or random experimentation, and, even if this were not so, there would always be accidents.

Repetitious accidents continue to occur despite the fact that the world view insists that they are disadvantageous. They would seem to represent some irreducible residue within the system. For instance, each time we pass a serious road accident we temporarily modify our actions (our vehicle speed) to conform more closely to the requirements of the value system but the value system remains unchanged. On the other hand, when an accident of a type that has never happened before occurs, then our value system may be modified on the basis of the perceived results. For instance, once certain deaths are seen to be the result of breathing asbestos particles (asbestosis) then the law relating to working conditions may be changed and hence the behaviour of the workers. Other first-time accidents may be perceived to have beneficial results and we are able, thanks to them, to enjoy benefits which otherwise would have remained unknown to us. Such happy accidents form an important element in creativity.

If we define creativity as that which alters world view, then we must recognize two types of creativity: first, that which alters the internal arrangement, but not the content, of the world view domain; second, that which alters the content of the domain (and also, perhaps, its internal arrangement). The first type will occur even without the feeds *b* and *d*. Consequently, it is the only sort of creativity recognized by transaction theory. Following its emphasis on the entrepreneur as creator, but reserving judgement on whether he is the prime integrator of culture, we may term this type of creativity 'entrepreneurial creativity'.

The second type of creativity involves the feeds *b* and *d*. Two factors are responsible for this. First, imperfect control by the monitor, particularly in the covert area. This is the type of creativity which involves rubbish. When that which was invisible and valueless becomes visible and valuable we may speak of 'wilderness creativity' (for example, the innovations heralded by 'the voice of one crying in the wilderness'; also, the idea of the artist with his feet in rubbish and of the journalist with his pencil in one hand and his muck-rake in the other). We have seen that an inevitable concomitant of this type of creativity is its negative aspect—something which was once visible and not rubbish becoming invisible and, should it intrude in any way, rubbish. This is the destruction of value or destructivity. To maintain terminological consistency, let us term this 'negative creativity'.

The second factor concerns serendipitous actions. These must be defined in broad terms, the accidents, irrational acts, and random experiments being seen as happy for the culture-bearers as a whole and not simply for the person involved (since we are seeking a sociological theory of creativity, not one in terms of individual psychology). Thus, for example, a person who for the first time eats a particular plant and finds it to be nutritious and enjoyable, and the person who for the first time eats another plant and finds it fatal, must both be considered to have performed serendipitous acts. Of course, the person who has eaten the poisonous plant has had a most unhappy accident yet, for the community as a whole, it is a happy one since they can in the future categorize that plant as toxic and, basing their food choices on this new constraint, avoid eating it. We may term this 'serendipitous creativity'.

These four kinds of creativity (entrepreneurial, wilderness, negative, and serendipitous) fully exhaust creative possibilities and

F

we can now fill in the labels on the various feeds to obtain the complete representation of the relationship between world view and action.

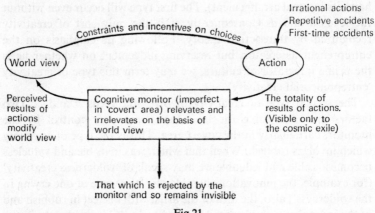

Fig.21

I must now pause to reveal my debt to an earlier monster-conserving theorist; not merely from politeness nor to deflect charges of plagiarism, but more particularly because it provides an opportunity for demonstrating the tyranny and suppression which the development of monster-excluding sociology has occasioned.

The fundamental distinction between that which alters the content of world view and that which alters only its internal arrangement provides the starting point for the theory of creativity advanced by Samuel Johnson.

The task of an author is, either to teach what is not known, or to recommend known truths by his manner of adorning them; either to let new light in upon the mind, and open new scenes to the prospect, or to vary the dress and situation of common objects, so as to give them fresh grace and more powerful attractions, to spread such flowers over the regions through which the intellect has already made its progress, as may tempt it to return, and take a second view of things hastily passed over or negligently regarded.[10]

[10] Samuel Johnson, *An Allegory on Criticism*, 27 March 1750. Republished in *The Rambler*, Vol. 1, 1800, p. 14.

Two hundred years later this distinction is no longer to be seen. The possibility of teaching what is not known is denied, and the only recognized region of creativity is that inhabited by transaction theory's entrepreneur who, by constructing new over-arching canons of value, ever reorganizes his parochialism so that it may become internally more consistent, systematized, and integrated.

One is compelled to ask how on earth it can happen that so noble a view of creativity, expressed with such clarity and force by so great a figure as Samuel Johnson, could ever come to be suppressed. The deed must appear all the more shocking to those who believe in the progress of knowledge; in the idea of scientists and scholars leaving no stone unturned in their unswerving determination to draw ever closer to the truth. For them, the path of sociology must present a sinister betrayal: a systematic channelling of enquiry in order to impel knowledge ever further from the truth; to prevent people from ever seeing how things really are—'le trahison des clercs'.

Johnson himself provides the answer. Knowledge should not be seen as an asymptotic approach to something called truth, but as little more than a side-effect of society:

Either of these labours [the two modes of creativity] is very difficult, because that they may not be fruitless, men must not only be persuaded of their errors, but reconciled to their guide; they must not only confess their ignorance, but, what is still less pleasing, must allow that he from whom they are to learn is more knowing than themselves.[11]

But, of course, he has not really provided the answer. Rather, his great achievement is that he has asked the right question: how is credibility generated and distributed, gained and lost? Catastrophe theory may allow us, belatedly, to come up with the answer.

[11] Ibid.

8 The geometry of credibility

The Republic of the United States of America is founded on the 'self-evident' truth that all men are created equal. The five hundred million Hindus of the Indian subcontinent are taught that men are fundamentally unequal. Why is one belief totally credible in the West and the contradictory belief totally credible in the East? Of course, before you can hope to answer this question you have to ask it, and this is something Western scholars have been very reluctant to do. The great Indianist, Louis Dumont, has castigated them for this mental sloth. In a scathing attack on Anglo-Saxon anthropology, he has disparagingly compared its practitioners with those indolent scholars of a previous age who, once fieldwork had become the established technique, continued to be satisfied with armchair research: 'One might say of our colleagues that the more they emphasize the political dimension, the less they stir out of their metaphysical armchairs, and the more comfortably they will remain with the fallacy which has dominated the nineteenth century ever since moral and political individualism was confused with the description of the life of man in society.'[1]

Dumont contrasted those societies wherein power and hierarchy vary independently with those in which power and hierarchy are aligned. The former is characterized by Indian society, the latter by contemporary Western society. In India the dominant ideology stresses society and the inequality of men: Homo Hierarchicus. In the West the dominant ideology stresses the individual and the equality of men: Homo Aequalis. Dumont argues that sociology, being essentially an elaboration of the ideology of Homo Aequalis, fails to grasp the significance of the contrasting ideology of Homo Hierarchicus, insists on imposing the Western interpretation upon

[1] Louis Dumont, Preface to the French edition of E. E. Evans-Pritchard, *The Nuer*. Translated by M. and J. Douglas in J. H. M. Beattie and R. G. Lienhardt (eds.), *Studies in Social Anthropology: Essays in Memory of E. E. Evans-Pritchard* (1975).

Indian society, and consequently is guilty of a crude and serious socio-centricity which erroneously assumes that the range of social experience of man in Western society fully exhausts his potential. The indictment is extended to philosophers such as Sartre, Marcuse, Weil, and Koyré who have 'a natural tendency to identify the social environment in which the philosophical tradition has developed with mankind as a whole'.[2]

This unquestioned assumption that power and hierarchy are always aligned also exists at less exalted intellectual levels within Western society. For instance, during the 1930s an irreverent and unsympathetic version of the The Red Flag included the lines:

> They treat us all like frogs and snails
> Why can't we all be Prince of Wales.

The first line, in which 'they' are perceived as oppressing 'us' in a most unpleasant manner, is clearly about the uneven distribution of power within society. The second line is about the uneven distribution of ceremonial or ritual status, that is, about hierarchy. The two lines together are only meaningful, and maliciously entertaining, if both lampooners and lampooned assume that power and hierarchy are always in alignment. In a society where power and hierarchy varied independently these lines would be pointless and quite lacking in humour.

Sociology, no matter how it develops and how it tries to examine itself, can never rid itself of this socio-centricity. The only way this can be done is by developing that other sociology appropriate to social systems where power and hierarchy vary independently, and then confronting the one with the other.

This is what Dumont has tried to do. He starts by exposing the tempting comfort of our metaphysical armchair upholstered with individuality and equality and turning its back on hierarchy and inequality. With fine asceticism he deliberately rejects the armchair and embarks on the development of that other sociology appropriate to Indian society. In his conclusion comes the confrontation in which he 'brings together two apparently incommensurable social types whilst rigorously preserving their differences', and looks at the relationship 'from right to left in order to consider India's reaction to the impact of the West, and from left to right to return to the

[2] Louis Dumont, *Homo Hierarchicus*, fn. 2d. (Paladin, London, 1970).

starting point'.[3] But he does not *quite* return to the starting point. He set out by leaving the comfortable armchair of the West and he returns to sit upon the hard wooden stool of the East. He leaves the final problem, the synthesis of these two contrasted sociologies, unresolved. Speaking of the right to left relationship, the impact of the West upon India, he asks: 'Who can say but that these changes have not built up their corrosive action in the dark, and that the caste order will not one day collapse like a piece of furniture gnawed from within by termites.' His rhetorical question assumes the answer 'no one', for 'the coarseness of our notions and methods of investigation and the absence of any precise idea of the former state of the system'[4] preclude the solution of this ultimate problem: the synthesis of East and West in a new and global sociology.

Dumont leaves us with two sociologies where previously we had only one. In the tradition of Kipling, he ends up saying that East is East and West is West and he offers no suggestions as to how the two might meet. Within the confines of Indian society this problem may well be, and remain, insoluble but the same confrontation now exists in a field where notions and methods of investigation are less coarse and where the former state of the system is more precisely known: the sociology of education.

Some recent work in the sociology of education has focused on the boundaries within educational systems. It is concerned, in the first instance, with the nature of the boundaries between categories; their clarity or fuzziness, and the manner in which the categories relate, or fail to relate, to one another; their connectedness or their disconnectedness. The more common concern with the contents of the categories—with what exactly it is that is being taught—is regarded as a foreground distraction, and relegated to second place. The same opposition between Homo Hierarchicus and Homo Aequalis—between rigidly imposed boundaries, clearly defined, highly respected, containing and controlling competition, and more flexible boundaries, more fuzzily defined, often reviled, sustaining and wholly contained by competition, which define Dumont's two parishes, the East and the West—is found within educational systems. As a result, whilst anthropologists stand around scratching their heads over the relationship of East and West and bemoaning their lack of data,

---

[3] Ibid. p. 282.   [4] Ibid. p. 266.

Basil Bernstein,[5] working entirely within the sociology of education, has almost solved the problem.

My starting point is one of the most imaginative of Bernstein's conclusions: the distinction between two fundamental types of curriculum, the 'collection curriculum' and the 'integrated curriculum' and, more important, the cyclical relationship between them, the 'curriculum cycle'. The collection curriculum is literally a collection of subjects. Each subject is taught without any reference to any other; it is self-sufficient and complete in itself. The clear separation of subjects and the elimination of criteria which might allow comparison and competition is enshrined in the timetable which specifies unchallengeably the temporal jurisdiction of each subject. The timetable is the embodiment of the vague faith in the God-like unity of the whole; vague because the unity of the whole can only be maintained by insisting on the clear separation of the parts. This is the 'purity rule' which insists that the whole of knowledge is encompassed by the various subjects and that the boundaries that define them are absolute. In the integrated curriculum, as the name implies, the emphasis is placed not on the autonomy of the various subjects but on the connections between them. Here the purity rule is rejected and the timetable no longer divides the day between subjects but, more flexibly, between 'themes'. There is no place here for self-sufficiency, the teacher must be prepared to argue the relevance of his specialism for others; to make his contribution to the shared task of presenting the theme to the pupils.

The parallel between, on the one hand, the collection and the integrated curricula, and on the other hand Homos Hierarchicus and Aequalis, is perhaps less immediately obvious, and is best approached in terms of the boundaries within educational systems. The relevant boundaries are those between teacher and taught and those between disciplines. These latter are laid out on two distinct levels: there are the boundaries between the various practitioners (the physicists, the classicists, the biologists and so on) and there are the boundaries which are drawn around the various fields to which the practitioners severally lay claim.

Homo Hierarchicus is the dominant ideology of the collection

[5] Basil Bernstein, *Class, Codes and Control: I, II, and III* (Routledge and Kegan Paul, London, 1971, 1973, 1975).

curriculum. Here the inequality of teacher and taught is emphasized. It is accepted that the teacher knows more, or rather, possesses more knowledge which he is prepared to a greater or lesser extent to impart to the pupil, provided he accepts the inequality of the relationship. Here the boundaries between disciplines are emphasized. Only in institutions based on the collection curriculum is one likely to hear the toast, 'to pure mathematics, may it never be of any use to anyone'. In the collection curriculum the prized virtues are specialization (knowing more and more about less and less) and scholarship (the meticulous plotting of one's course across the field of study).

In the collection curriculum, competition is contained by hierarchy, since the boundaries cannot be changed by politico-economic manœuvrings. Of course, the boundaries do change as the composition of the men at the top changes, but there is the conviction that each discipline is self-sustaining and can be evaluated only in its own terms. Cross-disciplinary comparison is not possible. Thus the boundary of a discipline cannot be changed, for example, by the demands of its united students or by inter-disciplinary intrusions: it is inviolate. It is not a case of, 'If you can't beat them join them'. There is no competition. You either join them on their own terms or you don't join them at all. Power is contained by hierarchy and boundaries exist above and beyond competition.

Homo Aequalis is the dominant ideology of the integrated curriculum. The inequality of teacher and taught becomes covert and their equality is emphasized (in staff/student committees and in the, apparent, acquiescence of university authorities to the demands for student participation). At the same time the boundaries between disciplines are fuzzy and transitory, often drawn more from administrative convenience than epistemological imperative. Indeed the boundaries between disciplines may be completely suppressed, courses may include all sorts of unlikely combinations, becoming organized around themes rather than subjects, and, in order to service these courses, the departmental arrangement by subjects is replaced by a more flexible framework of schools with vaguer titles (such as Behavioural Science, or Social Thought) culminating as some disenchanted misfits claim in the establishment of a Chair of Arbitrary Studies.

Within such a system competition is no longer contained by hierarchy. No boundaries are inviolate. All are provisional, open to criticism and subject to change. The breaking down of 'arbitrary' or 'repressive' divisions (for example, between staff and students and between disciplines) is encouraged. Disciplines are no longer self-sustaining and immune from outside criticism. Cross-disciplinary evaluations are possible and are made. The prized virtue is the ability to make lateral connections—to think for oneself. Disciplines must be prepared to justify themselves to others. It is a case of expand or perish—to swallow others or to be themselves swallowed, either to disappear without trace or to transform the swallowers in an 'iridescent metamorphosis'.[6] There is a progressive collapse of disciplinary autonomy, the members either deserting or finding themselves loyal to an ever-diminishing community. This residue argues, not as under the collection regime, about the position of the boundaries but over the best moment to allow themselves to be swallowed: some, refusing to accept the inevitable, maintaining that they should hold on, pull through and then, gaining strength, swallow others; others urging that they be swallowed now. This is the creative indigestion strategy of deliberately leaping, whilst life still lingers on, down the dominant discipline's gullet before it is quite ready for the meal, in the hope that the resultant heart-burn, by a process not envisaged even by Lamarck, will transform the morphology of the recipient.

Bernstein suggests that these two curricula are cyclically related: that a progressive collapse of boundaries will transform a collection curriculum into an integrated curriculum and that a progressive redefinition of boundaries will in turn transform an integrated curriculum into a (different) collection curriculum. The curriculum cycle may be represented diagrammatically (as shown in Fig. 22 overleaf).

This is a genuine cycle and not simply an oscillating linear system, since the route from collection curriculum to integrated curriculum is clearly separate from that from integrated curriculum to collection curriculum. The one is not simply the reverse of the other. Firstly, whilst the cycle brings us back to a collection, it is not the same collection from which we set out. There has been a change in the positions of the boundaries and of their contents. Secondly, the collapse from collection to integrated is headlong and irreversible, whilst the redefinition would appear to be a progressive building up.

[6] Needham has recommended this course of action for the discipline of anthropology. Rodney Needham, 'The Future of Social Anthropology' in *Anniversary Contributions to Anthropology* (E. J. Brill, Leiden, 1970).

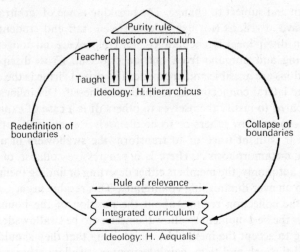

Fig.22

The collection curriculum, we know, can be stabilized; it is the curriculum with which most people are at present familiar. The integrated curriculum, it is suspected, is an unstable but essential intermediate form between successive collections. It would be pleasing to be able to investigate this suspicion, to discover whether the integrated curriculum really is an unstable intermediate form and whether this instability is an absolute condition or true only within limited specifiable ranges of conditions outside of which the integrated curriculum would be as stable as the collection curriculum. Whilst this investigation would be intellectually satisfying in itself there are also sound economic reasons for pursuing it.

It is no accident that, in the diagram of the cycle, the collection curriculum looks like a little Parthenon whilst the integrated curriculum resembles a diagrammatic representation of ribbon development. Architects, it would seem, are simple souls, and one should never overlook the blatantly obvious when seeking to understand their work. Butterfield, for example, designed Keble College Chapel as a physical representation of the rewards of hard work. The unseen foundations are laid in early youth and through the long hard years of toil the buttresses rise solid, yet plain and unremarkable, to blossom with patterned brickwork (OBEs) and ornate copings (knighthoods) only when their structural task is done. Educational buildings are the physical expressions of curricula. Tall buildings represent the collection curriculum, especially if they are plain and disparate low down, ornate and unified towards the top. Long low buildings, amorphous in plan, flexible, linked by glazed bridges and pedestrian walk-ways, represent the integrated curriculum. But buildings do more than just represent their curricula, they impose them. They act as blinkers, preventing those who inhabit them from ever seeing that things could be other than they are. Collection curriculum architecture emphasizes the vertical; integrated curriculum architecture emphasizes the horizontal. The most complete and perfect example of the former is the Radcliffe Camera in Oxford: a Parthenon-in-the-round, presenting a perfect façade in all directions. No neglected tradesman's entrance here where the despicable low-status boundary-crossing intruder can sneak in unnoticed. A fine example of the latter is the, as yet unrealized, Linear University:[7] a subtopian sprawl, its plan constrained along a single dimension, without fixed centre or clear-cut ends. New units may be plugged into the ends, obsolete units removed, the whole is simply the sum of its parts carried first this way then the other by the random tide of educational life, its centre nothing more than the transient mid-point between its ever-shifting open ends.

Assuming they could gain access, a boundary-builder would feel most uncomfortable in the Linear University and a boundary-demolisher equally ill at ease inside the Radcliffe Camera. In consequence, if there is a rapid shift in ideology amongst the inhabitants, it is only to be expected that their dissatisfaction with the existing curriculum, and their efforts to change it, will be conducted in the idiom of the construction and demolition industry. On the one hand we are urged to build centres of excellence (and to conserve what already exists): to accept that more is worse. On the other hand, we are asked to believe that Victorian and Edwardian schools (many of an astonishingly high standard of specification and workmanship) should be razed to the ground because the lavatories are outside, and there are not enough of them. The fact that the school and lavatories

---

[7] The brainchild of the Archigram group. There does exist a near-Linear University in Vancouver but it actually has an identifiable centre (which was selected as the appropriate place for a student occupation which, thanks to the linear plan, totally paralysed the institution).

could be enclosed in a geodesic dome for a fraction of the cost of demolishing and replacing with a new low-rise building, makes it clear that it is not the building but the curriculum that has become obsolete. There is much to be said for the despairing architect's plea that it would be easier (and cheaper) to design the educational policy to fit the existing buildings than *vice versa*, but to side with him would be to admit failure; cynically and erroneously to assume that educational policy and its implementation can never coincide.

Educational buildings represent a massive capital investment. Their expected life-span (when new) is considerable and they have a strong tendency, once they are built, to remain where they are and as they are. The disjunction of educational policy and implementation is the direct result of capital inertia brought about by unforeseen changes in the expected time-span of investments, both in buildings and equipment and in the recruitment and training of personnel. At present these changes in expected life-span are unforeseeable, but, if we can devise a methodological framework which permits the accurate prediction of changes in expected life-spans, the problem is solved, and the coincidence of policy and implementation is transferred from the fortune-teller's caravan (where it should be at present but is not) to the accountant's desk (where it is at present but shouldn't be).

Since in some circumstances it is the changes in the curriculum that render a building obsolete, thus cutting short its allotted span, whilst in other circumstances a long-obsolete building is demolished just as the curriculum having gone full cycle is about to grant it a new lease of life, it follows that the predictive framework we are looking for is that which determines changes in the curriculum. What is needed is nothing less than a model capable of generating a full account of the curriculum possibilities of educational systems.

I want to focus upon boundary changes and it will be convenient for this purpose to take an imaginary, but fairly conventional, institution of higher education. Two different kinds of boundary change can be isolated: first, boundary changes which, whilst they alter the form of the collection, do not involve an intermediate integrated stage; second, boundary changes which do involve the intermediate integrated stage. We could call the first 'evolutionary boundary changes' and the second 'revolutionary boundary changes'. Generally, but not always, the boundaries of a subject are not drawn so sharply and are not imposed so ruthlessly that there is no possibility for borderline activities and shifts of emphasis by some of its practitioners, and these gradual changes can give rise to gradual changes in the position of the boundary. But sometimes exactly the same sort of borderline changes cause the sudden total collapse of the collection curriculum and its replacement by the integrated curriculum. If a methodological framework can be devised which will allow both the description and prediction of these two kinds of change then this ultimate problem of sociology will have been solved.

The ideology of the collection system emphasizes purity and separation with some vague notion insisting on the unity of all the parts, that is, on the unity of knowledge. Consequently boundaries are sharply defined from the inside of each discipline/department and there is the belief that knowledge is private property and the behaviour appropriate to this belief. Slipping into the horticultural metaphor appropriate to the British educational system,[8] we could say

---

[8] Bernstein has entertainingly pointed out that the appropriate metaphor for the British system is horticultural, whilst, for the American, it is ejaculatory. Thus the successful British researcher may unfold or even blossom and perhaps eventually his tender plant may bear fruit. In the meantime his American colleague, having got it together and hardened up his ideas, will be coming on strong.

An American psychologist disenchanted with his calling describes his colleagues as 'potent but sterile rakes, leaving behind them a trail of ravaged virgins but no viable offspring'. Paul Meehl (June 1968), 'Theory testing in psychology and physics: a methodological paradox', *Journal of the Philosophy of Science*.

An Englishman, in a rather similar situation, puts it like this:

Meanwhile the mind, from pleasure less,
Withdraws into its happiness.
Annihilating all that's made
To a green thought in a green shade.
(from 'The Garden' by Andrew Marvell)

The horticultural metaphor evidently flourished in the (élitist) French educationa system:

'The buds which develop naturally are always the terminal buds—that is to say, those that are farthest from the parent trunk. It is only by pruning or layering that the sap is driven back and so forced to give life to those germs which are nearest the trunk and would otherwise have lain dormant. And in this manner, the most recalcitrant plants, which, if left to themselves, would no doubt produce nothing but leaves, are induced to bear fruit. Oh! an orchard or a garden is an excellent school! and a horticulturalist would make the best of pedagogues!' (Vincent in André Gide's *The Counterfeiters*, trans. D. Bussey, Penguin edn. 1973, pp. 135–6).

that the land is dotted with academic estates each contained within a well-maintained ring-fence, for in English law it is the landowner's responsibility to fence against the straying stock of his neighbours. Some of these estates may have common boundary fences but there is no reason to suppose that all land is enclosed. That which is covered in stones or prickly bushes and is of no value to anyone is ignored. Overlapping may sometimes occur but it is always clearly and unambiguously specified. One may have the right to graze another's stubble and so on. Thus a social psychologist, a linguist, a nutritionist and a social anthropologist can all, in theory, work simultaneously among the same tribe without coming to blows.

Usually members of a discipline define that discipline by appeals to the ideology: the legitimizing ancestors, for instance, and the boundaries that enclose it and set it apart from other disciplines. But also, especially at times of rapid boundary change, they may refer instead to the action frame of reference: for example, in the definition of mathematics as being what mathematicians do. To understand how boundaries change we must look at social action. We do not change a discipline's boundary by changing our minds. We have also to act on our new convictions.

The easiest way to change a boundary is to move the ring fence a little so that it takes in a piece of waste land. Three stages are involved. First, the actor must question his ideology sufficiently to be able himself to see the waste land as potentially fertile. That is, he must change his mind. Second, he must go out and cultivate his plot of waste land. This involves him in obtaining funds and support: no easy matter if the rest of the members of the discipline are concerned to exclude the plot he wishes to cultivate. An interesting inside/outside situation arises. The creative innovator on the outside sees his plot as fertile land which ought to be cultivated. Those on the inside see it as a plot against them. Third, having cultivated his plot he has to convince his colleagues that it is valuable land and should be incorporated. His colleagues will usually do this by explaining that, as a matter of fact, it was always within the fence but had simply been lying fallow. When all these conditions have been satisfied the boundary has been altered and ideology and action coincide once more.

If there are many extra-estate cultivators, then confusions and disagreements as to the exact position of the ring-fence will arise and, worse still, individuals from different estates may find themselves cultivating the same or adjacent plots of waste land and feel more affinity with one another than they do with their parent disciplines. Thus as the two outsiders become united by their shared endeavours and common opposition to their parents, the parents are at one another's throats in an acrimonious dispute over the ownership of the now valuable plot which their wayward children have co-cultivated.

Thus the ideology of a discipline, to a large extent, constrains the actions of its members, but those illegitimate actions which it does not, or cannot, prevent may in their turn alter the ideology. In this way a collection system can gradually transform itself without, as it were, realizing what it is doing. But in exactly the same sort of circumstances it may suddenly collapse to give an integrated system. Why?

I have already hinted, in rather crude terms, at the sort of mechanism which would appear to lead almost inevitably towards this sort of collapse: the case of the two co-cultivators who are driven ever-closer together by the same forces which bring their parent disciplines into conflict. In such a situation the horizontal links appropriate to an integrated system are being forged whilst the separation (the cat and dog non-relationship between disciplines so essential to the survival of the collection system) is called into question. It is reasonable to expect that a collection system can only cope with a limited number of such situations at any moment in time and that there is some critical level above which the whole Parthenon will crumble. This critical point might correspond to the moment when the rate at which boundaries are being established and reinforced is equalled by the rate at which they are being broken down and blurred. If we look at the location of research projects, some plots are clearly within the ring-fence of the discipline, others outside. Those within the fence cannot contribute to break-down, those outside can.

So we can say that boundary definition is a function of two variables: the number of research projects being carried out with the approval of the collection ideology and the number of research projects being carried out despite the collection ideology. Now imagine a situation where the number of projects approved by the ideology is declining whilst the number of projects despite the ideology is increasing. The last thing we can expect is gradual change—the continued stability of the collection system. Sooner or later something has got to give.

It is the sort of situation which occurs in the autobiographies of certain Nietzschean mountaineers. Describing their attempt on some hideous North Wall, they go higher and higher, the face gets steeper and steeper, the climbing harder and harder, the climbers tireder and tireder, hungrier and hungrier, thirstier and thirstier. At last comes the moment of truth. 'To go on was impossible, to turn back unthinkable.' Stability is the least likely outcome of all. They fall off.[9]

We are dealing with a system which in its generalized form is found in many phenomena, especially those which concern the social sciences. I have suggested that when two variables alter so the third variable, boundary maintenance, also varies. Sometimes it varies smoothly to give evolutionary change within a collection system. Sometimes it varies erratically to give revolutionary change involving the collapse of the collection system and its replacement by a (transitory?) integrated system.

How can we handle such phenomena? If things are changing gradually they can't be changing suddenly and if things are changing suddenly they can't be changing gradually. Since we need a description of the *switch* from one mode of change to the other, we cannot side-step this paradox by providing two separate descriptions, one in a gradualist language, the other in a suddenist language. This is where catastrophe theory comes in. Instead of resorting to contradictory languages, it draws for us a simple yet generalized and powerful picture of what is going on. The picture-drawing department of mathematics is called topology, and catastrophe theory is derived from a theorem in topology, first stated by René Thom, that, among other things, permits a non-contradictory description of both gradual and sudden change. In French the word *catastrophe* does not carry the catastrophic overtones of the same word in English, and it should be emphasized that catastrophe theory is so named simply on account of its ability to handle sudden and discontinuous change at the same time as it copes with gradual and smooth change.

The topological description appropriate to the curriculum cycle can be built up in the following way. A three-dimensional graph showing the relationship between the level of boundary mainten-

---

[9] I am indebted to the late Dr Tom Patey for this analogy. Lest the reader is puzzled as to how, after falling off, the climber is able to write his autobiography, I should explain that, thanks to modern protection techniques, only quite a small proportion of mountaineering falls are fatal.

ance, the forces upholding the boundaries, and the forces eroding the boundaries will depict the full range of curriculum possibilities within which the curriculum cycle proposed by Bernstein should emerge as one specific sequence of possibilities.

These variables can be expressed, in forms which it should be possible to operationalize, as follows:

x axis: Rate of research projects with approval of collection ideology.

y axis: Rate of projects despite the collection ideology. This is roughly equivalent to the rate of projects with the approval of the integrated ideology, and thus the x and y axes together depict the partial contradiction of these two ideologies.

z axis: An index of boundary maintenance. Under a collection system this would be compounded from the total number of boundaries within the system weighted for their intensity, that is, their clarity or fuzziness, their permeability or impermeability. Under an integrated system all such boundaries should disappear to be replaced by only one, that separating what shall be included from what shall be excluded: a boundary imposed by the rule, not of purity, but of relevance.

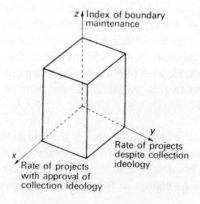

Fig.23

At any moment in time the research situation can be described, in terms of x and y, as a point on the base of the cube. A changing research situation can be described as a sequence of such points to give a two-dimensional graph with an arrow to indicate the direction of change. This x, y plane (the base of the cube) acts as the *control space*. It is called the control space, not because we control it but because changes in the values of x and y result in changes in the effectiveness of the boundary. Thus changes in x and y control the 'behaviour' of z. For this reason the z axis is called the *behaviour dimension*. So the z axis does not represent human behaviour but rather the behaviour of a system of which humans are an essential part. The human behaviour provides the mechanism which ensures that changes in the control space do result in changes along the behaviour dimension. This mechanism is nothing other than the monster-conserving model of the relationship between world view and action, and the crucial component in this model is the intelligent individual continuously reassessing his values in the light of the perceived results of his actions and then choosing between his future options of the basis of those modified values. Aggregate changes in the nature of the boundary occur because most of the component individuals strive, most of the time, to modify their values so as to minimize the discrepancy between the expected (or hoped for) results of their actions and the actual results that they see.

This sort of mechanism is called *the dynamic* and we can build up the three-dimensional graph that will depict the full relationship between the three variables, x, y, and z, by considering what sort of aggregate changes in z are likely as the situation in terms of x and y is gradually modified in various ways. If we take some initial situation in this control space then it will, thanks to the dynamic, have a certain most probable level of boundary maintenance associated with it. What happens to this *probability distribution* as the values of x and y are varied?

(i) Neither x nor y increasing: this is the situation where there is no change in the relative strengths of the forces upholding and eroding the boundaries and thus the most likely outcome is that there will be no change in the level of boundary maintenance.

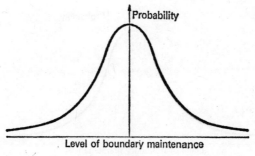

Fig.24

(ii) x increasing, y constant: if there are more and more research projects within the ring-fence but no change in the number outside then the most likely outcome is that the level of boundary maintenance will be increased. This is the sort of situation one would expect to find as Bernstein's unstable integrated system was giving way to a new collection system. There is a tightening up of boundaries and a re-imposition of hierarchy.

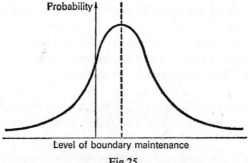

Fig.25

(iii) y increasing, x is constant: if there are more and more research projects outside the ring-fence but no change in the numbers inside then inevitably boundaries are increasingly under attack and the most likely outcome is a decrease in the level of boundary maintenance. This is the sort of situation one would expect to find as Bernstein's collection system was moving towards its collapse and replacement by an integrated system (see Fig. 26 overleaf).

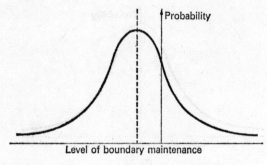

Fig.26

(iv) Both x and y increasing: if just x was increasing we would
expect z to rise. If just y was increasing we would expect z to fall.
If they both increase then the opposing forces acting upon the
boundary will be progressively magnified and the likelihood of
their remaining balanced (quite probable, initially) will be
correspondingly diminished. (After all, the situation in which
they remain balanced and when the most likely outcome is no
change at all corresponds to that in which neither x nor y is
increasing.)

Thus as x and y are increased so the likelihood of the situation
swinging one way or the other increases (and correspondingly,
the size of this swing) and so the likelihood of nothing happening
dimimishes. This is the sort of situation that would exist within a
fairly tolerant collection system which was suddenly subjected to
an exponential growth in knowledge, research projects, person-

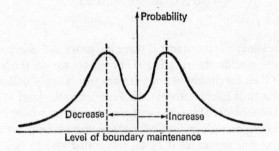

Fig.27

nel and departments: a rough characterization, that is, of the general educational situation to which Bernstein's analysis applies and within which it has emerged.

Now it might appear that all these axes and probability distributions are just a ridiculously elaborate way of restating the obvious and that the effort in expounding them, on the one hand, and comprehending them, on the other, is not going to be repaid by any firmer grasp upon the phenomena. But appearances can be deceptive, and Thom's theorem gives the astonishing result that the most and least likely levels of boundary maintenance (that is, the maxima and minima) for all possible situations on the control space must lie within a single smooth surface which, by virtue of the twin-humped probability distribution, must contain a curious overhanging section called the 'cusp catastrophe'. It will, in fact, look something like Fig. 28 overleaf.

The task now is to see whether Bernstein's curriculum cycle can be fitted to this graph and then, if it can, to provide a convincing translation in social terms of what such a geometrical description entails. This translation should be on two levels. First, it should provide a dispassionate, outside observer's description of what is going on. Second, it should provide an insider's description of what it is like to be caught up in it all.

The extreme left and the extreme right (looking from the origin) edges of the graph (the curvy surface containing the cusp catastrophe) represent, quite appropriately, what might be termed the totalitarian conditions of the system. Along the right edge all research projects lie within the existing ring-fences and as the number of projects increases so those fences are reinforced and the index of boundary maintenance increases. This represents the extreme form of the collection system within which the only tenable and tolerated ideology is that of Homo Hierarchicus. Indeed so total is the control imposed via this ideology that not a single research project is permitted outside the established limits. The high level of order, clarity, and predictability of such a condition is balanced by its total inability to change to meet changing external circumstances and the rarefied and sterile scholasticism that inevitably ensues. Along the left edge all projects conform to the requirements of the ideology appropriate to the integrated curriculum, that of Homo Aequalis. Thus as the rate of projects increases there is no increase in the index

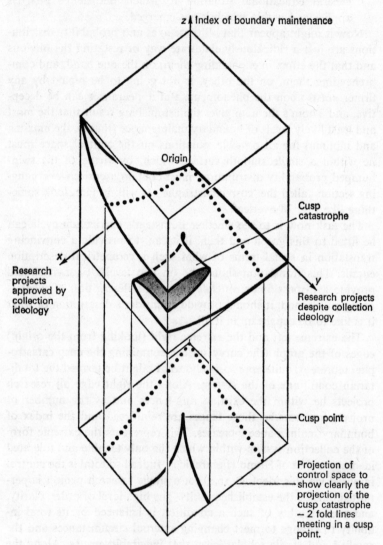

Fig.28 The Possibilities of the Curriculum

of boundary maintenance for none of the projects that would cause such an increase, that is, projects which straying from the rule of relevance might quietly sketch in the outlines for a collection curriculum, are permitted. Again the control exercised via the ideology is so total that any deviationist or revisionist project is nipped in the bud. The survival of such an extreme condition, once established, is problematical for it would seem to entail a once-and-for-all definition of relevance.

Moving in a little from these extreme conditions we come to those represented by the two dotted lines within the surface. Along these lines a small proportion of projects that are not in conformity with the dominant ideology are permitted or, at any rate, not effectively legislated against. Such a condition may be stabilized if the rate at which these diverging projects are being incorporated into the ideology equals the rate at which they are occurring. This may be done in the case of the collection curriculum by gradually moving the position of the relevant ring-fence and, in the case of the integrated curriculum, by altering the criteria which define relevance. In this way the dominant ideology retains its high degree of control but at the same time is modified in response to those pressures which it does not, or cannot, control. Such a balanced and stable situation, whilst it may certainly occur, is in no way specially privileged and it is much more likely that changes in the locations of research projects will cause either the weakening or the strengthening of the dominant ideology. That is, the situation will begin to move towards one or other of the extremes, and in so doing may enter and, perhaps, pass through the cusp.

Let us take, as an example of such a path, Bernstein's curriculum cycle (see Fig. 29, page 174). Initially, when a collection system is being created, we can assume that most research projects are approved by the ideology. In another sense they are giving substance to the ideology. As the cycle proceeds a crucial difference between the two variables x and y begins to make itself felt. Within any collection system the area inside a discipline's ring-fence at any moment in time is finite, whilst the area outside is infinite. Under conditions of long-run growth, to stand still is to perish. Each department must aim to expand at least as quickly as the others. So more and more research projects are initiated, all or almost all within the ring-fence which, thanks to these very projects, is becoming more and more clearly defined. On the control space, the initial situation lies outside the cusp and some distance from the extreme right (point A on Fig. 29). As the boundaries become more and more clearly defined by the increased number of research projects, so the situation moves towards, and may even reach, the extreme right (point B on the diagram).

The pressure on available land within the ring-fences now builds up explosively since there are more and more researchers and each successful research project leaves its particular plot exhausted. At the same time there is no pressure at all on land outside the ring-fences since its area is infinite. Increasingly research within the fences becomes crowded and unsatisfying. Virgin plots (mixing the metaphors) are in extremely short supply and those that do present themselves tend to be 'old maids'. Thus everything points to the plots outside the ring-fences. The number of research projects in each department must increase if only to keep up with the others. Almost inevitably the controls are relaxed and this increase takes place mostly outside the ring-fences. In the early stages of this process the extra-estate researchers will tend to be rather shamefaced and apologetic about the location of their plots and anxious to bring them within the ring-fence as quickly as possible. Their supervisors, and more conformist colleagues who have remained inside, will, probably more from a desire to regularize an anomalous state of affairs than out of sympathy, be eager to facilitate these shifts in the position of the ring-fence. In other words they all still subscribe to the collection ideology. Even so, they cannot stem the tide and their discipline becomes less disciplined with every expedient move they make.

On the control space the situation has turned away from the right edge and, with the rate of research projects still increasing, is heading towards the cusp (point C on the diagram). These complex forces that propel the situation from A to B to C and onwards are *in toto* the dynamic of the curriculum cycle. The easiest way to understand all the different things that are happening as a result of this dynamic is to plot the cycle ABC . . . initially on the projected control space (that is, just in terms of x and y in the location of research projects). Then, in order to see what is happening to boundary maintenance, this cycle has to be projected upwards until it cuts the three-dimensional graph $A^1B^1C^1$ . . . We can see that from A^1 to B^1 there was a considerable increase in boundary maintenance and from B^1 to C^1 a considerable falling off.

At C^1, for the first time, the situation encounters a 'splitting factor'. That is, as the situation moves beyond C^1 into the cusp there are suddenly two most probable values of z for each situation (x, y) and as we go further into the cusp so these values ever diverge. The translation of this topological description into a sociological description is crucial. The acceptance by sociology of topological methodologies and of the profound implications they entail will occur only if this translation can be clearly and convincingly achieved.

Fortunately, I have already provided this sociological description of the splitting factor. It is the situation in which the extra-estate cultivators begin to feel more affinity with one another than they do with their parent disciplines. The splitting factor resides in the fact that the same force that drives them ever closer together is responsible for the dispute between their parent disciplines. At the same time the first fragile horizontal links appropriate to the integrated curriculum are being forged whilst the dispute between the parent disciplines transgresses the purity rule which insists on the clear separation of the parts, on their non-accountability to one another except through the mediation of the vague notion of the unity of the whole.

The extra-estate researchers begin, for the first time, to question the desirability of moving back inside their disciplines. They feel less apologetic about the location of their projects, becoming increasingly proud of, and strident about, what they are doing. They begin to feel that it is not for them to move back into their disciplines but for their disciplines to make the adjustment. And this adjustment is not simply the small shift in the ring-fence that would incorporate the valuable plot into one discipline or the other but the complete dismantling of those fences and their replacement by the framework of horizontal links that would proclaim and legitimize the 'true' nature of their shared achievement.

At the same time those inside the respective ring-fences begin, for the first time, to question the desirability of incorporating these troublesome outsiders. They begin to call for an end to expediency and for a stand on principle. They are aware, quite correctly, that the boundaries that sustain the collection system to which they belong have been progressively and dangerously weakened by such expedients and that if it is to survive they must be strengthened. What

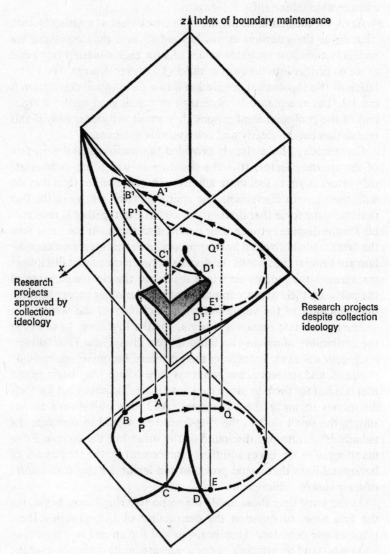

Fig.29 The Curriculum Cycle

better way to strengthen these boundaries than to stand firm and refuse to welcome these threatening outsiders who, anyway, are only prepared to be accepted on their own terms? A polarization has occurred: those inside striving to impose a stronger control via the still dominant collection ideology to which they subscribe; those outside refusing to accept this situation and trying to change it so that it may come to resemble more closely the state of affairs consistent with the still submerged integrated ideology which they now unashamedly profess.

Initially this polarization involves only a tiny proportion of researchers and this, combined with the dominant position held by the collection ideology, means that the full seriousness of the changed situation (indeed, the fact that it has changed) is not appreciated by those who are caught up in it. Unaware of the Rubicon they are crossing they are unable to pull back and, amid growing confusion and acrimony, they carry on across the cusp and into catastrophe. In terms of the graph, the dominance of the collection ideology means that the situation remains precariously on the upper sheet whilst the splitting factor, gradually affecting more and more of those caught up in the system, drives its wedge between the diminishing numbers of those loyal to the old ideology and the increasing numbers of those who embrace the new. The situation moves from C to D. At D the polarization fills the entire academic arena, the collection ideology can no longer claim dominance, and just one more research project outside the ring-fences, or one more case of co-cultivation, brings about the revolution which those inside the boundaries had so much dreaded yet, by their supposedly prophylactic action, had ensured. The balance of ideological power is suddenly shifted, the integrated ideology of Homo Aequalis becomes dominant and that of Homo Hierarchicus becomes submerged. As the situation moves out of the cusp from D towards E the index of boundary maintenance collapses catastrophically.

A world view based on the ideology that made such sense of the collection system becomes nonsensical and that appropriate to the integrated system suddenly becomes spectacularly meaningful. When the path ABCDE . . . is projected up to cut the graph, the catastrophic implications of this tiny step from D towards E is instantly apparent in the sudden massive collapse of boundary maintenance from the upper sheet (of which the collection ideology makes such sense) to the lower sheet (of which the integrated ideology makes such sense). Thus the cusp provides a geometrical representation of the partial contradiction of these two ideologies. Had the situation been propelled by a less frantic dynamic involving a slower, or even negative, growth rate it might have avoided the cusp altogether (travelling, say, from P to Q) and making the transition from collection to integrated curriculum in a smooth evolutionary manner avoiding both the polarization of personnel and the catastrophic collapse of boundaries. Those familiar with the histories of Hornsey and Guildford Schools of Art in Britain and of Columbia University in the States can be in no doubt that the path taken by them was through the cusp.

This sudden collapse at D^1 constitutes 'the maoist moment' and is extraordinarily exhilarating for the integrated ideologists as they experience the instantaneous, and virtually total, disappearance of all the irksome boundaries that have repressed them for so long. In this sense, we might call this discontinuous change from the top sheet of the cusp to the lower a 'revolution of the left'. This is not the only sort of discontinuous change that is possible. If a dynamic were propelling the situation through the cusp in the reverse direction then there would be a sudden and massive imposition of boundaries as the situation leapt from the lower sheet to the upper sheet. Such a change might be called a 'revolution of the right'. Topologists refer to these upper and lower sheets of the cusp catastrophe as 'attractors'; each trying to capture the situation, with the middle sheet, representing the least likely outcome, acting as a 'repeller'. It would be quite wrong to regard such revolutionary changes simply as rather large fluctuations about a mean.

At, or shortly after, E the dynamic becomes somewhat hypothetical. The autonomy of the institution is invaded, the guard-dogs move in, the gates are closed and the staff purged. When the gates reopen the situation, drastically revised, is somewhere around A or B once more. This invasion is possible because those inside any educational institution are not wholly isolated from those outside. They rely upon the outside world for both funds and students and those who pay the fiddler will, sooner or later, call the tune. And the tune they call is the Unity of Knowledge and the words are those of Sweet Economic Reason. Here is a modern rendering by the visiting fiddler of the London School of Economics.

Only the economist faces up squarely to the everyday fact that university education has never been and can never be a free commodity. . . .

Think what would happen if, say, Harrods were to operate on the assumption that consumers do not buy, sales staff do not sell and owners do not control. Chaos would at once become the order of the day, and violence would soon triumph at the expense of all that is reasonable and natural.

Yet it is precisely this weirdly irrational pattern of exchange that we discern in the world of higher education today. . . .

Consumers, the students, do not pay the full economic cost of the services they receive; producers, the faculty, do not sell the services they give; and those who foot the bill for this largesse, the taxpayers, are dutifully denied control over the services they finance.[10]

This instability of the integrated curriculum is not the result of something intrinsic to the educational system but is due to the intervention of the outside world which insists on the unity of knowledge. One of the advantages of using this topological model is that it provides a geometrical description of this distinction between intrinsic and extrinsic properties. If we look at the control space, the non-hypothetical section of the dynamic is a sector of a smooth ellipse whilst the extrinsic intervention has to be represented as a sharp interruption.[11]

The model itself prompts the next question: what would happen if the outside world did not intervene? Would the dynamic conform to the broken line that would smoothly complete the established part of the ellipse? What would be involved in this hypothetical journey from E to F to A and what would it feel like to be caught up in it? (See Fig. 30 overleaf.)

First of all, throughout this sector of the dynamic there is a continuous falling off in the total number of research projects, from the

[10] Professor Devletoglou, 1974. Address to The Hellenic Society, London (as reported in *The Times*).

[11] Of course, this means that we have not yet got the complete picture representing the relationship between the educational system and the wider social system within which it is embedded. This, presumably, will involve more dimensions and a more complex catastrophe that will depict and predict this discontinuous change resulting from the 'extrinsic intervention'. This indicates the direction of future research. This is not some system of Chinese boxes with this complex catastrophe nestling inside another even more complex. This is the largest box: there is no cosmic police force for us to call upon for extrinsic intervention in the total social system.

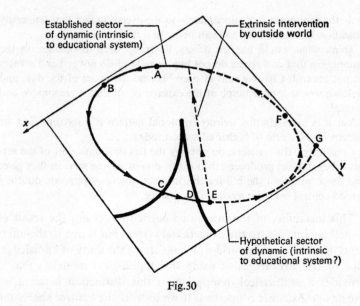

Established sector
of dynamic (intrinsic
to educational system)

Extrinsic intervention
by outside world

Hypothetical sector
of dynamic (intrinsic
to educational system?)

Fig.30

all-time high round about D to the return to the initial modest number at A. But this falling off is not equally distributed between those projects approved by the collection ideology and those despite it. Secondly, looking at the behaviour space (see Fig. 29), we can see that the variation in the index of boundary maintenance is slight: that its value, already low at E^1, declines even further eventually reaching a minimal value. After this it begins to increase, slowly at first but then more rapidly, until it reaches the quite high value at A^1.

Again, the problem is to translate from topological to sociological description. At E^1 the educational institution has just experienced the trauma of a sudden catastrophic collapse of boundary maintenance and the resultant reversal of the dominant ideology from that consistent with the collection curriculum to that consistent with the integrated curriculum. At the same time the benign approval of the outside world, the wider social context of the institution, is withdrawn and The New Men are faced with the task of organizing and implementing a thorough-going integrated curriculum, and of purging the surviving remnants of the collection curriculum, within a context of external suspicion, disapproval, and overt hostility. Those inside the institution can no longer count upon the outside for continued support in terms of funds and personnel. In such a confused situation immediately following the bitterness, disruption, and rapid change of the revolution of the left, the initial optimism and wild euphoria of the maoist moment soon evaporate. In consequence, the elimination of irrelevant research projects initiated under the former regime, and the fostering of the relevant new projects that will give substance to the integrated ideology, all take place against a background of resignations, fund withdrawals, and recommendations by headmasters to their more able pupils to apply to other less radical institutions. This is the combination of circumstances that causes the instability and inevitable collapse of this hypothetical sector of the dynamic, but, even if these external forces were not present, there would still be an overall falling-off in the number of research projects as irrelevant projects were eliminated more rapidly than relevant ones were initiated. If no other forces intervened the situation would move rapidly from E, along the hypothetical segment initially, before diverging tangentially to reach the extreme totalitarian condition at G and then stay there (see Fig. 30).

The reason why this would not happen, and why it would be prevented by a falling-off in research projects even if they are approved by the integrated ideology and even if there were no external hostility, is that it would seem inevitable that disagreements would arise as to the definition of relevance and that, in the absence of any vague unifying principle for moderating and containing such disagreements, a power struggle between the different factions, each trying to impose its own definition of relevance, would inevitably develop and, increasingly absorbing time and energy, cause a cutback in research projects. How can people get on with the difficult task of achieving the aim if there is no agreement as to what that aim should be? The situation moves to F, the nearest it can get to the implementation of policies derived from the ideology of Homo Aequalis.

Leaving for the moment the question of whether it is possible to stabilize the system at or about this point, we require a sociological description of the turning point and of how the situation moves gradually and smoothly away from the integrated system at F towards the fairly tolerant collection system at A. As the disagreement about the definition of relevance increases, so the attractions of doing relevant research diminish. In such a climate manipulators and opportunists flourish. In the absence of any unifying principle the individual or group that can attract the most adherents will win the day and those who move away from the obsession with relevance and towards some sort of purity, becoming interested not in the relevant questions (since no one will agree on what they are) but in the difficult questions (which are always present even if masked), are able to offer a measure of order, discipline, and status, where others compete with different kinds of disorder, indiscipline, and equality. In this way these persons, gathering strength unto themselves, gradually sketch in the outlines of the new collection system.

In this sense it would seem that hierarchy and separation are the inevitable concomitants of the academic enterprise and that they will always have a tendency to flourish especially where the possibility of their existence is denied. They are like weeds: always present unless continual action is taken to prevent them from being there. During the debate about the definition of relevance such actions are not taken, for the debate is about which plants should be considered to be flowers in the integrated garden, and if you cannot decide which plants are flowers neither can you decide which ones are weeds.

Even so, it would seem that there are ways in which the integrated curriculum might be stabilized, by avoiding the fruitless debate on relevance which is responsible for the turning point. In the external intervention that prevents the integrated sector of the cycle from occurring at all, it is the outside world's insistence on the unity of knowledge that is crucial. Thus it seems likely that if this requirement were removed the integrated system could be stabilized. In place of the unity of knowledge we would have the multiplicity of knowledge, with knowledge and relevance defined by context, most probably occupational context. Thus one sort of knowledge would be deemed relevant for manual workers, another for white-collar workers, and so on. An example is the training of London taxi-drivers who before they are allowed to practise must pass a gruelling examination on London's street plan, one-way systems, hotels, hospitals, shortest and quickest routes and the like. Within the trade this is called 'doing the knowledge'. The knowledge in this case is defined by occupational context: it does not (yet) form part of any university degree course. If knowledge is allowed to be multiple in this way then relevance is unambiguously defined by (occupational) context and any educational system may be stabilized permanently with its integrated curriculum perfectly reflected by its ideology of Homo Aequalis. There is some evidence that in certain educational institutions that are isolated from the demands of the national economy (special schools for the handicapped, for instance) such stabilized conditions do exist.

Both the ideology of Homo Aequalis and the multiplicity of knowledge have been advocated by the radical educationist Ivan Illich.[12] But if the unity of knowledge is deposed, then occupational status must become paramount. Can this really be what the de-schoolers want? It looks suspiciously like Aldous Huxley's *Brave New World*. The topological model shows that the state of affairs so passionately advocated by Illich is not likely to be attained. This is because, in order to satisfy his two conditions (the multiplicity of knowledge and an ideology of Homo Aequalis, not just within each occupationally relevant system of knowledge but also between all those diverse systems), there would have to be an overall definition of relevance. But such a definition is not possible for, in order to stabilize the integrated curricula, relevance has to be defined differently for each occupational context. It follows that occupational contexts can only be related in terms of inequality. The hewers of wood and the drawers of water are likely to be less equal than others. Another way of putting this is to say that there is no position on the three-dimensional surface that satisfies Illich's conditions and that, since this surface depicts all probable situations, Illich's ideals are likely to prove unattainable. The model thus provides a way of distinguishing between attainable and unattainable ideals: a way of sorting 'possible entities' from 'so-called possible entities' on a basis of something other than personal prejudice. For instance, the model has allowed the detailed consideration of situations (those in the hypothetical sector of the curriculum cycle) which, though there are no examples to refer to, are nevertheless perfectly possible.

It is clear that topological (monster conserving) sociology is far removed from the more familiar empirical (monster excluding) form. Returning to Dumont's rhetorical question (about the synthesis of East and West) that provided the starting point of this analysis, we can see that the normal progression from fact to theory has been completely reversed.

---

[12] Ivan Illich, *Deschooling Society* (Calder, London, 1971).

Dumont is concerned with how gradual changes may undermine a dominant ideology and ultimately lead to its gradual or sudden replacement by another, partially contradictory, ideology which until that moment was either submerged or absent. He provides, in informal language, a description of a 'dynamic' propelling a situation by gradual changes in the control space into and finally through the cusp to give a sudden discontinuous change in the behaviour dimension and in the ideology associated with it. The dominant ideology, Homo Hierarchicus, is Dumont's wooden stool; the 'dynamic' is the gradual gnawing of the termites inside, hidden by the darkness because the ideology that would relevate such gnawings, that of Homo Aequalis, is submerged. At last the situation enters and moves through the cusp until one tiny gradual change in the control space, one more chomp of a single termite's jaws, causes the catastrophic collapse of the dominant ideology. The stool disintegrates into dust and is instantly replaced by the comfortable armchair of the West. In crying, 'Who can say but that these changes have not built up their corrosive power in the dark, and that the caste order will not one day collapse like a piece of furniture gnawed from within by termites', Dumont is asking the right rhetorical question. Unfortunately he assumes the wrong answer. It is not 'no one' but 'anyone' and I must now take back my words to the effect that, within the confines of Indian society, Dumont may well be right. Just because we are ignorant of some of history's details, or just because something, though perfectly possible, has not happened yet, it does not follow that we cannot describe how it must have been or predict how it is bound to be.

A dynamic phenomenon such as a curriculum has associated with it a particular picture (or *morphology*). That morphology is a description not just of such fragments of the phenomenon as we may have observed or about which we may happen to have historical data. It is a description of all the possibilities of that dynamic phenomenon. Of course, we have to start with some empirical data. We make some investigations and we carry out some observations and these, plotted in terms of some variables, gives us a cloud of points in a euclidean space. Provided there are enough of these, and provided that not all of them are wrong, we can with the aid of catastrophe theory discover the morphology of which they constitute a few tiny and inaccurate fragments. Once we have this morphology we know all the possibilities of that phenomenon. Not only can we describe possibilities that have not yet happened and reconstruct history that is inadequately recorded, we can also return to and correct our initial empirical data, discarding these points that are obviously wrong and adjusting those that have been poorly observed or distorted by the investigator's bias. Description no longer has to wait upon empirical evidence: theory need no longer be constructed only in hindsight.

9 The geometry of confidence[1]

The treatment of the curriculum cycle in the previous chapter, though purely qualitative and very metaphorical, does I hope give some indication of the way in which catastrophe theory may be able to help in the understanding of cyclical phenomena. Cyclical phenomena are dynamic in that they are constantly changing, yet at the same time persistent in that they exhibit repetitive regularities. Constantly changing phenomena that do not repeat themselves are likely to pass unnoticed, for if we don't see them the first time they happen we don't get another opportunity. So the chances are that the phenomena that are noticed are those that display recurrent regularities—either just the same sort of thing happening again and again or else the same sort of sequence of things happening again and again. The trouble with directing our attention to phenomena is that they present themselves to us pre-selected in this way, for we can only hope to deal with those phenomena that we notice and these will inevitably tend to include the recurrent and exclude the one-off.

Catastrophe theory is the tool that allows us to transfer attention from the level of phenomena to the level of the possibility of phenomena and so enables us to give some sort of description of, and to make some sort of allowance for, those phenomena which though present do not come to our notice. For instance, if we look at curriculum phenomena and see just collection curricula or just integrated curricula and no connections, no paths, from one to the other, then we are seeing static regularities: the same sort of thing happening again and again. In other words we are just seeing isolated points within the upper and lower sheets of the graph containing the cusp catastrophe. Our vision is perfectly correct in that it recognizes

[1] A more detailed and technical version of this chapter appears in J. Clyde Mitchell (ed.), *Numerical Techniques in Anthropology* (Institute for the Study of Human Issues, Philadelphia, 1979). In addition to a more extended discussion of ceremonial exchange, it contains a fairly comprehensive list of references.

the qualitative distinction between these two types of curriculum, but sadly restricted in that it gives no indication of the ways in which they are related. If, on the other hand, we look at curriculum phenomena and see the collection curriculum and the integrated curriculum *and* the cyclical connections between them we are seeing both dynamic change and recurrent regularities: the same sort of sequence of things happening again and again. In other words we are seeing the cyclical route linking the upper and lower sheets of the graph by two clearly separate paths, one passing smoothly outside the cusp, the other passing discontinuously through the cusp. The combination of this, the widest vision we are ever likely to enjoy, with Thom's theorem allows us to fill in the entire surface with its cusp catastrophe. That is, cyclical phenomena, unlike straightforward repetitive phenomena, can provide us with a slice out of the surface that furnishes sufficient information for us, equipped with Thom's theorem, to sketch in the entire surface. The slice out of the surface describes the phenomena: the whole surface describes the possibility of phenomena. Thus the catastrophe theory approach to the study of cyclical phenomena is pre-eminently suitable as a way of transferring our attention from phenomena to their possibility.

This sort of approach is likely to give its largest pay-offs in the so-called soft sciences for it provides a qualitative technique for discovering hitherto unsuspected connections, identities, and family resemblances. The connection I would now like to investigate is that between the trade cycle of the Industrial West and the cyclical ceremonial exchange of pigs in the New Guinea Highlands. These are phenomena that are not usually bracketed together. The trade cycle, the periodic alternation of boom and slump, is normally seen as resulting from advanced industrialization and convincingly annexed by economics. By contrast, ceremonial exchange is one of the delights of anthropology. It is something of which we in the Industrial West have very little but of which primitive societies tend to have a lot. Both economics and anthropology, I feel, stand to gain from the eradication of this invalid distinction between the West and the Rest: between Us and Them.

The phenomenon, which I have called 'the pig cycle', is an elaborate system of ceremonial exchange in the Central Highlands of New Guinea. Gold-lip shells, feathers, stone axes and the like feature in the exchanges but their main component is pigs (and to a lesser extent pork). The system extends over 150 miles of mountainous terrain and so passes through several different cultures. Thus parts of the system have been described by anthropologists, in so far as they related to the particular peoples they worked among, but there is no comprehensive account of the total system. The view which the various peoples caught up in the system have of the system is as restricted as that of their ethnographers. The Enga call the system the *te* and see it as a linear system with exchanges coming into and going out of their area. The Kyaka, who are at one end of the system, call it the *moka* and see it rather differently from the Enga since, whilst it is open at one end, it is for them closed at the other.

It is probably no exaggeration to say that the pig cycle is a phenomenon so extraordinary that, if it were not for the fact that it exists, no one would have believed it possible. The most amazing feature of this exchange system is its periodicity. It is not a steady flow, nor is it a seasonal flow. Every four years or so it builds up to a tremendous climax. Elkin, the anthropologist who first stumbled upon it, happened to arrive in the Wabag area of the Highlands just as one of these spectacular climaxes occurred. He found the landing strip covered with thousands of pigs all tethered to neat lines of stakes. Between these serried ranks the individuals whose energies had brought all these pigs together presided, in all their birds-of-paradise finery, over their dispersal.

This periodicity creates problems in observation, since a full account would require the anthropologist's fieldwork to extend over four years. But even this would not be adequate because in the subsequent four-year period all the exchanges flow in the opposite direction. So, to observe a truly complete cycle he would have to stay there for at least eight years. The description that follows has been pieced together from the accounts of many different field workers.

When looked at in more detail, the cycle can be divided into a number of distinct phases (distinct both to the observer and to the people involved). The cycle, of course, is continuous, but the description must start somewhere and it is convenient to take the moment just after the climax in which the thousands of pigs have been exchanged and most of them eaten, leaving only a minimal population of pigs to start breeding from again.

Phase A. Solicitory gifts (*kenju*), legs of pork, live pigs, pearl shells, and axes are passed from partner to partner in the direction of the main prestations (a technical term useful for describing one half of a delayed exchange) in the previous half of the cycle. This phase lasts from several months to over a year.

Phase B. The main prestations (*kuma pilyanin*, literally 'true moka') come in the opposite direction. These are much more substantial gifts in the order of 8 or 10 pigs per solicitory unit. This phase takes place consecutively in each clan along the sequence, and two types of festival may be distinguished: the internal *moka* between members of one clan, and the much more spectacular external *moka* between members of different clans.

Phase C. This phase starts when the main festivals have reached the last clans in the 150-mile chain. The pigs, or the majority of them, are then killed and cooked and the pork passed back once more from partner to partner, leaving in its wake an epidemic of gastric disorders.

Phase D. Solicitory gifts as in Phase A but in the opposite direction.

Phase E. Main prestations as in Phase B but in the opposite direction.

Phase F. Cooked pork as in Phase C but in the opposite direction.

The cycle is now complete, the seventh phase being identical with Phase A.

Although the *te/moka* appears to be a unique phenomenon, the various cultures through which it passes seem to be fairly similar, and fairly typical of the New Guinea Highlands in general. They are settled agriculturalists with economies based mainly on sweet-potato cultivation and pig-breeding. They are territorially and politically organized on the basis of a segmentary type of lineage framework, similar to that of the Nuer, the Tiv, or the Kuma, and including in its widest span (the clan) anywhere between roughly one thousand and five thousand persons. There is considerable variation in the rigidity with which territorial and political organization are tied to the segmentary lineage system, and also in the extent to which ancestors may be 'fiddled'. Attempts to relate variations in the rigidity and flexibility of the segmentary lineage system to variations in the density of population, the pressure on land, or on land available for sweet-potato cultivation, have met with little success, and one of the leading ethnographers[2] has suggested that, within any one lineage, there is a fairly regular and predictable variation in these properties over time deriving from the effects of a celebrated New Guinea political figure, the 'big man'.

'Big man' is pidgin for the shrewd, forceful, and energetic entrepreneurs who are so influential a feature of Highlands life. New Guinea Highlands society is highly individualistic, competitive, and materialistic. This competition is normally conducted in terms of shell money, elaborate dress and ornaments, and, most of all, pigs. The breeding of pigs requires firstly the services of wives and secondly the support of followers, the securing of which depend on the personal qualities and drive of the aspiring 'big man'. As one typically materialistic 'big man' put it: 'All I care for in my life are my pigs, my wives, my shell money and my sweet potatoes.' Most men never achieve the status of 'big man' and those who do can only sustain it during their prime. No man who reaches a ripe old age can hope to die a 'big man'.

The *te/moka* ceremonial exchange system is cyclical in that there are periodic destructions of pigs, but it also conforms to a pattern of linear oscillation between the two extremities, places called Talembais and Minyip. Elsewhere in the New Guinea Highlands the cycle exists without the linear oscillation. Further afield (in the islands off south-east New Guinea and among aborigines of Northern Australia) there exist exchange systems which are linear but which are not associated with either a cycle or oscillation. This particular system, the *te/moka,* is thus the most complex and presents three separate problems: the cycle, the linearity, and the oscillation.

The linear flow of goods such that an individual or group is simply one link in a chain of exchanges or partnerships often extending for hundreds of miles is a familiar phenomenon in economic anthropology and may readily be understood as resulting from an evenly spread demand for goods from localized centres of production. For example, in the Northern Australian exchanges European goods such as calico which originate in the Darwin area tend to flow southwards in exchange for stone spear-heads, pearl shells, and boomerangs, the centres of production of which lie far to the south.

---

[2] M. J. Meggitt, 'The Pattern of Leadership among the Mae-Enga of New Guinea', *Anthropological Forum,* Vol. II, No. 1, 1967.

By contrast, *churinga* (sacred carved wooden boards), the production of which is not localized, pass in either direction. Thus linearity is to be expected in any exchange situation where raw materials and/or special skills are localized. Topographical features which dictate lines of communication and settlement patterns will merely serve to accentuate this linear nature of the exchange sequences. Such systems may appear to both the ethnographer and the native, who can both see only a small segment of the total system, to be essentially similar. But it is what happens to the ends of the linear sequence, beyond these limits of observation, that determines the crucial property of the system—its behaviour over time.

There are three possibilities concerning the ends: a linear sequence can come to a dead end, it can feed into a larger and more complex system of exchanges, or it can bend around and eventually join up with its other end to form a ring. Thus any system, however complex, can be reduced to linear sequences (with either open or closed ends) and ring sequences. (The open end is, of course, simply a heuristic device and must ultimately reduce to closed ends and rings.) In the case of the Northern Australian exchanges any surplus that arises at the open ends is readily absorbed by the larger and more complex systems that they connect with and so the volume of flow will normally remain fairly constant over time. It is a steady-state system. (A fundamental distinction is made in communications engineering between 'steady-state' and 'generative' systems. A steady state is exhibited by a system of interdependent variables which show no progressive or irreversible change. In a generative state progressive and irreversible changes occur. If the input is constant and the progessive and irreversible change takes the form of a decrease in output we can describe the system as 'degenerative'. If the change takes the form of an increase in output we can describe the system as 'regenerative'.)

In the case of the *te/moka* the volume of flow at any point in the sequence will remain constant, but the system as a whole will not be steady-state but regenerative since there will be a steadily increasing pile-up of goods at the two closed ends. Such a regenerative system, left to itself, would eventually either break down or transform itself, since only a steady-state system can hope to survive unchanged over time. However, there are some possible modifications which can be applied to a closed-ended linear system which, even if they do not transform the system to a steady state, can at least contain its fluctuations within a steady-state envelope. If, instead of a steady flow, the goods were transmitted periodically in 'packets', then when the pile-up occurred at one end it would be possible to reverse the direction of flow to drain away the accumulated goods. Such oscillating systems are common enough in electronics and there is no reason why they should not occur in the communication of goods as well. Such a system, once it has been set in oscillation, will continue to oscillate with a constant period and amplitude so long as the reversed flow from one end does not reach the other end, thereby progressively increasing the size of the pile-ups. This condition is met by the *te/moka* where the cooked pork never passes all the way from one extremity (Minyip) to the other (Talembais). The transformation of the pile-up of live, comparatively durable, pigs into dead and auto-destructive cooked pork may be seen as a secondary modification for insuring that the envelope containing the pig-cycle remains steady-state.

Moreover, the odd number of phases—the three types of prestation, solicitory gifts, main prestations, cooked pork, each phase being the signal for initiating the reciprocal phase in the opposite direction—ensures the regular reversal of flow direction. An even number of phases could never provide the switching mechanism for reversing the flow directions and so could never give rise to an oscillating system.

Thus some exchange systems in primitive societies are undoubtedly generative phenomena and can never be adequately accounted for by steady-state theory. Unfortunately, all present attempts to account for economic phenomena in such societies rely on steady-state theory. Economic anthropologists are all agreed on one (and only one) point, that Keynesian economic theory is quite inapplicable in primitive societies. In holding to this view they stand out like living fossils beside the community of economists who are all Keynesians now (not in the sense that they subscribe to a specific set of concepts but in the sense that they subscribe to a body of theory that can handle both steady-state and generative phenomena).

Classical economists saw the trade cycle as a steady-state phenomenon. Admittedly there was an alternation, an upswing and a downswing, but the whole was contained within a steady-state envelope, and the possibility of a regenerative or degenerative trend was not entertained (a view which Keynes scathingly criticized as predicting that when the storm has passed the sea will be calm once more). Keynes did not assume a steady state. He started out by accepting that economic phenomena are likely to be generative, and that only at one specific set of parameters will they be steady-state and so appear to fit the classic model.

Economic anthropologists are divided into two camps. There are the 'neo-classicists' who hold that classical theory, suitably modified, is applicable in primitive societies; and there are the 'substantivists' who reject such an approach on the grounds that economic relationships in primitive societies are of a totally different nature from those in Western society. One of the leading substantivists has actually used the supposed inapplicability of Keynesian theory as a stick with which to beat the neo-classicists.

... if it is thought that Western price theory is relevant to primitive economy, why not other branches of Western theory—say Keynesian income and employment theory—as well? The answer, perhaps, is that in the attempt to apply Keynesian theory to primitive economy it would become evident that the assumptions of functional similarity of economic organization between the primitive and the West is empirically indefensible. In a word, it cannot be done.[3]

The neo-classicist reply to this *reductio ad absurdum* is, 'Precisely, but then no one said it could.'[4] I regard this challenge to apply Keynesian theory to primitive society not as a *reductio ad absurdum* but as a perfectly reasonable and proper step to take: in a word, it can be done. Indeed, since anthropologists have got a lot of catching up to do, it had better be done.

The curve for the pig cycle, plotting total pig population against time, can be deduced in qualitative terms from various invariants of New Guinea pig-husbandry, such as average litter size, the availability of lactating women for the supplementary suckling of runts, and the porcine gestation period. Without going into these fascinating but technical and time-consuming details, the curve turns out to be something like Fig. 31 overleaf.

---

[3] George Dalton, 'Economic Theory and Primitive Society', *American Anthropologist*, Vol. 62, 1961, p. 16.
[4] Ronald Frankenberg, 'Economic Anthropology' in Association of Social Anthropologists Monograph No. 6, *Theories in Economic Anthropology*.

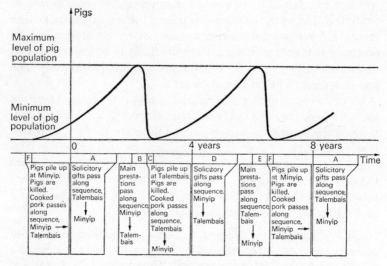

Fig.31 Pig Population

Leaving aside, for a few moments, the consideration and subsequent rejection of various explanations that either have been or could be advanced for the pig cycle, I will boldly state that the only wholly satisfactory account must be in terms of the causal relationship between the pig cycle and the aggregate level of credit.

As well as the visible, tangible, cyclical fluctuations in pig population, there is a parallel invisible, intangible credit cycle. The enormous growth in the pig population during the early part of the cycle coincides with the period during which aspiring 'big men' are building up their followings, using their energy, dynamism, and rhetoric to inspire confidence among their fellow men. Once this confidence is created they can convert their fellow men into followers by the extension of credit. The extension of credit creates a larger following, the size of the 'big man's' following promotes confidence in him among those who are still uncommitted, and they in their turn become his followers. This tremendous upsurge in confidence results in an enormous increase in the pig population. Similarly, a decay of confidence will lead to the calling-in of debts and, at the very least, to a rapid fall-off in the growth rate of the pig population. If this turning point also involves ruthless competition in which some men are ruined by bankruptcy whilst others, presiding first over the presentation of thousands of pigs and then over the feasts in which these thousands of pigs are consumed, survive triumphantly, then there will actually be a sharp drop in the total pig population.

This hypothetical credit cycle would be of the same period as the pig cycle, but its turning points would be displaced in such a way as to anticipate the turning points in the total pig population; this displacement being due, at the lower turning point, to the time it takes to convert the gaining of confidence and the granting of credit into live pigs, and, at the upper turning point, to the time it takes to convert a loss of confidence and a calling-in of credit into cooked pork. The two curves, the pig cycle (expressed in real pigs) and the hypothetical credit cycle (expressed in promised pigs), will look like this.

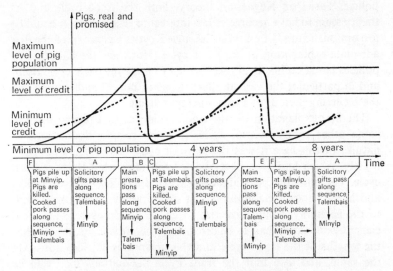

Fig.32 Pig Population: Level of Credit

I must now pause to explain how it is that the hypothesis contained in the relationship between these two curves provides an explanation of the pig cycle and also how it is that this explanation is essentially Keynesian.

Cyclical fluctuations have been familiar to economists almost since the birth of their discipline, and the development of economic theory has, to a considerable extent, derived from successive attempts to explain these fluctuations. The fluctuations have come to be known as the 'trade cycle' or the 'business cycle' and the body of theory seeking to explain the fluctuations is called 'trade cycle theory'. The trade cycle fluctuations were first noticed (or, at any rate, considered worthy of explanation) in the nineteenth century, and the first explanation was provided by Jevons in 1878. From then until comparatively recently the trade cycle and the problem of its explanation have been central to economic theory. In particular, Keynesian theory largely derives from problems of the trade cycle, and provides an explanation where classic economic theory was inadequate. Since the economic revolution which came with the adoption by, in particular, the United States and Great Britain of economic policies based on Keynesian theory, both the trade cycle and its theory seem to have become of less interest to economists. It could be too optimistic to say that this is because Keynes has provided the first adequate explanation of the trade cycle. However, the adoption of policies based on his theory has helped to tame the trade cycle itself, and in particular the violent alternations of booms and slumps and the recurring periods of heavy unemployment.

The first explanation for the trade cycle was that its cause lay in some other environmental cycle, in some regular fluctuations in nature. In this case it was the sunspot cycle (seven years approximately) which had been observed to coincide with a thunderstorm cycle. This climatic cycle might be expected to affect the crop yields, and hence, since agriculture was at that time the main component of the economy, would give rise to an economic cycle. This most elegant explanation had to be discarded when it was discovered that the lengths of the trade cycle and the sunspot cycle were not quite the same, and also that the trade cycle fluctuations increased as agriculture decreased as a component in the economy. The fact that the period of the pig cycle is between six and eight years suggests that it is not caused by any natural cycle in the environment and this conclusion gains confirmation when we find that the period of the cycle has changed over the years and that there are similar cycles elsewhere in the New Guinea Highlands, some with longer and some with shorter periods.

Recently, there has been a resurgence of the Jevons type of explanation: the intervention of some external and natural constraint. Roy Rappaport[5] has advanced an ecological explanation for another pig cycle in New Guinea in terms of the homoeostasis between the pig and its environment and the pig parasite and its environment (the pig). It is difficult to know what to say about such ecological explanations since they are concerned primarily with delineating the natural limits to human activities and not with understanding the possible forms which these human activities can take. Providing there are no flaws in such ecological arguments I have no quarrel with them: they are simply irrelevant to my concern in the sense that if the human activities I wish to study were not ecologically possible they simply wouldn't be there.

Most economic explanations that have been advanced for the trade cycle have been of this type; based on the idea that people pursue their cultural values until collectively they bump up against some natural limit. These theories rely on buffers; sometimes two buffers with the variable bouncing back and forth between them, sometimes just one, a ceiling or a floor with either a balloon- or ball-like variable. But there is one explanation, the Hansen-Samuelson model of the trade cycle, which shows how economic fluctuations will occur even in the total absence of natural limits or restraints. In this model the cycle is derived solely from the interaction of those two Keynesian concepts: the Multiplier and the Accelerator.

Fortunately there is no need to go into the technicalities of the Hansen-Samuelson model. It is sufficient for my present purpose to explain that the Multiplier involved Keynes in propounding his celebrated fundamental psychological law, 'That men are disposed as a rule and on the average to increase their consumption as their income increases but not by as much as the increase in their income.' Thus Keynes found it necessary to take individual motivation into economic account but conveniently and, alas, erroneously was able to treat it as a constant.

The Accelerator is more technical. It is based on the notion that in a representative industry there is a ratio between the value of capital and annual output. More simply, it is the idea that there is a ratio

---

[5] Roy A. Rappaport, *Pigs for the Ancestors: Ritual in the Ecology of a New Guinea People* (Yale University Press, New Haven, Conn., 1967).

between the number of machines in a factory and the number of goods produced by that factory. Of course, you can over-use or under-use machines but the ratio is taken to be that optimum state of affairs where the machines are neither so over-used that they and their operators are subjected to undue strain nor so under-used that a proportion of the capital tied up in them is in effect lying idle. The next step in the Accelerator is the idea that as the level of demand for the products of the factory varies, as inevitably it will, the factory owner strives continuously to adjust his stock of capital, by buying more machines, or postponing the buying of more machines, or *in extremis* selling off machines, so as always to remain as close as he possibly can to this optimum ratio. This he will do by seeing how things are going, which actually means seeing how things have gone, for this feedback of information as to how well or badly his products are selling is inevitably subject to a time lag. Stripped to its essentials, the Accelerator is based upon the lagged relationship between plant and product, and is applicable to any process in which the production of one sort of good is governed by the production of another sort of good. Pig-husbandry is one such process: the production of what we may call 'disposable pigs' is governed by the production of 'breeding pigs'. The Accelerator is a formalized description of the rational decision-making process that determines why this little piggy goes to market and this little piggy stays at home.

The Hansen-Samuelson model of the trade cycle incorporates this very simple feedback mechanism—inevitably time-lagged feedback of information concerning levels of demand—and gives rise to cycles even in the absence of buffers. These cycles will, in general, be generative: either damped (settling down and dying away) or anti-damped (getting worse and worse) and only at one specific set of parameters will they be of constant amplitude. The Hansen-Samuelson model incidentally provides a neat condensation of the Keynesian spirit: the insistence that economic phenomena are in general generative and only steady-state in the special case; the focusing of attention on real world processes such as the factory with its machines and its products; and above all, the conviction that the totality must be understood as the aggregation of individual contributions each in itself rational in terms of that individual's situation.

The way in which cyclical fluctuations result from these lagged adjustments is most easily explained by a famous mechanical example of exactly the same sort of process. Imagine a rather badly designed central-heating system in which the supply of fuel to the boiler is regulated by a thermostat in one of the rooms. If the temperature of the room falls below the desired level the thermostat will cause more fuel to be fed into the boiler but, of course, the benefit of this will not be felt immediately since it takes some time for this additional fuel to raise the temperature of the room. So the thermostat causes more fuel to be fed into the boiler even though that which it is already receiving would be sufficient, given time, to raise the room temperature to the desired level. The room overheats and the thermostat then reacts by cutting down the supply of fuel to the boiler. But, of course, it takes some time for this cut-back of fuel to have much effect on the temperature of the room and so the thermostat cuts back the fuel further with the result that the room becomes too cold, the thermostat over-reacts and away the cycle goes again. If the system is really badly designed these cycles may be anti-damped and the boiler will eventually explode. If it is not too badly designed the cycle will be damped down until it oscillates between more or less tolerable extremes of temperature.

If you were to plot, on the same graph, the variation with time of both the fuel added to the boiler and the temperature of the room you would obtain two oscillating curves that remained in step with one another but with the peaks and troughs of the fuel curve always anticipating those of the temperature curve: the anticipation at the trough reflecting the time taken for an addition of fuel to be converted into an increase in room temperature, and the anticipation at the peak reflecting the time taken for a reduction of fuel to be converted into a drop in room temperature.

It is not too difficult to deduce qualitatively what the curves for the disposable pig population and the breeding pig population must be in the case of the pig cycle and they turn out to be something like Fig. 33 overleaf.

'Aha!' or even 'eureka!' one cries—curves with exactly the same characteristics as those for the central-heating system. It is just a matter of playing around with the parameters until one obtains a near-perfect fit between the pig cycle and the Hansen-Samuelson model. But there is a snag, and a serious snag at that!

A pig-breeder will at any moment in time mentally divide his herd into those pigs which he reserves for breeding and those which he regards as disposable, but this division is not fixed (except in the case of castrated male pigs) and he can if he likes convert a breeding pig into a disposable pig or *vice versa* in a twinkling, as it were, simply by changing his mind. Now, in the pig cycle this is what happens. Near the top of the upswing individual pig-breeders are faced with critical and difficult decisions about just when to start converting into disposable pigs those breeding pigs that will not be able to produce a mature litter in time for the main prestations. The decision is critical because he must have as many mature disposable pigs as possible available for the main prestations, and difficult because though he knows the time of the main prestations is approaching, he cannot tell just when exactly it will arrive.

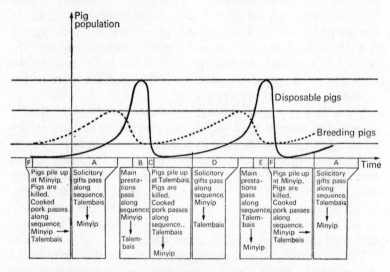

Fig.33 *Note*. These two curves added together give the total pig population curve in Fig. 31

Now this sort of thing is not reconcilable with a feedback mechanism. To return to the mechanical analogy of the feedback system in which the temperature of the room governs the amount of fuel added to the boiler via the mediating device of a thermostat, we find that converting breeding pigs into disposable pigs is equivalent to converting the excess heat in the room directly into unburnt fuel—an impossible process that would completely do away with the need for any thermostat. Feedback mechanisms are based upon the feedback of information—of temperature in the case of the room and boiler, of knowledge about changes in levels of investment in the case of the trade cycle. The thermostat is the device that does this in the first case; the entrepreneur adjusting his actual stock of capital to his desired stock of capital is the device in the second case. The feedback mechanism will only function so long as the two parts of the system which it mediates between are mutually non-convertible. This is certainly so in the case of the room and boiler, but certainly not so in the case of the breeding pig and the disposable pig.

What we have got is something that looks just like an oscillating and feedback system but isn't. What then *is* the fuel that drives the pig cycle? It is the aggregated confidence of the individual pig-breeders. If their confidence is high they will be eager to extend credit (if they are aspiring 'big men') and to accept credit (if they are the followers of the 'big men'). If their confidence falls they will respectively be eager to call in this credit and to pay off these alarming debts.

It is now, I hope, clear why it is that the only wholly satisfactory explanation must be one in terms of the causal relationship between the pig cycle and the aggregate level of credit. Turning back to the hypothetical diagram of this relationship (Fig. 32) it can be seen that the curves are exactly of the type that are associated with an oscillating system deriving from a feedback mechanism. In this case, credit can only be converted into pigs via the pig-husbandry process, the time scale of which is determined by invariants associated with the human breeding cycle, the pig-breeding cycle, the sweet-potato growth rate, the cycle of the seasons, and so on; that is, invariants deriving from the ecosystem. Thus, the credit-into-pigs transformation can only be effected through this mechanism, and with this time lag, and so, if it can be shown that the credit cycle must be of this form, then the form of the pig cycle is also determined.

The expansive style of operation of the 'big man' would seem to validate the upswing of this hypothetical credit cycle, but what of the turning point and the downswing? A clue to the explanation of the turning point is provided by one of the parting shots in the fruitless debate on the variations in rigidity and flexibility of New Guinea lineage systems.

Meggitt,[6] in discusssing political aspects of Enga organization, has suggested that, within any lineage, a cyclical pattern is generated by the interaction of the 'big man' system and the segmentary lineage system. He insists that within the life history of each clan there is a fairly predictable alternation in the style of operation of the 'big men': expansive optimism giving way to defensive pessimism, and periods of peace alternating with outbreaks of war.

I do not wish to suggest that the cyclical alternations of the pig cycle and the cyclical alternations of lineage fortunes proposed by Meggitt are one and the same. Rather they should be seen as two possibilities that can be generated by the relationship between two partially conflicting ideologies, that deriving from the 'big man' and that deriving from the segmentary lineage structure. The conflict between these two coexisting ideologies resides in the simple distinction that the 'big man' ideology is ego-focused whilst the lineage ideology is not. The former provides an admirable validating framework for the maximization of individual advantage but can furnish no basis for co-operation for the benefit of the whole. The 'big man' ideology is basically that of 'might is right'. The lineage ideology similarly provides a validating framework for the maximization of individual advantage but *within certain limits*. Exactly what these limits are is an undecidable question, for the rigidity/flexibility of the lineage framework varies spatially (that is, from one society to another) and temporally (that is, within any given society, over time). Ideally the lineage framework provides a ranking of claims for support between any one man and all his fellows, this ranking being a function of the genealogical distances between him and his fellows. In practice, however, this rating is never absolute since there frequently exists the possibility of restructuring the lineage framework in such a manner that a linkage particularly desired for the maximization of some individual advantage is promoted to the top position in the ranking. Nevertheless the simple fact that the framework, though continually transformed, persists through time, is proof that not all such possible restructurings are equally probable and that considerable constraints upon the avenues whereby individual advantage may be maximized do exist.

These conditions are met by the social systems involved in the pig

[6] Op. cit.

cycle. The 'big man' is always there, sometimes riding flamboyantly on the crest of a wave, whipped up by his own exuberance, at other times shortening sail, calling in his loans and wondering how he can weather the storm which his rapid translation from wave-crest to wave-trough has precipitated. And throughout all these ups and downs, there persists in some form or other, at times practically submerged, the lineage framework which the 'big man' has so forcefully used and abused, in his single-minded pursuit of pig-power.

The problem now is to obtain a description of the range of possibilities which the relationship between these two coexisting and partially conflicting ideologies can generate. Such a description can be expressed in terms of person to person credit relationships, both those within a discrete section of the system and those crossing from that section to the rest of the system. By taking as this section the clan, which is the widest grouping encompassed by the segmentary lineage framework, we can be sure that all those credit links that are forged between the section and the rest of the system must be validated only by the 'big man' ideology, since they extend beyond the widest scope of the lineage framework.

During the course of the pig cycle there are significant aggregate variations in these credit relationships, both in terms of their density (reflected in the total number of such relationships both within and across the boundary of the clan) and in their intensity (reflected in the total credit load imposed upon these relationships). All credit relationships are forged in response to the perceived advantages of the participants but only some are, in addition, validated by the lineage ideology (they represent the 'big man's' use of the lineage ideology). Other relationships (including all those across the clan boundary) are formed in spite of the lineage ideology (they represent the 'big man's' abuse of it). Three variables can be isolated.

1. The level of credit.

2. The number of credit relationships validated by the lineage ideology.

3. The number of credit relationships forged despite the lineage ideology.

These variables can be rearranged as follows.

1a. The level of credit.

2a. Total number of credit relationships.

3a. The ratio, total amount of credit extended through relationships created despite the lineage ideology : total amount of credit extended through relationships validated by the lineage ideology.

A three-dimensional graph in terms of these variables will provide the description we are seeking; the manner in which the credit cycle (1a), the entrepreneurial activities of the 'big man' (2a), and the partial contradiction of the two ideologies (3a) are related.

The first two variables are self-explanatory but the third requires some elaboration. The assumption here is that the degree of conflict depends upon the relative credit load between validating and non-validating relationships. (This would seem to be a reasonable assumption since the 'big man' who has, say, half his relationships despite the lineage ideology but only, say, one-quarter of his credit, is surely creating less confusion than another who has, say, three-quarters of his credit extended through the same proportion of relationships.) The significance of this variable expressing the degree of ideological conflict resides in the fact that the 'big man' ideology, being ego-focused, confirms the world view characterized by Hobbes's notion of a war of all against all, whilst the lineage ideology insists that this war is confined only to certain areas of the world and that there are regions to which it can never spread and which, in consequence, stand out as fixed islands of certainty set in the turbulent sea of unpredictability. If one is prepared to accept this philosophical

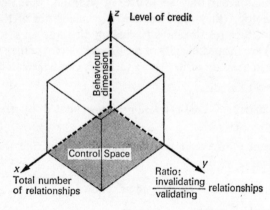

Fig.34

position then the rate of change of this third variable becomes an expression of the degree to which certainty is being destroyed (or, if its value is negative, the degree to which certainty is being created).

Such profound speculations apart, and despite the total absence of quantitative data, it is still possible to state some geometrical properties concerning these three variables. As with the curriculum cycle, the relationship must be contained in a three-dimensional space with axes as in Fig. 34.

The procedure now is exactly the same as that followed for the curriculum cycle:

(i) In the case where neither x nor y is increasing, the most likely outcome is that there will be no change in the level of credit.

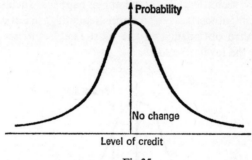

Fig.35

(ii) When x is increasing but y remains constant, we have a situation where more credit links are being forged but where there is no erosion of certainty. That is, the gulf between people's expectations, based on their references to the lineage framework, and what actually happens is neither widened nor narrowed. In such a situation the most likely outcome is an increase in the level of credit (see Fig. 36 overleaf).

(iii) When y is increasing but x remains constant we have a situation in which no more links are being forged but there is a progressive transfer of credit from those relationships validated by the lineage ideology to those created despite this ideology. In other words certainty is being steadily eroded and people's expecta-

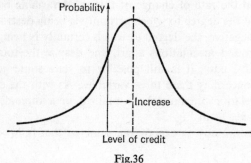

Fig.36

tions based on their references to their genealogies are progressively confounded by what actually happens. Increasingly that which seems least likely to happen happens. Such situations of increasing uncertainty and unpredictability are not conducive to expansive optimism and the most likely outcome is a decrease in the level of credit.

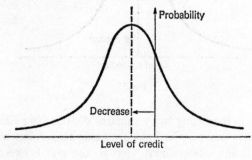

Fig.37

(iv) In the situation where both x and y are increasing more links are being forged and therefore more credit is being extended, but at the same time these new links are increasingly made despite the lineage framework. Here the two ideologies are increasingly in conflict, the 'big man' ideology constantly encouraging the forging of new relationships and the lavish extension of credit whilst at the same time eroding certainty at an ever-quickening pace and so increasing unpredictability as progressively to encourage the calling-in of credit. There can be no justification for assuming any kind of balance between the extension and the calling-in of credit (except in the very early stages) and as the process continues, so increasingly must the pendulum swing one way or the other, and, progressively, the likelihood that there will be no change in the level of credit decreases.

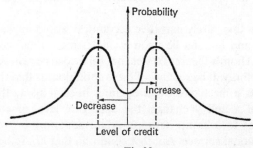

Fig.38

In the absence of any quantitative data it is not possible to say anything about the exact shape and size of these probability distributions and any description derived from these data must be based solely on qualitative facts such as, whether there are one or two maxima, one or no minima, whether these indicate no change, increase, or decrease in the level of credit, and their position relative to earlier or later situations.

For instance, as the rate of increase of x and y changes in examples (ii) and (iii) so the maxima will be displaced to give greater increases and decreases respectively in the level of credit and, moreover, though the relationship is probably not linear it is certainly smooth and continuous: gradual changes in the rates give rise to gradual shifts in the positions of the maxima. Similarly there is a continuous sequence of changes linking examples (i) and (iv) from zero change in both x and y through a steady increase in both rates, and as this occurs the single maximum in example (i) will become progressively flattened and then form a shallow minimum which as the sequence proceeds is gradually deepened whilst the maxima which it separates become more and more laterally displaced. In the same way, a gradual variation in the mix of the rates of change of x and y in example (iv) will result in progressive asymmetry in the probability distribution with one or other maximum becoming smaller, with their being displaced increasingly unequal amounts from the neutral position and with a corresponding displacement of the minimum until, at some point along these sequences, the minimum will disappear and at the limits, where the rate of increase of y approaches zero and that of x approaches zero, the distribution will become congruent with one of the configurations of examples (ii) and (iii) respectively.

Thus, from this purely narrative account, it would appear that all the maxima and minima lie upon a single smooth and continuous surface, and Thom's theorem states that (provided certain conditions are satisfied) this will be so. One of these conditions is that there must be a dynamic, a mechanism that operates in such a way that, when the values of x and y change, the aggregate level of credit also changes so as to take up its appropriate new position within the three-dimensional surface. Another condition that has to be satisfied is that this dynamic has to be effective. For instance, it would be no use having a dynamic that operated on the same sort of time scale as the changes on the control space (the values of x and y). If this happened, then the appropriate position in the surface would keep changing long before the dynamic had brought the level of credit to the right value. So, for a dynamic to be effective, it has to operate in a faster time than the changes in the control space. We need to ask two questions about the dynamic. First, how is the change in the level of credit (indicated by the shifts in the positions of the maxima) effected? Second, what happens in the last case (iv) where two opposite changes are indicated?

Credit is extended through myriad relationships between credit givers (and callers-in)—'big men'; and credit receivers (and repayers) —the 'big men's' followers. The level of credit within the society is the aggregation of individual borrowings. Each individual will, at any moment, have an idea of his desired level of borrowing—the optimists wishing to increase the level, the pessimists wishing to decrease the level. The probability distributions depict this range of individually desired borrowings.

The 'big men' (the credit givers and callers-in) strive at all times to maximize their followers which means that they constantly adjust their extension of credit so that it accords more closely with the most popularly desired level among the receivers. Now, of course, the granting of this credit and the activities of the 'big men' influence individual receivers and cause them to revise their desired level of borrowing. In consequence, the probability distribution changes shape again, and the 'big men' extend or call in credit so as to maximize their followings by adjusting to the new position of the peak.

In this way, the relationships between the 'big man' and his followers provide the dynamic which effectively ensures the continuous smooth process whereby the 'big man' constantly strives to position himself at the maximum: to extend (or call in) credit by an amount that will give him access to the largest number of followers. His behaviour is thus very local—chasing his peak as it changes position —and he has to ignore the global situation: what is happening elsewhere along the distribution. But the peak does not just change position: it changes shape as well, and in certain circumstances it disappears completely. What happens then?

The 'big man' continuously adjusts to his local maximum and so is unaware that this is becoming less pronounced and that another peak has appeared at a very much lower level of credit. If this new peak grows whilst his local peak declines then there will come a moment when it (the local peak) flattens out. In this situation there is no longer a local maximum for him to adjust to and he has no option but to make the sudden and discontinuous jump to the new maximum at the much lower level of credit. For instance, take the sequence of changes described by this curve in the control space.

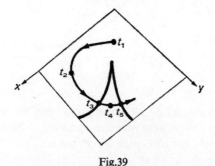

Fig.39

As the values of x and y change in this way the dynamic performs the following operations (Fig. 40).

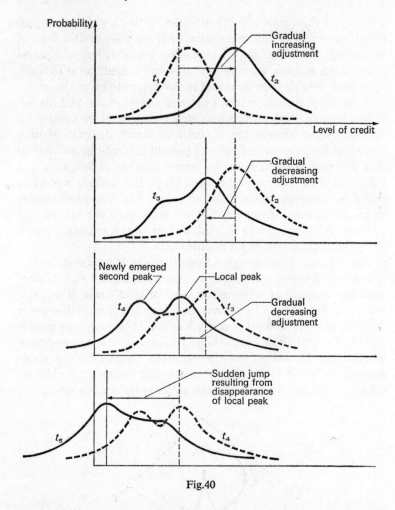

Fig.40

It results in the sudden discontinuous jump from the upper sheet to the lower sheet of the cusp catastrophe occurring at the moment when the situation on the control space leaves the cusp.

The question now is: what are the probabilities in the pig cycle? What sorts of changes in the values of x and y are happening there? Once again, despite the absence of quantitative data it is still possible to say something about the qualitative changes that will occur. First, there is a finite, and indeed quite small, number of potential relationships that are validated by the lineage ideology, whilst there is in theory an infinite and in practice a very large number of potential relationships that are not validated by it. Second, it would seem reasonable that a man who is trying to maximize his control over pigs will, in the first instance, try to activate those potential relationships that are validated by the lineage ideology, and that only when he has done this will he seek to activate those that are, to some extent, disputed, and then those that are not validated at all. The ethnographies tend to support this assumption. A consequence of these two qualitative factors is that, as the pig cycle develops, the relationship between x and y must be of the following type.

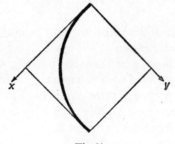

Fig.41

This amounts to saying that as the density and intensity of credit relationships increases so increasingly will this growth be among those relationships that are not validated by the lineage ideology. This means that inevitably, sooner or later, the situation will move into the cusp. Here we can expect sudden discontinuous change; in this case, a sudden reduction in the level of credit such as occurs during the main prestations phase of the cycle. If we assume that unactivated credit relationships, like talents, atrophy then this sudden reduction in the level of credit will be followed by a rapid diminution in the density and intensity of relationships, especially those that are not validated by the lineage ideology. It is in such gloomy unpredictable times that one discovers who one's friends really are, and it is in the nature of these things that, blood being thicker than water, they turn out to be those whose closeness to oneself is enshrined in the genealogies. As a result the total number of credit relationships diminish and increasingly those that remain are validated by the lineage ideology. The situation returns to its starting point. In terms of x and y the situation follows a cyclical career that cuts the cusp once.

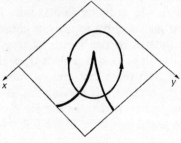

Fig.42

For the total picture of this career we must go into three dimensions, projecting this two-dimensional cycle upwards until it cuts the surface of the three-dimensional graph (as shown in Fig. 43 opposite).

This is the description of what is happening in any one clan in the *te/moka* sequence. A cycle of three phases (A, B, and C or D, E, and F) takes about four years. During such a cycle the level of credit builds up quite steeply from its lowest level until it flattens out at its peak, the time of the main prestations. This is the point where the situation passes out of the cusp and, at this moment, all loans are called in and the level of credit drops suddenly to its lowest value (see Fig. 44 on page 212).

For the total picture it is necessary to sum all the clans. The main prestations occur in one clan after another along the sequence over a period of several months and this means that the graph of credit level against time for the entire system will be somewhat softened and, in particular, the odd feature, the instantaneous switch from peak to trough, will disappear and be replaced by a steep slope. That is, we will obtain the hypothetical curve for the credit cycle (see Fig. 32).

The existence of the turning point is now explained without any recourse to external intervention. The actions of individual pig-breeders, in aggregate, transform the system to which each belongs, yet which is nothing other than the totality of such individual contributions. This transformation propels the system into, and through, the cusp, and in consequence the most likely outcome, before it leaves the cusp, is a sudden catastrophic collapse in the level of

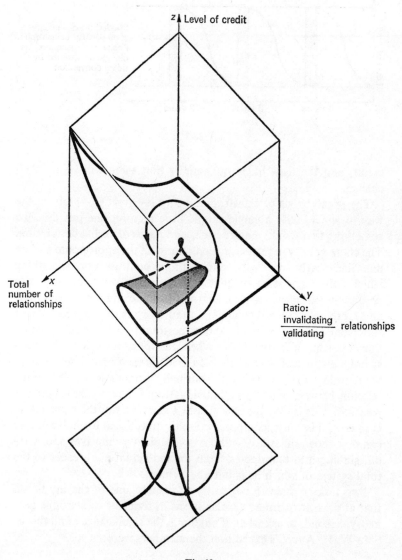

Fig.43

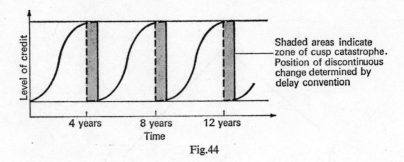

Fig.44

credit, and the least likely outcome is that there will be no such change.

The protagonists of catastrophe theory lay great emphasis on the way in which, with a single simple little picture, one can describe something that would require pages and pages of verbal description. The claim goes even further, for one can with the appropriate picture describe clearly, concisely, and without contradiction something which either cannot be adequately described in words at all or else requires a verbal description that is full of seeming contradictions and tautologies. One such apparent tautology is the very Keynesian statement I have just made about the totality being nothing other than the sum of its parts. But when one looks instead to the catastrophe picture, of which this is so inadequate a verbal description, the tautology disappears and the normally intractable problem of the relation between micro (the individual) and macro (the totality) is resolved. This is why the catastrophe theory part of the explanation is so crucial because, equipped with this topological formulation, we can now move smoothly, without contradicting ourselves and without sinking into tautologies, from the individual pig-breeder to the total system of which he is but one element.

Two tasks remain. First, to try to dispel some of the mysticism that at present surrounds explanations in terms of catastrophe geometry. Second, to ask what, if anything, the significance of all this is.

In W. H. Auden's expedition the members were:

> ... sound on Expectation
> Had there been situations to be in;
> Unluckily they were their situation:
>
> > (from 'The Quest')

The same is true of the New Guinea pig-breeder. The cusp catastrophe with its dynamic is a powerful and condensed way of describing just this sort of relationship between actor and situation. The graph provides a way of depicting the probabilities of certain social phenomena, these phenomena being, in general, social actions in relation to which there can exist partially contradictory ideologies. The cyclical career traces out a particular sequence of such probabilities, each of which, so far as any pig-breeder is concerned, defines his situation. It follows, therefore, that the answer to the question, 'what forces constrain the situation to pass through the particular sequence of probabilities described by this career?' is: 'the rational maximizing behaviour of the individual pig-breeders'. In other words, catastrophe theory allows us to draw a picture of two different kinds of blinker: a picture, that is, of the irreducible contradiction between co-existing ideologies. It then describes how some people come to acquire one kind of blinker and some the other kind of blinker, and it goes on to show how and why a person may change from one kind of blinker to the other. It shows how intelligent and thinking individuals, as their situations change, come to change the bases for their rational behaviour, and it shows how that rational behaviour, in aggregate, transforms their individual situations.

In trying to assess what, if anything, the significance of all this is (apart from the sheer delight involved in trying to solve difficult problems) it occurs to me that though this catastrophe theory approach succeeds where even the Hansen-Samuelson model fails, it is nevertheless wholly in the spirit of Keynes. Thus, if it has any implications, they should have the effect of improving upon Keynes rather than rejecting him (which, with our post-Keynesian ills, is the popular trend at present).

Keynes quite deliberately entitled his great work *The general theory of employment, interest and money* so as to parallel Einstein's *General theory of relativity* for he saw his theory as subsuming classical economics as a special case in the same way that Einstein's subsumed Newtonian mechanics. Catastrophe theory holds out the prospect of doing a Keynes on Keynes. Keynes made an expedient assumption—his famous fundamental psychological law—concerning the point at which economic theory must take note of social considerations, and chose to regard that input as a constant. As the pig cycle goes through its violent ups and downs it is all too evident

H

that the Enga pig-breeders are not disposed 'by and large and on the average' to save a constant proportion of any increase in income that they may receive. The marginal propensity to consume is a constant only in the special case. In general it varies as a result not of economic forces but of the social and cultural forces related to changes in the amount of certainty within the system—the tug-of-Hobbesian-war. Anthropologists have been remiss in not trying very hard to discover what these forces might be but now, rather belatedly, it looks as though catastrophe theory will allow us to write the general equation of which Keynesian theory, with its social constant, is the special case. This, it seems to me, is what we stand to gain by bringing together the West and the Rest: economics and anthropology.

10 The needle's eye

I began by making the brash claim that the anthropologist, by study-ing rubbish, could furnish a deeper understanding of man's relation to his environment than could either the ecologist or the economist. Let me finish, more modestly, by suggesting that catastrophe theory, by clarifying the contradictions rubbish theory reveals, provides the hypothesis that may lead us to that deeper understanding.

The ecologist's insistence on the connectedness of everything has to coexist with the knowledge that we can never take everything into account. The economist's confident stance on the firm ground of scarcity is shaken once he realizes that his feet are actually sinking into the shifting sands of cultural values. When people begin to feel inadequate they become defensive. This is an understandable reac-tion but an unfortunate one, for the only intellectual style that will lead the ecologist and the economist out of their common plight is expansive improvident optimism; something that does not come easily to belt-tightening, theory-hoarding pessimists. They should throw caution and, if need be, long-cherished concepts to the wind. The ecologist should take a deep breath and then address himself to some very different questions about connectedness. What sort of connection exists between the urge to understand the connectedness of everything and the social context, the social constraints and freedoms, of the person who feels that urge? And how does this social context differ from that of the individual who feels no such urge? Why is one person encouraged to seek comfort through increasing certainty, the other to profit by the erosion of that cer-tainty? What is the connection between these two contexts: what sorts of odysseys await the individuals who undertake the journey from one context to the other? The economist for his part would be well advised to gain some understanding of the dynamic properties of the cultural sands that threaten to engulf him. Since the ecologist and the economist, in view of their current predicaments, are unlikely to be able to do anything about all this themselves I have taken the liberty, in a rather roundabout way, of doing it for them.

The catastrophe theory hypothesis is essentially a novel way of approaching the central mystery of the social sciences: the relationship between category and action, between culture and society, between values and behaviour. It puts forward the idea that cultural categories, whilst they are to some extent socially negotiable, also exhibit a certain toughness. Though they can be pushed, they cannot be pushed just anywhere. This in itself is not a very novel idea and most, if not all, social scientists would probably agree with it. However, this agreement is always expressed in informal language. As the language is tightened up, becoming more precise, more formal, and less tolerant of contradictions, so the idea of the relationship is squeezed towards one extreme or the other. Either culture becomes so plastic as to be infinitely negotiable, just an epi-phenomenon of social action; or it becomes so rigid that negotiation is impossible—culture then determines social action. At this point the social scientist, suddenly slipping back into informality, will admit that, really, it's a bit of both. Well, actually, it's neither.

The student of segmentary lineage systems will surface every now and then from the depths of his analysis to make the conventional announcement: 'Among the So-and-so, politics are conducted in the idiom of kinship.' The assumption here is that there are two autonomous domains, kinship (category) and politics (action), related to one another in the manner of the medium and the message, or the rules of chess and the playing of chess, and, in relation to any particular event, this analogy is valid. It is the next step in the conventional argument that is not valid. This holds that, if there are two autonomous domains in relation to this event and two autonomous domains in relation to the next event, then there are two autonomous domains in relation to both events. This is the convenient fallacy which Whitehead, with his philosophy of the eternal object, was concerned to expose and rectify.

The error arises in the following manner: the event relates the two domains and so, during the event, the two domains cannot remain fully separated (though they may not be, and very often are not, fully merged). After the event there are two separate domains once more, but it cannot be assumed that they are the same domains. Only in the special case where the merged portion happens to split into segments identical with those from which it was formed is this assumption valid. This is the special case where there is persistence and no change. So I am suggesting that there exists, as yet, no formal language within which the concepts of persistence and change may be handled, though of course it is perfectly possible to talk about it all informally.

In making his assumption the social scientist is singling out two polar special cases from the generality they straddle without giving any reason as to why they should be privileged in this way. That there are no 'privileged moments' is a guiding principle for astronomers. Would that it were also held by those who gaze upon humanity.

Once the social scientist has made his dubious assumption of separation, he can analyse a process in terms of either one domain or the other. He can then speak, not with forked tongue, but with two tongues. One says that cultural categories are the reflection, or the by-product, of social action; the other says that culture is the rule-book that specifies what actions are possible. He then claims to be able to stitch his two tongues back together again without imposing any speech impediment on either of them. This stitched-up tongue says that, of course, cognitive frameworks do not just spring up in isolation. It says that a world view is always closely tied to the social context that it renders meaningful. But it has to be a special sort of tie: the two parts, world view and social context, have to be perfectly balanced. In other words, the two tongues can only wag together in perfect harmony in the special case where there is persistence and no change. If world view could sometimes alter social context, and if social context could sometimes alter world view, then his stitched-up tongue would cause him some very distressing speech impediments.

It seems that, once we rightly insist that viable principles of classi-fication should not be studied in isolation but should be seen to be closely connected with viable social patterns, the very nature of the language that we use leads us to see that relationship as rigidly self-perpetuating. Of course, there must be a self-perpetuating element within the relationship or else there would be no recurrent regularities to call the relationship to our attention in the first place. It is in this sense of having some recognizable persistence through social experience that I use the term viable. But the sort of language that we use to describe these viable relationships, chicken-and-egg statements like 'we shape our buildings and our buildings shape us', assumes not just some recognizable persistence but eternal repetition.

But our buildings were not always as they are now, nor were we always as we are now, and in using such a formula we impose a static understanding upon a changing reality. Like latter-day, if unwitting, Canutes we try to stem the flood of social and cultural change. Words, when it comes to dynamic processes, are a snare and a delusion even to the wary. Pictures are much better.

This Canute-like behaviour is the direct result of the monster-excluding style that inevitably follows from this assumption of separation, and it has some serious consequences. The monster conserver, not wishing to make this assumption of separation, might try to adopt what is sometimes called a phenomenological approach and, looking at the range and variety of social behaviour, might try to uncover the range and variety of the tastes which would make sense of that behaviour. He could then look to see which tastes enjoy social acceptance and which tastes are rejected, and whether acceptance and rejection derive from internal or external factors. This is the line of enquiry followed by Ruth Benedict. Since then (the 1930s) monster conservers seem to have disappeared from the social sciences.

She takes issue both with the extreme categorists who 'like Durkheim have cried, "the individual does not exist"' and with the extreme actionists who argue that 'society is not and never can be anything over and above the individual minds that compose it'.[1] She maintains that this is a false antagonism deriving not from any intrinsic irreconcilability between category theory and action theory but merely from the contingent circumstances of anthropologists and sociologists.

The argument between those who have thought it necessary to conceive of the group as more than the sum of its individuals and those who have not, has been largely between students handling different kinds of data. Durkheim, starting from an easy familiarity with the diversity of cultures and especially the culture of Australia, reiterated, often in vague phraseology, the necessity of studies of culture. Sociologists, on the other hand, dealing rather with our own standardised culture, have attempted to demolish a methodology the need for which simply did not occur in their work.[2]

[1] Ruth Benedict, *Patterns of Culture* (Routledge & Kegan Paul, London, 1935), p. 166.
[2] Ibid. p. 167.

Benedict, too, had an easy familiarity with the diversity of cultures but, confronted with their bewildering variety, she did not (like Wittgenstein) fall back on the doctrine of cultural relativity. She felt that culture should not be studied in isolation but should be seen as closely connected with viable social patterns. This means that she had within her grasp the means of rejecting cultural relativism without having to embrace cultural universalism. Each culture might be unique but this was of little consequence since the requirement of viability meant that cultures inevitably took up certain limited and specifiable configurations: there were 'patterns of culture'. So these patterns, and not the unique cultures that like different-coloured inks were simply the media in which the patterns were drawn, were what the anthropologist should aim to describe and understand. 'In all studies of social action, the crux of the matter is that the behaviour under consideration must pass through the needle's eye of social acceptance.'[3] With success in her hands, she threw it away: '. . . only history in its widest sense can give an account of these social acceptances and rejections.'[4] Her fatal flaw was her conviction that there was no contradiction between category theory and action theory: that anthropology and sociology could be reconciled without at the same time being transformed beyond all recognition. She thought that they were both true and that their antagonism was false, but it is the other way around. The antagonism is true and they are both false.

The process at the needle's eye is the key to the relationship between persistence and change. If there was no process, if nothing ever passed through the eye of the needle, then that which was persistent would remain persistent and that which was ephemeral would remain ephemeral. If there is a process at the needle's eye, if some things once persistent become ephemeral and if some other things once ephemeral become persistent, then this process will explain why in general what is traditional now is not exactly the same as what was traditional before. Monster-excluding anthropologists have either to deny the existence of the needle's eye, in which case they assume that culture does not change, or else they acknowledge its existence but donate it to some other discipline (to physiology, psychology, or natural and physical sciences. Benedict, finding that

[3] Ibid.   [4] Ibid.

the needle's eye is still within her orbit, loses her nerve at the last minute and offloads it on to 'history in its widest sense'). They usually excuse their conduct in giving away this burdensome portion of their birthright by falling back on Wittgenstein's plea that it does no real harm. Like Wittgenstein claiming that the fact that the rules of composition change does not matter because they change so slowly, they argue that the process at the needle's eye is so gradual that it is of little consequence. So, for monster excluders, the contradiction involved in defining tradition as that which does not change and then, in the next breath, talking about 'changing tradition' is rendered harmless by the assumption of gradualism. What better way, then, of emphasizing the harmful consequences of this contradiction, than by questioning this assumption?

This is how, in 1972, a series of seminars devoted to 'tradition' was introduced.

... the idea of a temporal process of accumulation and selection in which some elements survive, others fade away, new ones emerge and take a place in the context of what has survived. It is an image of a process through time in which a pattern both persists and changes. A dominant 'theme' or pattern pervades the persistent and affects the new elements; meanwhile the prior 'theme' itself changes under the impact of the new elements so that the prior 'theme' fades and is replaced by another theme. This process of accumulation, selection and fading away exists in every sphere of social and cultural life. . . .[5]

This same gradualist viewpoint is often favoured by art and architectural historians. For example, the 'classical tradition' in English architecture is often presented in this manner, with its themes of 'taste'[6] and 'balance' merging and altering in response to social, technological, and intellectual changes, as we proceed from the exciting innovations of Inigo Jones freely interpreting the work of Palladio, to the restricted range of options available to the neo-classicists pedantically insisting on archaeological exactitude. This is undoubtedly a useful descriptive framework but its usefulness, and validity, vary in inverse proportion to the

[5] From the cyclostyled introductory notes circulated by the chairman, Professor E. Shils.

[6] Confusingly, not 'taste' in the usual sense but in the specialized eighteenth-century sense of the exclusive, snobbish recognition of certain fixed values by certain people.

rate of change of tradition. If we look at what was happening in the early years of the nineteenth century we find that, rather than one theme gradually replacing the prior theme which is then supposed to fade away, two themes were present in direct opposition to one another. Those whom we now call neo-classicists (Soane, Cockerell, Wilkins, Smirke, Adams) considered themselves to be simply classicists. Those subscribing to the rival theme called them pseudo-classicists. Gradualism is a poor way of describing a process that divided even nuclear families; Sir John Soane and his architectural journalist son were in opposing camps. As the rival themes developed and the English countryside was strewn with the massive piles of emphatic architectural statement, the gradualist viewpoint became increasingly unattainable and the inevitable showdown, when it came, was dramatic, total, and virtually instantaneous. It was 'The Revolution against Taste': the sudden complete overthrow of the classical tradition by the rival theme at the moment when it finally attained dominance.

Too often, this phenomenon is represented merely as a pietistic intensification of the antiquarian revival of Gothic. It was far more than that. Its intuition was deep and formidable, perhaps more clearly conscious of what it wanted to destroy than what it wanted to build. To disrupt the rule of taste was the first objective, performed with incredible ease. The three-centuries-old fabric collapsed within ten years of the publication of Pugin's *Contrasts* in 1836; the common stuff of early Victorian architecture was made up out of its ruins. What to create in its place was the problem which baffled and puzzled three generations of architects.[7]

Here then is the limiting case where gradualism is wholly invalid; where one single event (the publication of a book) changes totally the framework that is supposed to contain it, leaving in its place a wasteland of architectural anomie. Instead of gradualism, a lot of tradition and a little change, we find we have suddenism, no tradition and all change. So it would seem that the changes resulting from the process at the needle's eye can be sudden, discontinuous, and sometimes very large. It follows that the gradualist viewpoint can only be approximated to by adopting a sufficiently distant position. At the limit, where all is change, such a viewpoint does not exist.

[7] John Summerson, *Georgian London* (1945; Pelican edition 1962), p. 292.

If gradualism and suddenism are both present in the phenomena we study how can we take them both into account? The solution is provided by what is called 'non-Hamiltonian mathematics', and the distinction between this and Hamiltonian mathematics also serves to demonstrate the present dominance of an intellectual tradition (the cartesian) the theme of which is gradualism *or* suddenism, and its suppression of the rival tradition (the Heraclitean) the theme of which is gradualism *and* suddenism.

Hamiltonian mathematics are gradualist mathematics in which 'marginal changes now cause only marginal changes later'.[8] The physical sciences rely almost entirely upon Hamiltonian mathematics (for example, calculus) and their predictive success has been so impressive that applied mathematics has become largely dominated by the physical sciences with the result that Hamiltonian mathematics and mathematics have, understandably but erroneously, tended to be seen as one and the same. However, the physical sciences (as well as the biological and social sciences) contain many examples of sudden discontinuous change in response to marginal changes, as, for example, when liquid water changes into gaseous steam, and these phenomena are dealt with (but not explained or described) by means of an explicit justification termed a convention.[9] A convention is simply a rule of thumb whereby the scientist automatically switches from a gradualist to a suddenist viewpoint (or *vice versa*). So long as the conventions are clearly visible, and the requisite procedures for crossing them unquestioningly obeyed, they permit the coexistence of the mutually contradictory themes of gradualism and suddenism.

Such explicit justification and scrupulous use of conventions is vastly superior to the way these themes are handled in the social sciences where the convention is concealed, either by denying its existence, ruling it out of court, or leaping back and forth between formal and informal languages all the while maintaining that they are one and the same. However, once this sloppy state of affairs has been

---

[8] E. C. Zeeman, 'The Geometry of Catastrophe', *Times Literary Supplement*, 10 Dec. 1971.

[9] Examples are the 'Maxwell convention' in the kinetic theory of gases, 'shock waves' in fluid dynamics, and the 'Neumannian cut' in elementary particle physics. The 'delay convention' in catastrophe theory is misnamed and is, in fact, a theorem.

recognized and the conventions of the social sciences have been made explicit, both the physical sciences and the social sciences are in the same boat and may be subjected to the same critique. In using an explicit convention the physicist is saying 'a gas is always a gas except when it is something else, such as a liquid or a solid'. In using an implicit assumption the social scientist is saying either 'if things stay as they are there'll be no change' or 'if things do change it's no concern of mine'. These dishearteningly trivial conclusions could be avoided if we could find a descriptive and predictive framework capable of handling both gradual change and sudden change, because then the need for conventions would disappear. Catastrophe theory provides this framework.

But first the problem must be cast in suitable form. Whilst it is valid to talk about the persistent and the ephemeral in relation to any one event it is not possible to do this in relation to a sequence of events, since it frequently happens that an event will change the contents of the persistent and ephemeral categories. No such objections are raised if we take as our focus, not the categories, but the boundary between them. This boundary exists so long as there are some things that are persistent and some that are ephemeral, and the changes that occur to the contents of these categories are recorded as transmissions across this boundary. Thus the boundary may be visualized as enclosing a finite category of things that are persistent, surrounded by an infinite ocean of ephemerality. This boundary is not fixed but is itself a variable dependent upon two other variables, transmissions from the ephemeral to the persistent and transmissions from the persistent to the ephemeral. These two variables cause the boundary to vary both as regards its clarity or fuzziness and as regards its position. We have already given qualitative expression to this sort of boundary variation in the notion of the index of boundary maintenance. The way in which these variables are related can be explained with the help of a simple example.

Some years ago, when the 'troubles' at Guildford and Hornsey Art Schools were at their peak, I was interviewed for a post as a lecturer in Liberal Studies at a College of Art in the West Country. The Principal explained to me that, when he was himself a student, long before the war, he had only one hero (Monet or Cézanne, I forget which) throughout his many years at provincial and London colleges. His fellow students, too, he said, though they did not have the same hero as him, remained loyal to the ones they had. But nowadays students, feeding on journalistic and therefore ephemeral publications (such as *Studio International* and *Art Forum*), frequently had different heroes at the end of one term from those they had at its beginning, or even from one week's end to the next. Such a rapid heroic turnover was clearly abhorrent to him and he wished to know if, by teaching them anthropology, I could hold out something firm and lasting for them to cling to.

Clearly, he felt, first, the need for tradition; second, that tradition was being eroded and that this was a bad thing; third, that this process of erosion should be retarded and if possible halted and reversed. What is more, he was in a position to do something about it and, without going into the nature of my reply, I can reveal that I did not obtain the post and that it was subsequently re-advertised and went, eventually, to an archaeologist.

Many boundary forces are acting upon 'the fixed centre of things'[10] in art education: the cavalier transmissions of artists into, out of, and sometimes virtually straight through it by the students, the often unsuccessful efforts by the Establishment to prevent these transfers, the editorial policies of art periodicals, and the monitoring of job-applicants in favour of those who are tradition-minded. The summation of all these component forces weighted both by the strength of commitment of the individual and his access to monitoring controls is no easy task, but for present purposes it need not be attempted, and we may simply infer that a certain total force is being exerted the effect of which is to uphold the boundary, and a certain total force is being exerted the effect of which is to erode the bound-

---

[10] A graphic phrase coined by Georg Simmel which, whilst inaccurate in its assumption of fixity, serves to emphasize both the crucial role of tradition and its location within space-time and not simply within the temporal dimension. That is, tradition is invoked in the assertion 'we have always done that' *and* in the assertion 'everyone does that'. The impossibility, in anthropology, of treating time and space as fully separable variables follows inevitably from the fact that the basic component of any human social system, the individual human being, cannot be in two places at the same time. The formal recognition of this nursery fact is the basis of the recently developed 'time geography'. The informal expression of the same sentiment was provided by Barbara Stanwyck on board the *Queen Elizabeth* in the 1930s when she asked 'What time does this place get to New York?' See Georg Simmel, 'Fashion' in *International Quarterly*, New York, 1904. Reprinted in *The American Journal of Sociology*, Vol. LXII, No. 6, 1957.

ary. Stability, the special case where the boundary is unaffected, is clearly the least likely outcome of all (even if it were the conscious aim of the majority of those involved in art education, which it most certainly is not).

This unjustified assumption of boundary stability sometimes receives more formal expression in the notion of a contract. An example, within the sociology of education, is the 'pedagogic contract' which forms the basic concept in the software of computer-based teaching systems. This contract between teacher and taught is assumed to be a necessary condition for pedagogy: it is the mutually agreed frame within which the teaching process occurs, though it is possible (so the argument runs), if there is agreement on both sides, to modify the framework as the process proceeds. Such a contract is yet another concealed convention which denies the dynamic relationship between category and action by insisting that they are autonomous domains.[11] In reality, the 'contract', far from being a mutually agreed framework changeable only by unanimous consent, is the ever-shifting outcome of conflicting and contradictory attitudes to 'the fixed centre of things'. Even an Art School Principal might feel that the pedagogic contract imposed upon the Gurkha mercenary recruit who addresses his corporal drill-instructor as 'Guruji' ('O great and learned teacher') exceeds his wildest dreams of student discipline, and the recent history of higher education is best seen, not as a cosy working together of staff and students under a mutually agreed contract based on enlightened self-interest, but as a long-drawn-out conflict in which the goodwill and much of the capital of the educational system has been squandered in acrimonious clause-by-clause litigation over the contract's validity.

This relationship between persistence and change involves three variables: the total force acting to uphold the existing boundary, the total force acting to erode the boundary, and the index of boundary maintenance. It follows that it must be possible to depict this relationship, whatever it might be, within a three-dimensional space.

[11] There is no serious objection to this idea of the pedagogic contract (or 'experimental contract' as Pask calls it) when it is used to design short-term teaching systems. It is a useful approximation. The objection arises when the model is believed to describe what teaching is. Pask himself is well aware of this danger and distinguishes between 'goal-seeking' (teaching systems) and 'goal-setting' (social systems). See Gordon Pask, *Goal-seeking and Goal-setting* (Systems Research Publications Ltd.).

The assumption of boundary stability (as is found in action theory and in category theory) requires that any graph drawn in this space is a horizontal plane, since any other type of surface would involve changes in the value of boundary maintenance (i.e. boundary instability).

The plane appropriate to the military education of the Gurkha recruit will be near the top of the vertical axis, having a high index of boundary maintenance; that appropriate to British art education will be much lower as a result of the frequent boundary violations.

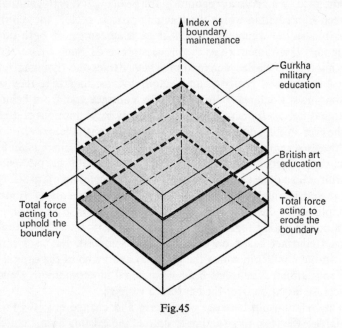

Fig.45

There are two important consequences to this assumption of boundary stability. First, there can be no explanation or description of how the one plane may be transformed into the other; that is, of how the British art education system might come to resemble the Gurkha system or *vice versa*. Such a description would require the two to be linked by a continuous surface, an impossibility if boundaries are always stable. Second, such changes, if they occur, can only be represented as discontinuous leaps from one plane to the other. That is, they can only be dealt with by a convention.

In discarding the assumption of boundary stability it might appear that we are leaping out of a precise but inadequate frying-pan into a meaningless fire. Instead of a beautifully structured *mille-feuille*, each layer characterized by a particular level of boundary maintenance and related to each other layer by specific conventions, we appear to have a completely chaotic cube of scrambled egg within which there are no discontinuities and a million and one ways of getting from the British to the Gurkha system.

Appearances can be deceptive. Thom's theorem proves that graphs in any number of dimensions are composed of only a limited and specifiable range of ingredients. Further, ordinary and exceptional ingredients may be distinguished by the criterion of smooth or discontinuous change. Ordinary ingredients involve gradual change, exceptional ingredients discontinuous change. It follows that the graph representing the relationship between persistence and change, a relationship which we know sometimes involves continuous change and sometimes discontinuous change, must contain the exceptional ingredient appropriate to three dimensions, the cusp catastrophe. So, when we look inside the cube we find, I suggest, not scrambled egg but something like this.

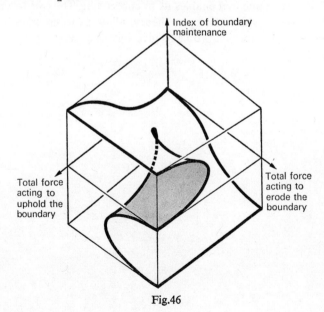

Fig.46

The simplicity of this hypothesis, the fact that most of the cube is uninhabited and that the inhabited regions all lie within one smooth and continuous surface, tends (paradoxically) to obscure its implications which are that, for the first time, we can handle formally both gradualism *and* suddenism, both evolution *and* revolution, both category *and* action, both persistence *and* change. This Heraclitean hypothesis emerges as greatly superior to the cartesian, for it replaces an infinite number of special-case stable two-dimensional graphs, related to one another by an infinite number of conventions (the *mille-feuille*), with a single three-dimensional graph that involves no assumptions of stability and entails no conventions.

I set out posing riddles about snot and I have ended up discussing cubes filled with scrambled egg. What, if anything, is the connection? What has rubbish theory got to do with catastrophe theory? Probably the simplest way of answering these questions is to say that in serious adult thought rubbish is an excluded monster and that, since the processes and contradictions involved in that monster are crucial to social life, its exclusion is regrettable. Rubbish theory provides the description of the monster; catastrophe theory provides the technique that enables us to conserve it. The two together, rubbish theory and catastrophe theory, allow us to embrace a less repressive style in which problems give way to capabilities.